Early Islam and the Birth of Capitalism

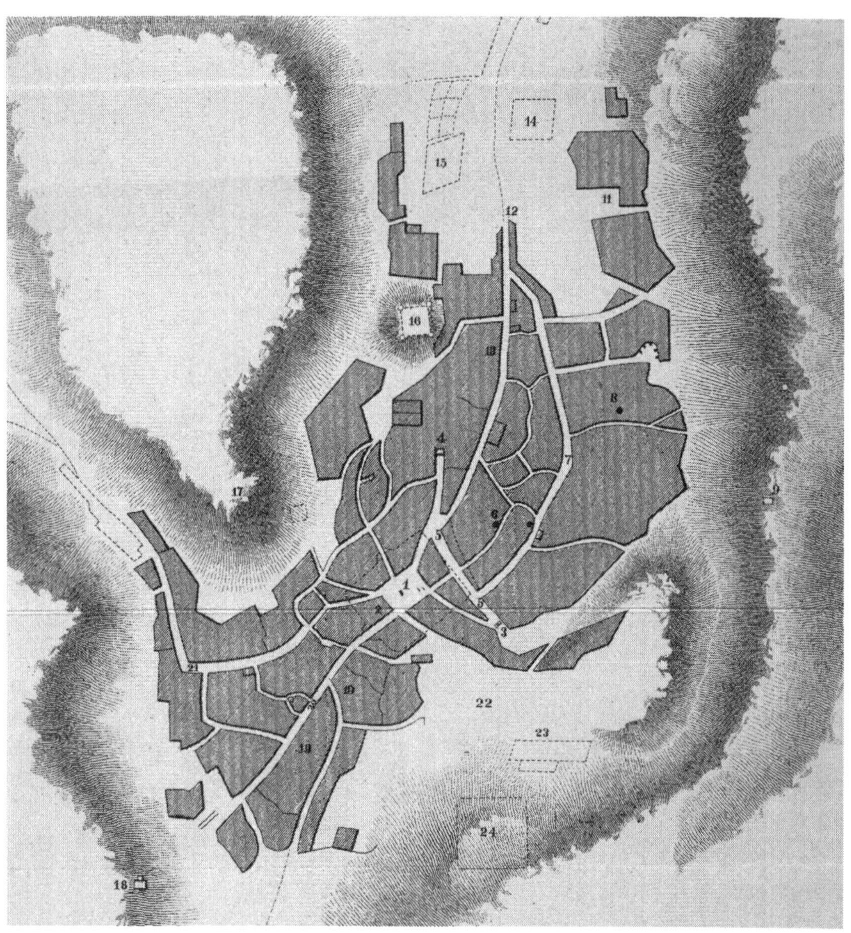

Map of Mecca based on the *Chronicles of Mecca*.
Places of interest include the Kaaba (No. 1), Muhammad's marital home (No. 6), and his birthplace (No. 8).

Early Islam and the Birth of Capitalism

Benedikt Koehler

LEXINGTON BOOKS
Lanham • Boulder • New York • London

Front cover, *Audience of Venetian Ambassadors in Damascus*, painting by Circle of Giovanni Mansueti (1460–1526), Paris, Louvre Museum.

Published by Lexington Books
An imprint of The Rowman & Littlefield Publishing Group, Inc.
4501 Forbes Boulevard, Suite 200, Lanham, Maryland 20706
www.rowman.com

16 Carlisle Street, London W1D 3BT, United Kingdom

British Library Cataloguing in Publication Information Available

Library of Congress Cataloging-in-Publication Data
Koehler, Benedikt.
Early Islam and the birth of capitalism / Benedikt Koehler.
pages cm
Includes bibliographical references and index.
ISBN 978-0-7391-8882-8 (cloth : alk. paper) -- ISBN 978-0-7391-8883-5 (electronic)
1. Islam--Economic aspects. 2. Capitalism--Religious aspects--Islam. 3. Economics--Religious aspects--Islam. I. Title.
BP173.75.K645 2014
330.12'2091767--dc23
2014016716
ISBN 978-0-7391-9745-5 (pbk : alk. paper)

∞ ™ The paper used in this publication meets the minimum requirements of American National Standard for Information Sciences Permanence of Paper for Printed Library Materials, ANSI/NISO Z39.48-1992.

Printed in the United States of America

Contents

Chapter One

The Richest Man in Arabia

First Arabs made a name for themselves in business; their reputation for religious zeal came later. The Bible has Arabs trading in luxury goods; the Roman Pliny thought Arabs "are the richest nations in the world, seeing that such vast wealth flows in upon them from both the Roman and the Parthian Empires."[1] Such memories were erased when Islam burst out of Arabia, out of what seemed a giant void, in the shape of invaders who spread despair over the end of an established order and fear of a new one dominated by religion and war. The Arabs from then on were seen as warriors rather than traders, and the trait that once had been commonplace was overlooked until the nineteenth-century orientalist Aloys Sprenger pointed out Arabs were "inventors of world trade."[2] The origins of Arab culture in commerce then came into focus.

Muhammad ibn Abdullah, Islam's founder, was proud of his descent from Arabia's most respected tribe, the Quraysh, who owed their standing to success in business rather than in battle. Muhammad even at the peak of his career was pleased when he heard praise for his own financial accomplishments; he smiled when his deputy Abu Sufyan ibn Harb complimented him, "you have become the most wealthy of the Quraysh!" Abu Sufyan's fawning accolade was not empty flattery, far from it, because Muhammad by then earned annual rents exceeding ten thousand ounces of gold (in today's terms, commensurate with several million dollars). Muhammad was the richest Arab of his time.

Long before Muhammad was born in Mecca (in 570), Arabs had been trading between Europe, India, and China, manning trade expeditions that were big (up to 2,500 camels) and went far (caravans mostly went to Gaza, ships sailed as far as Korea). Such ventures involved considerable logistical challenges: readying goods, selecting staff, equipping camels and ships. But they also required complex financial arrangements: trade expeditions had to be funded, and caravan managers and investors wished to know in advance how to share profits. Meccan traders operated firms with terms that let investors spread their risks and gave managers pre-agreed bonus shares. These companies were structured like venture capital companies and Muhammad had intimate knowledge of how they were set up and worked—his wife Khadija bint Khuwaylid was Mecca's most prominent venture capitalist. In fact, Khadija first met Muhammad when she invested in a caravan he managed, and Khadija after they married continued managing her investment portfolio while Muhammad set up in the leather trade; the couple owned a home in Mecca's most desirable neighborhood. Muhammad for twenty-five years of married life had daily insight into the practical challenges of running a business.

Khadija was the first convert to Islam. The majority of merchants in Mecca, on the other hand, were hostile to the new creed. The city each year hosted pilgrims of some two hundred denominations and if, as Muhammad wished, worship were reserved for Allah they were liable to stay away. Islam constituted a threat to Mecca's business model. The business community first tried to bribe Muhammad to moderate his demands (they offered to make him the richest man in town) but when that failed, boycotted him and drove him out of the city. Muhammad emigrated to Medina and Mecca was left in control by his adversary Abu Sufyan ibn Harb.

In Medina Muhammad shaped two institutions that became in every Islamic city the hubs of civic life: the mosque and the market. Muhammad put several decades of commercial experience into effect by issuing a range of fiscal and commercial provisions; he declared trade on the Medina market exempt from tax and introduced taxes to fund social security payments. He also set a host of commercial incentives: he improved consumer protection; gave guidelines on how commercial contracts were to be drafted; and banned insider trading. The list could go on. But Muhammad's flair for commerce in early Islam was not unique; his first three successors all were former professional merchants who adapted commercial conventions as the realm of Islam scaled up from a small-scale civic community to an empire.

The Islamic Empire was successively ruled from three capitals: Medina, Damascus, and Baghdad—and evolved into a trade zone bounded by China and the Atlantic where senior officials were appointed without regard to their religious affiliation. In Medina, formerly Byzantine officials introduced a government budget that entitled each Muslim to a fixed annual stipend: this was the world's first government pension plan. In Damascus, Christian tax officials were instrumental in launching the Islamic gold dinar: a single currency for a single market. In Baghdad, by the early tenth century a fully fledged banking sector had come into being: exchanging gold and silver coins and lending money to government and to merchants who were able to pay money into accounts in one city and draw money in another. These drafts had several names—one of them was the Persian word *čak* that has come down to us as *check.*

The money being made in Baghdad was staggering; the caliph Muqtadir's favorite bauble was a silver bird made of 50,000 ounces of silver. But wealth percolating into Baghdad society bred a taste for spending money intelligently. The caliph al Mamun founded a *House of Wisdom* that gathered and translated works written by Greek philosophers (but for this initiative these works would have been lost to posterity). Muslims also looked East; they explored the religions of India and advanced the study of medicine, mathematics, and geography. To a society that grew rich from trading with distant lands, geography was plainly useful, as was mathematics because counting was very important to run a business. The world's first accounts that show how to work out compound interest appear in tenth-century Baghdad.

BEGINNINGS

Islamic elites very early achieved enormous wealth and knew what to do with it. Washington Irving, the nineteenth-century novelist whose biography of Muhammad even today does not read dated, noted

> One almost regards with incredulity the stories of immense sums passing from hand to hand among these Arab conquerors, as freely as bags of dates in their native deserts; but it must be recollected they had the plundering of the rich Empires of the East, and as yet were flush with the spoils of recent conquests. [3]

Irving was right, but only in parts. Victory spoils were one of the sources of Muslim wealth, but not the only one. Early Islam's capacity for wealth creation was remarkable. The Islamic single market promoted entrepreneurship, global trade, and new forms of corporate enterprise. Economic innovations abound: they include a new monetary regime, the invention of charitable trusts, offshore trade centers, and venture capital partnerships. Islam promoted property rights of women, of religious minorities, and of foreigners. Rules for fair trade promoted consumer protection and banned monopolies.

Arabs within decades after Muhammad's death ousted Persian and Byzantine rule from the Middle East and Egypt. Explanations for this sweeping victory variously adduce some mix of martial vigor, avarice, and plain luck. Even assuming these factors fully explain why Arabs could make a success of invasions, they fall short of showing why their rule proved durable, let alone help deduce how Islamic societies within a short span of time launched a trajectory of economic growth sustained for centuries. From the start, an attitude enabling economic growth was evident in Islam. Max Weber, the sociologist of religion, pointed out Islam's conspicuous emphasis on material gratification, encouraging the acquisition of "wealth, power, and honour."[4] Pursuing prosperity, and knowing how to do so, accompanied the drive for supremacy and glory.

An Arab entrepreneur was the model for one of world literature's most famous protagonists. The *Arabian Nights* introduce Sindbad the Sailor who described what drove him to forgo the comfort of his familiar surroundings and again and again seek the thrill of taking risks:

> It was while my life was at its most pleasant that I felt a pernicious urge to travel to foreign parts, to associate with different races and to trade and make a profit. Having thought this over, I bought more valuable goods, suitable for a voyage, than I had ever taken before, packing them into bales. When I had gone down from Baghdad to Basra I loaded them on a ship, taking with me a number of the leading Basran merchants. We put out.[5]

Sindbad embodies the quintessential Arabian entrepreneur, an intrepid adventurer who leaves the comforts of his home to set sail to foreign climes. He soon rues his decision when disaster strikes and he loses his money and very nearly his life, but then, fortune reverses and he returns, healthy, wealthy—but none the wiser. Sindbad finds domestic tranquillity so boring he soon needs to set out again and then the plot repeats. Arab merchants honed the quintessential skill of entrepreneurs, weighing risks. The *jahiliyya* poet Shansara celebrated the entrepreneurial temper, because "riches are only in reach of someone who has no fear of danger or exile."[6] Rewards came at extraordinary risk and could be lost in a flash. The Arab word for these risks, *azar*, has come down to us as *hazard*. Real-world Sindbads ran risks to earn extraordinary returns. Arabia's mercantile class was multi-ethnic: Sindbad's name points to his origin in Sind (today in Pakistan).

Islam originated in Mecca, a city with a long tradition as a center of religious devotion and of trade. In most societies, markets have been shaped by government, but in Mecca, government was shaped by markets. Entrepreneurs had shaped the city that raised Muhammad, and Muhammad's distinguished ancestral dynasty of entrepreneurs is repeatedly mentioned in the Koran. Muhammad was a prophet who brought to his vocation some thirty years of business experience. To most religious leaders, such as Abraham, Jesus, or Buddha, economics mattered little. Muhammad, by contrast, along with shaping every other aspect of the Muslim way of life, cast rules for trade and tax, in the process preserving or reforming many pre-Islamic commercial practices. Through adapting these rules to an economic sphere that was enlarged by conquests, early Islamic societies became the most innovative economies of their age.

The orientalist Aloys Sprenger tracked back to the dynamic of the Arabian economy before Islam was born. Accordingly, Arab trade created a link between Europe and Asia. Arabs had not only spotted the business opportunity of connecting distant markets, but also the profit potential of supplying those goods that had the highest profit margins: jewels, pearls, ivory, incense, and gold. Arabs looked back on a long track record of successful commercial venturing, were commercially astute and had a grasp of the mechanics of cross-border trade, gold mining, agriculture, and trading. Muhammad harnessed these competitive strengths. For nearly two centuries Muhammad's hometown, Mecca, had been the focal point of religious devotion and, as a spin-off benefit, of trade. The Meccan economy had working relationships with partners in Europe and Asia long before Muhammad was born.

THE DESCENT OF MARKETS

The defining characteristic of Arabia's shapeless pre-Islamic society was commercial acumen, and early Islamic institutions set free market dynamics throughout Islam's realm and in neighboring countries. Just how stark was this contrast between Islamic societies and their Christian neighbors became apparent when in the Middle East crusaders arrived in numbers. The Islamic Empire's single market had spin-off benefits for Europe: Islam and Christendom were enemies in politics but partners in commerce. Europe's nascent capitalism emerged once Europeans imported this know-how and replicated Islamic economic institutions.

The dynamic of Islam's approach to economics is thrown into relief by comparison with the state of economies in Europe, where a thousand years had lapsed without progress in material culture. Although intuition suggests markets would have flourished alongside the states that housed them, facts do not bear out this assumption: empires in Europe expanded but markets stagnated. Europeans were slow to discover how trade creates wealth. The first European to describe how a market comes into being was the inquisitive ancient Greek traveler and historian Herodotus. He told of Carthaginians sailing along the African coast where they deposited goods on a beach, then after retreating to their boats by smoke signal invited customers to come forward and inspect the goods. Prospective buyers placed an amount of gold next to offered goods showing how much they were prepared to pay and then in turn withdrew. Then, bargaining began. If Carthaginians considered the bid fair, they collected the gold and departed, else returned aboard and gave their customers time to raise their bid. Bargains were struck through wordless communication.[7] Herodotus identified three elements that constitute a market: buyers and sellers are assured of personal safety (they never come face to face); cheating is policed (nobody would ever again trade with a thief); and prices are agreed through bargaining. Herodotus showed the precise moment from which markets issue—the discovery how to set prices through bargaining. Herodotus anticipated insights of the economist Friedrich von Hayek, who pointed out where to look for the wellspring of economic activity: "The price system is just one of those formations which man has learned to use . . . after he had stumbled upon it without understanding it . . . man has been able to develop that division of labour on which civilization is based because he happened to stumble upon a method which made it possible."[8] Herodotus also had a collateral insight that pre-empted Hayek: not only did merchants, rather than governments, create markets, but Herodotus also asserted governments may even prevent markets. In the Persian Empire, Herodotus wrote, markets were "a custom unknown to the Persians, who never make purchases in open markets, and indeed do not have a single marketplace in their whole country."[9] Contempt for commerce also pervaded the upper classes of the Roman Empire who were barred from pursuing careers in business. Rome's anticommercial bias is thrown into relief by comparing Herodotus's description of a silent market with that by Pliny:

> It was to the effect that the merchandise on sale was left by them upon the opposite bank of a river on their coast, and it was then removed by the natives, if they thought proper to deal on terms of exchange. On no grounds ought luxury with greater reason to be detested by us, than if we only transport our thoughts to these scenes, and then reflect, what are its demands, to what distant spots it sends in order to satisfy them, and for how mean and how unworthy an end![10]

Herodotus's intuition how markets emerge did not have an impact on ancient Greece or Rome. Antiquity's most constructive economic policymaker may have been Alexander the Great, who founded Alexandria and populated the city with a multicultural mix of Egyptians, Greeks, and Jews and vested in it a large degree of municipal autonomy. Alexandria was a separate fiscal entity to the rest of Egypt and in effect became an offshore trade center. Antiquity's largest city and political capital was Rome; Alexandria, politically inconsequential but mercantile, was the second largest city and the capital of trade. Alexandria was living proof that for prosperity, trade mattered more than power. But the insights and initiatives of Herodotus and Alexander the Great remained isolated exceptions. Ancient Greece and Rome bequeathed no economic literature of consequence; by the end of the Middle Ages Europe's standard of living was only marginally higher than at the beginning. Great empires rose and fell for thousands of years without advancing our knowledge how markets come about and how to run them. It is astonishing that in Europe Herodotus's inquiry into how markets evolve remained the last word on the subject for over 2,500 years. Adam Smith, for example, who thought deeply about the workings of markets, is silent on how they began.

Analyses of the dynamics that actuate markets emerged notably in the work of Friedrich Engels and Max Weber. Engels, like Herodotus, asserted commercial middlemen are crucial for markets at the origin and mapped out a subsequent pathway for the evolution of markets and, as a second round effect, of states:

> Now for the first time a class appears which, without in any way participating in production, captures the direction of production as a whole and economically subjugates the producers; which makes itself an indispensable middleman between two producers and exploits them both. Under the pretext that they save the producers the trouble and risk of exchange, extend the sale of their products to distant markets and are therefore the most useful class of the population, a class of parasites comes into being, genuine social sycophants, who, as a reward for their actually very insignificant services, skim all the cream off production at home and abroad, rapidly amass enormous wealth and a corresponding social influence, and for that reason receive under civilisation ever higher honours and ever greater control of production.[11]

Engels's argumentation has flaws. Accordingly, merchants link distant markets, in the process amass wealth and come to dominate society (for doing very little). However, Engels did not elaborate, for example, why producers acquiesce to overpay commercial middlemen; why competitors do not come forward and whittle away their profits; and crucially, Engels was silent on how merchants came by the information that set them in motion in the first place. Engels leaves in the dark how the first market came into being.

Max Weber challenged Engels. Markets, according to Weber, incubate in a particular mental predisposition of certain individuals who care little about short-term comfort and adjust their actions to earn long-term material gain. Individuals with this value set existed in all eras, but their way of life came to dominate social norms through the advent of Protestantism that made commercial enterprise ethically meritorious. Weber's theory that capitalism results from specific behaviors and attitudes has remained dominant. But his assertion that Protestantism was midwife to nascent capitalism was overturned by a review of empirical facts. Werner Sombart pointed out Europe's economic growth trends had begun curving up prior to the advent of Protestantism, specifically in medieval Italian mercantile republics such as Venice and Genoa. There, growth ensued from discoveries of how to pool investment capital, to set up trading ventures, to send money abroad, and to exchange foreign currency, and from these communities, ruled by businessmen rather than princes or priests, entrepreneurial energy rippled across Europe, became self-sustaining, and permeated society and culture more widely. A spirit of innovation gathered strength throughout Europe—in England, where jurists developed the Common Law, in Iberia, where navigators set forth to find promising trade routes to Asia and America, in Germany, where unshackled intellectual inquiry led to the Reformation. Werner Sombart left unresolved why capitalism, a particular frame of mind congenial with Protestantism, emerged in Italy, a country where Catholicism set the gaze of adherents on the next world. The trigger that stirred market forces dormant in Europe for so long, this book argues, was the adaptation of Islamic institutional templates.

THE CULTURE OF COMMERCE IN ITALY

"Traffic" is a familiar term in the English language but not a native one. The term was imported from Italy where merchants to describe commercial dealing coined the term *trafico*, a concept originating in the Arabic word *tafriq* that connotes distribution. Arabs supplied a host of other common terms in trade and finance, such as *tariff*, *check*, or *carat*. Another familiar word, *hazard*, derives from the Arab term to describe the risk of caravan travel, *azar*; *razzia* comes from the Arab word for raids, *ghazi* ('gh' is sounded as 'r'). Novel commercial terms and concepts arrived through Italians because they were close to Islamic markets. The Mediterranean Sea was an exterritorial expanse as lawless and dangerous as were the deserts of Arabia. The prospect of rapid profit tempted Arab pirates to negotiate its waters to prey on cities along the French and Italian coastlines, but gradually, however, it transpired recurring business promised greater gain than one-off raids. The lesson that commerce is more lucrative than theft was learned and unlearned over and over—the process from which market conventions issued suffered many reversals and took centuries. But when entrepreneurs supplanted pirates, trade between Muslims and Christians became a conduit for importing into Europe new approaches to commercial institutions and frameworks. Capitalism in Europe through this process came into being.

The trajectory of a tiny city south of Naples, Amalfi, demonstrated how a community could progress from banditry to the position of partner of the most powerful authorities of the time. Many Italian cities, even Rome, had suffered Muslim raids, but Amalfi, although in easy striking distance from Muslim Sicily, was left untouched, and for this reason: Amalfitans, rather than oppose Muslim pirates, joined up with them—to the exasperation of the Vatican that promised Amalfitans favorable trade terms on condition they renounce their support for infidels sacking Rome's churches. The Vatican's offer fell on deaf ears; piracy was more lucrative than anything the pope could offer. But eventually, Amalfi's merchants abandoned piracy in favor of a more stable business model: to their trading post in Constantinople (to which as subjects of the Byzantine emperor they were entitled) they added another one in Cairo (a concession granted by Egypt's Fatimid rulers), and rounded off their portfolio of outposts with a hospital in Jerusalem. Amalfi enjoyed first mover advantage in a three-way traffic between Italy, the Byzantine and Muslim Empires. The city's merchants, once they became prosperous, demonstrated their commercial success through generous benefactions, including to churches in the city their ancestors helped raid, Rome. Loyalties were as elastic as business flows.

Amalfi's success attracted competitors. Pisa, Genoa, and Venice fought each other over markets as fiercely as did crusaders and Muslims over battlefields, in the process blurring the distinction between commerce and piracy. Amalfi's harbor was spared by Arabs but torched by Pisans. Venetians, sailing to Palestine for the first crusade, fought their first military engagement against Pisans to exclude them from the race to claim stakes in the Holy Land. Venice, Genoa, and Pisa controlled swaths of cities in Palestine that were exempt from tax; effectively, these were tax havens. Venetians perfected a business model whereby they conveyed crusaders and pilgrims to Palestine (for a fee) and provided military assets to crusaders (in return for tax concessions in occupied territories). Venice, a nominal subject of the Byzantine emperor, in 1204 directed a crusade to Constantinople and there installed a political puppet on the Byzantine throne. Venice's apogee consisted of a reverse takeover of her sovereign.

The crusades did not upset the balance of power in the Mediterranean. The Arab military occupied North Africa and large swaths of Spain, Southern Italy, and Sicily. Muslims and Christians pursued a twin track policy: in politics bellicose, pacific in commerce. Muslim authorities never embargoed trade with Italy (nor, for that matter, with Constantinople), and commercial relations between Italian and Levantine communities continued seamlessly after the last Byzantine soldier departed from the region. Venetian patricians evolved the same business model as Meccan plutocrats—convoys issued across seas, as did caravans across deserts. Venture capital companies funded convoys whose fixed departure dates set the city's annual rhythm of financial and mercantile life.

Italian mercantile republics were one of several conduits into Europe of goods imported from the Islamic realm and, of no less importance, of ideas. Another important avenue was via the presence Europeans established in the Middle East. In the midst of many Muslim cities, Muslim authorities licensed European merchants to open self-contained, walled trading outposts, called *funduqs,* affording incoming merchants accommodation and storage areas. *Funduqs* were dotted across the maps of the Middle East and North Africa. Muslims enjoyed reciprocal arrangements in Europe, albeit on a smaller scale. Constantinople in the eighth century licensed a Muslim trading post in (and attached to), a mosque; Venice in the late Middle Ages licensed a *Fondaco dei Turchi.*

Commercial knowhow gained through dealing with Islamic business partners by the thirteenth century was a catalyst for original European contributions to the study of law and economics. The Pisan Leonardo Fibonacci in 1202 wrote a book, the *Liber Abaci*, which was the first of a new genre of business manual showing how commercial arithmetic is key to making money. (Herewith an example: "*A man went on business to Lucca, next to Florence, and then back to Pisa, and he made double in each city, and in each city he spent 12 denari, and in the end, nothing was left for him. It is sought how much he had at the beginning.*")[12] Fibonacci's book was a success because he wrote for readers eager to improve their numeracy, which demonstrates the remarkable progress in commercial culture over the previous two centuries. In tenth-century Venice, commercial documents show that few merchants at that time could even provide a signature, let alone perform calculations in writing. Literacy and numeracy had progressed by 1204 such that Venice, on imposing her mastery on Constantinople, declared herself "*ruler over 3/8 of the Byzantine Empire.*" A new mentality gained ground, one that calculated and evaluated costs and benefits, efficiencies and improvements, and when applied to spheres such as architecture and painting enabled Renaissance rationalism.

While Fibonacci broke new ground in the study of how to accumulate goods, his contemporary Francis of Assisi brought into focus a complementary question, namely what constitutes an ethical approach to fair distribution of goods. Fibonacci and Francis occupied opposite poles of medieval law and economics, but for both Islamic approaches to law and economics were formative. The influence was direct on Fibonacci, who in his autobiography thanked his Arab teachers for training him. In Francis's case, the creative adaptation of Islamic institutional templates occurred over a longer period of time and was mediated through Franciscan friars.

The lifestyle of Franciscan friars, one of voluntary poverty, posed a dilemma for jurists. On the one hand, Franciscans abjured possession of material objects, but on the other hand, they inhabited buildings that constituted a form of property. It was difficult to reconcile the contradiction, until at last the Vatican cast a suitable legal construct, an entity with a distinct legal personality but distinct from its members—a fictive abstract person called *universitas*. The concept had ramifications beyond settling the legal status of Franciscan property holdings; scholars invoked it to constitute institutions of higher learning (and in due course, it provided the basis for evolution of the corporation). The fine distinction between owning and using a property had a precedent, however, in Islamic law, where benefactions were channelled into so-called *waqfs*. Islamic precedent also foreshadowed another institutional innovation of the time, English institutions of higher learning. The organizational structure of Merton College in Oxford and of Peterhouse in Cambridge replicated Islamic self-governing schools of jurisprudence, *madrasas*, which were endowed with benefactions managed at arm's length from donors. A third significant innovation of the time occurred in Genoa with the launch of a gold currency. Islamic precedents foreshadowed innovations in commercial, legal, academic, and monetary spheres. Capitalist society in Europe emerged from a confluence of strands that originated in early Islam: beginnings were discernible when in Medina Muhammad deregulated prices.

"PRICES ARE IN THE HAND OF GOD"

Muhammad grew up in a society where many economic conventions had gone unquestioned from Babylonian times. Throughout the Middle East, markets for daily necessities, such as food, were strictly regulated: prices were set by market supervisors rather than by vendors. There were variants how far regulation extended; Judaic law, for example, even capped a trader's profit margin (at one sixth of production costs). If sellers raised prices above official rates, say, to take advantage of food shortages during famines, customers were entitled to file complaints and to demand market supervisors intervene. Muhammad's capacity to instigate radical reform is thrown into relief against this backdrop of market conventions by his decision to disband regulation of food prices.

Traditions relate the circumstances of this event. A famine bore down on the community and rising food prices exacerbated hardship. In keeping with standard practice for seeking redress, Muhammad was petitioned to intervene and set a price cap. This request, however, met with Muhammad's refusal—for his adherents, an incomprehensible decision. Not only was this decision at odds with established trade conventions, it also seemed incompatible with Muhammad's reputation as compassionate guardian of the indigent. Just how contentious was this decision is shown by what happened next: Muhammad's decisions were rarely challenged, but on this occasion there appeared opposition and his adherents deputed a speaker to prevail once more on him to reverse his decision. Muhammad sensed he could not enforce his decision through personal authority alone and thereupon withdrew to solitude, to seek in communion with Allah whether he should revoke his non-interventionist stance. On his return, however, he faced his adherents and declared that his prayers for authority to set prices had gone unanswered. Therefore, to intervene in prices, he declared, by implication was not in his gift: "Prices," Muhammad proclaimed, "are in the hand of God."

On first blush, deregulating prices in a seventh-century Arabian market for food staples may appear a matter of little consequence. But the economist Friedrich von Hayek would disagree. If the price mechanism "were the result of deliberate human design," Hayek averred, "it would have been acclaimed as one of the greatest triumphs of the human mind."[13] When an economy driven by markets rather by governments comes into being, the ramifications are endless, because taking price-setting out of the hand of government and giving it to the invisible hand of markets has ripple effects on economic incentives—when entrepreneurs rather than officials determine how to allocate resources, economic rationality permeates all spheres of economic life. Herodotus, Muhammad, and Hayek recognized the importance of the price mechanism to economic activity.

SOURCES

A word on sources. The extent of information passed down on Muhammad is immense. These stories, called *hadith*, were an inexhaustible trove for Islamic histories and lore, religious and legal literature; they run into tens of thousands of anecdotes, ranging from poignant evocations of profound emotion to unabashedly preposterous yarns. Islamic scholars gathered every scrap of information, however minute, about Muhammad, his successors, and many other personalities and events of the early Islamic era. No other religion's origins, Muslims asserted, was as thoroughly evidenced as those of Islam.[14]

Doubts have been raised whether Islamic sources are reliable, however, for the following reason: Muhammad's first biography was not written until over a century after his death and because accounts until then were passed on orally, Islamic historians lacked the means to sift distortions and fabrications promulgated by interested parties in the intervening period. Islamic historiography from the outset, therefore, unavoidably mingled fact and fiction. However, Aloys Sprenger disposed of these contentions and his refutation bears repeating.[15]

Muhammad indeed was adamant the written word was the exclusive preserve of the Koran. His confidant and successor Umar recalled the Prophet had passed a ban on written documentation and censored him for copying a book ("The prophet got very angry, so much so that he got quite red.")[16] Muhammad's aversion against any document other than the Koran kept in writing, as Max Weber pointed out, accords with his status as a prophet, because prophets receive divine revelation through oral communion and in turn pass on their teaching personally rather than through paper or parchment. (Jesus, for comparison, acted likewise.)[17] Umar, once elected as Muhammad's successor, was urged to lift the ban on written accounts. Umar was a decisive personality and displayed hesitation only in exceptional circumstances. However, on this occasion he deliberated an entire month, which evinces the fact views differed widely and Muhammad's injunction must have been observed in the breach. Finally, Umar confirmed Muhammad's ban because "the nations who have been before you, have written books, and trusted upon them, and left the book of God."[18] But Umar was unable to enforce a proscription that had already been flouted when Muhammad was alive; Sprenger infers Muhammad's and Umar's injunctions were openly ignored from around the fortieth year after Muhammad's emigration to Medina because relatively few testimonies have been left by companions of Muhammad who died theretofore.[19] Therefore, discounting Islamic historiography based on the alleged absence of written sources does not seem persuasive until facts that stand in opposition to Sprenger's refutation have been produced. (For the sake of comparison, the gospels have been dated to some sixty years after the crucifixion.)

Early Islamic historians had at their disposal a colossal accumulation of narratives; sifting them was a challenge for them (and us). A single example may suffice as illustration. The traditionist Bukhari relates a *hadith* that Muhammad had sex with each of his eleven wives in a single day.[20] This extravagant claim produces a gasp of surprise in any reader. Even the most credulous readers will hardly concede the veracity of this assertion; but not a few will be inclined to sense its truth in parts; and almost all will be persuaded no such story ever could have circulated unless Muhammad in fact would have been known as a man of extraordinary energies. To anyone willing to read between the lines, Arab lore and the *hadiths* on which they are based are invaluable testimonies. Islam affected the way of life of all levels of society, and the world of commerce was no exception. The pattern as much as the particulars of individual stories open to view how Muhammad and his successors set free a commercial revolution whose benefits are still felt today.

NOTES

1. Book of Ezechiel, 27:22. Pliny the Elder, *Natural History*, Book 6, Chapter 32.
2. Sprenger, *Die alte Geographie Arabiens*, 299.
3. Irving, *Mahomet and His Successors*, Vol. 2, 374.
4. Weber, *Wirtschaft und Gesellschaft*, Vol. 1, 358.
5. *Arabian Nights*, Night 550.
6. Weil, *Die poetische Literatur der Araber*, 12.
7. Herodotus, *The Histories*, Book 4, Chapter 196.
8. Hayek, "The Use of Knowledge in Society," 52.
9. Herodotus, *The Histories*, Book 1, Chapter 153.
10. Pliny, *Natural History*, Book 6, Chapter 24.
11. Engels, *The Origins of the Family, Private Property and the State*, Harmondsworth, 1985, 203–4.
12. Fibonacci, *Liber Abaci*, 460.
13. Hayek, "The Use of Knowledge in Society," 527.
14. Ibn Kotaibah, cited in Sprenger, "Über das Traditionswesen bei den Arabern," 1.
15. Sprenger asked, "Had Ibn Ishaq merely oral sources of the biography of Mohammed or written ones? It is necessary to show whether the Moslims, during the first century after the Hijrah, did write books at all" ("Origin and Progress," 304). He set out his findings in *Life of Mohammed*, 66–68; "Origin and Progress of Writing Down Historical Facts," 380–81; "Alfred

von Kremer's Edition of Waqidy," 211–12; *Das Leben und die Lehre des Mohammad*, Vol. 3, 82.

16. Sprenger, "Origin and Progress," 310.
17. Weber, *Wirtschaft und Gesellschaft,* 459–60.
18. Sprenger, "Origin and Progress," 310.
19. Sprenger, "Origin and Progress," 380; Sprenger, *Das Leben und die Lehre des Mohammad*, Vol. 3, 82.
20. Caetani, *Annali dell'Islam*, Vol. 1, 141.

Chapter Two

Markets without Government

Business as usual would resume in Arabia once short-lived disturbances in Medina had run their course—such might have been the forecast in the world's principal capitals when in 632 news arrived of the passing of Muhammad ibn Abdullah, an Arab potentate who several years earlier had demanded world leaders acknowledge his status as Apostle of Allah and submit to Islam. To issue an ultimatum to a Byzantine emperor may have seemed an overconfident gesture. But the correspondence as such, on the other hand, was by no means a breach of diplomatic protocol, quite the opposite. In Muhammad's family, corresponding with heads of state went back several generations and diplomacy and trade ran in the family. Hashim ibn Abd Manaf, Muhammad's great-grandfather, had concluded international trade treaties, and Abd al Mutallib, his grandfather, was so conspicuously wealthy that three kilograms of gold were afforded for his burial garment. Muhammad, too, originally followed family tradition and pursued a career in business before he broke with family tradition when he found his vocation in religion rather than in trade. The Byzantine emperor did not take Muhammad's fiery letter lightly and thought it prudent to gather intelligence about him. Abu Sufyan ibn Harb, Muhammad's main Arabian adversary, briefed Byzantine authorities that, yes, Muhammad attracted many followers, but his fledgling religion appealed mainly to the lower classes, the ranks of the young, the poor, and women. The wily Abu Sufyan left it to his listeners to infer that a religion professed by such inconsequential constituencies most likely was a passing phenomenon. Abu Sufyan's assessment, however, was difficult to reconcile with Muhammad's remarkable career, and Byzantines had every reason to keep a watching brief on Muhammad ibn Abdullah, at the very least for reasons of trade diplomacy—this scion of a dynasty of entrepreneurs was the richest man in Arabia.

Muhammad's wealth late in life did not come from trade. The once successful entrepreneur had been effectively bankrupted when his Meccan compatriots imposed a boycott on his business and drove him out of Mecca. However, Muhammad went on to earn an even larger fortune from his position as Messenger of Allah, which together with military and political prerogatives included the right to lay rules for tax in times of war and peace. In war, the lion's share of victory spoils went to Muhammad, in peace, he collected tax on wealth; this revenue he managed as he saw fit. This fiscal framework threatened to unravel after Muhammad's death. Communities all over Arabia gave notice they now considered tax treaties defunct and Medina itself threatened to split into a confederation of two separate communities, Muslims and non-Muslims, each electing their own chiefs. Most alarming was that at this moment of crisis, Muhammad's closest circle was torn because Muhammad had died without appointing a successor and it was unclear who could claim inheritance to his power, his property, or both. All three trouble spots—across Arabia, within Medina, and among Muhammad's inner circle—needed to be resolved promptly, if Islam were not to expire along with its Apostle. Observers looking ahead at the moment of Muhammad's death might have forecast Muhammad would be remembered, if at all, as a failure who should have stuck to his business career.

This was not the first time Islam faced extinction. Ten years earlier, Muhammad had escaped from Mecca on the run from assassins and was lucky to be alive. Muhammad's preaching had alienated Mecca's leading merchants who boycotted his business and ruined his social standing, and the once successful businessman at the low point of his career arrived in Medina as an impoverished refugee. But from that point, Muhammad embarked on a success story as a religious leader, political force, and ruler of his hometown and most of Arabia. To achieve Arabia's political unification within a decade was remarkable, even more so that unity against all odds proved durable. Muhammad's refugee community in Medina was the nucleus of an empire that within a century reached from China to the Atlantic. Religion held this community together. One of Muhammad's immediate actions on arrival in Medina was to site a mosque; but almost concurrently, however, another story began to unfold: Muhammad soon after siting a mosque established a market and then proceeded to lay rules for fair trade. Muhammad gave his community along with a new religion a framework for its economy. Muhammad's economic policy promoted entrepreneurial initiative, efficient distribution of resources, and wealth creation, a framework for creating wealth that lasted centuries. To Muhammad's followers his attention to the practicalities of business and to regulations for trading and tax came as no surprise; they would have expected no less from a successful businessman who came from a family with a long tradition of entrepreneurial drive. At the moment of Muhammad's death, however, his community was without a leader and Islam's fate once again hung in the balance. Rebels aimed to overturn the imposition of a new single faith, leader, and tax regime. Muhammad's successor Abu Bakr, elected in haste, faced insurrections all over Arabia, and but for his success in overcoming them, Islam's history may have followed a familiar sequence in Arab history—religious fervor erupting into political turmoil and fizzling out as quickly as it began. But against all odds, Islam survived. Business would never be the same again, not in Arabia, not elsewhere.

Muhammad's career, his family heritage, and his familiarity with Arabia's commercial conventions equipped him to frame the economy he was to build. Muhammad's early followers in Mecca had given up everything to follow their leader into exile in Medina, but they knew they had embarked on a venture promising extraordinary rewards. Muhammad was optimistic they would survive and prosper. When he heard his adherent Suheib had left behind substantial property in Mecca to follow his leader into exile, Muhammad said: "Suheib, verily has made a profitable bargain."[1] The assets Muhammad brought with him to build a new community in Medina consisted of his self-belief and his business experience, and Muhammad was not the only early Muslim to die a rich man. Many of his close companions were set soon to accumulate considerable wealth, if they had not done so already. Casting a light on the economist Muhammad's success story requires tracking back to what went before.

ARABIA'S ECONOMY

Arabia's skies and soil are hostile to farmers and Arabs ever understood their hopes of prosperity hinged on finding trade partners abroad. The mainstay of Arab exports was staples, such as leather and textiles, and luxury goods sourced from remote frontiers—from Yemen came frankincense, a fragrance essential for dignifying pagan and Christian rituals; from the waters around Bahrain, pearls; and from mines throughout Arabia the most valuable commodity of all, gold, which was valued so highly by foreign dignitaries that King Solomon built a naval base on the Red Sea to facilitate imports.[2] Getting hold of pearls and gold was grueling, but worth the effort because luxury goods were less bulky to transport and earned higher profit margins.

Arab trade was conducted in size. Caravans issuing from Mecca comprised up to 2,500 camels, and Mecca's leading merchant would be in charge of coordinating and equipping these large enterprises. Caravan managers faced exacting demands. Physical stamina was essential; Abdullah, Muhammad's father, succumbed on a caravan journey and his fate was hardly exceptional. Additionally, managers needed commercial nous. Caravans provided safety in numbers and economies of scale, but commercial risks, on the other hand, were borne by individuals. Substantial rewards beckoned those who could overcome the chief obstacles, distance and danger; investors and producers pooled funds and wares, and offered caravan managers a share in profits. Abu Sufyan, who led caravans in Muhammad's day, boasted his ventures were backed by all sections of society: "I swear, I didn't know anyone in Mecca, man or woman, who did not consign goods to me."[3] The monetary value of Mecca's caravans was huge. A caravan of one thousand camels, leaving before the Battle of Badr, "contained significant wealth, for there was not a man or woman from the Quraysh in Mecca who had some wealth accruing, but it was sent in the caravan. Even the woman who had a paltry sum sent it. Some said that it contained fifty thousand dinar, though others said there was less."[4]

Overland caravans heading west constituted one leg of Arab trade; another was seaborne trade to the east. Arabs sailed to India, Indonesia, China and Korea, and in some Asian locations settled in numbers. Arab merchants returned from China with a Chinese monopoly product, silk, coveted already by ancient Romans; the Roman emperor Marcus Aurelius considered the import of silk sufficiently important to warrant sending a Roman trade delegation to China. Most silk traveled from China to Europe by land and by sea along the overland Silk Road controlled by Persians who imposed tariffs on caravans passing through. Arab entrepreneurs, however, opted for an alternative route, by sea, which although more dangerous, had the advantage of avoiding Persian sales taxes. Arabs ran risks and backed their commercial judgment to overcome the chief barriers to trade, distance and danger, and further expanded their market share when they came to control lands bordering on the Indian Ocean. Umar founded Basra as a gateway to trade with Asia, and Chinese records in 651 noted their emperor received a delegation from the *Han mi mo ni*, a Chinese version of the *Emir al-muminin*, Commander of the Faithful.

HOW NEIGHBORS SAW ARABS

Foreigners did not know what to make of Arabs. The high quality of goods issuing from Arabia was difficult to reconcile with the forbidding landscape whence they came and the frugal appearance of the people who lived there. Outsiders rarely ventured into Arabia's deserts, rarely met Arabs, and for the most part based their views on second hand accounts from neighboring Israelites or Syrians. Information on Arabs was scarce, but the Bible and Greek and Roman authors gave reports on how they made a living. The Bible noted Arab exports to Egypt (likely to have included slaves) and that they sold Israelites "spices, precious stones, and gold."[5] Making up for lack of first-hand knowledge, hearsay was exaggerated. A Greek geographer, a certain

Agatharchides, claimed Arabs mined gold nuggets the size of olives and that trade with India had made Arabs one of the richest people in the world. But it remained a mystery how this wealth came about. Pliny the Elder thought Arabs equally suited to business and brigandage and was irked Arabs extracted extravagant profit margins from wares "which are sold among us at fully one hundred times their prime cost."[6] Diodorus Siculus, another Roman, thought making money from exports accounted for the wealth of Arabs: "Commercial pursuits are the chief cause of their greater prosperity. For many of the tribe follow the business of transporting frankincense, myrrh, and other costly spices to the Mediterranean."[7] The wealth of Arabs, Romans knew, came from trade.

Neighbors were tempted to take control of trade routes through Arabia but had little to show for their efforts. A Roman seaborne invasion, for example, was so ineffectual it left no trace in Arab records. Persians and Byzantines would have liked to prevent Arabs from outflanking their trade routes and undercutting prices for silk but their diplomacy never advanced beyond establishing client relationships with tribes across their empires' borders. The only foothold established inside Arabia was that of the Abyssinian king who temporarily controlled Yemen, but otherwise, no foreign power ever succeeded in installing a compliant regional puppet inside Arabia. However, one other salient fact about Arabs trickled out to the outside world: religious devotion seemed central in their communal life. Herodotus had heard of a deity, by the name of Alilat, whose religious rituals, somehow, seemed to involve stones.[8]

THE CHRONICLES OF MECCA

Mecca in Muhammad's day had perhaps 15,000 inhabitants. At the time Herodotus wrote down what he had heard, any community settling there must have been far smaller. Between the lives of Herodotus and Muhammad, a millennium elapsed, and most of the intervening period is opaque. However, the medieval *Chronicles of Mecca* showed how early Islamic historians tried to shed light on how by insensible steps Mecca emerged from myth into history.[9]

Accordingly, Adam after his expulsion from Eden built a temple in the valley of Becca using as its cornerstone a black rock. When, much later, Abraham and his son Ishmael strayed into Becca, they found this rock and incorporated it in a square structure, the *Kaaba* (meaning square or cube). Abraham introduced the custom of circumambulating the *Kaaba* as an act of devotion, and the angel Gabriel providentially directed Abraham also to dig a hollow inside the sacred precinct for storing gifts and valuables. Soon the *Kaaba* attracted nomads who joined the descendants of Ishmael to worship there. Although the *Kaaba* was distinctive because no other site in Arabia could trace its origins back to Adam and Abraham, idolatry emerged, for the following reason. One of the tribes inhabiting Becca, the Chuza, wherever they traveled would take along a black rock as a reminder of the *Kaaba* and perform a ritual circumambulation on each night of their journey. Over time, they became indifferent whether they were worshipping the original or the copy, and of a time they were on a trade mission to Mesopotamia they asked their hosts to gift them a statue of a local deity, Hubal, which on their return they set up next to the *Kaaba*. The entry of Hubal into the precinct of the *Kaaba* set a precedent: other tribes henceforth brought statues of their own particular deities, and over time no other site in Arabia came to host so many faiths. Religious differences did not spark rivalries, and every tribe had free choice among deities; the Quraysh chose for their patron a deity named Hubal, the Thakif chose another, El-lat.

Becca valley, a landscape so forbidding nobody actually settled there, had as its single natural asset that attracted nomads the *Kaaba*. Roaming tribes shared access to the *Kaaba*, camping in the vicinity on whatever spot their camels could find grass; they would congregate during the day and at dusk repair to their herds and their tents.[10] That pattern changed when Kossai ibn Kalib, leader of the Quraysh, became guardian of the *Kaaba* and secured permanent control by the Quraysh by erecting homes surrounding the *Kaaba*. Becca valley, hitherto uninhabited, now had a city, Mecca, and the *Kaaba* was guarded by the Quraysh.[11]

The skill of the Quraysh at cutting advantageous deals came to be proverbial in Arabia. An Arab saying for someone who has suffered a great commercial loss, namely "losing more than Abu Gubchan," according to the Arab author Masudi, was inspired by Kossai, who acquired the right to guard the *Kaaba* from a certain Gubchan in exchange for a camel and a goatskin of wine.[12] Kossai's gain from trading with the hapless Gubchan was extraordinary, but he failed to extend his advantages, however, when he asked his fellow tribesmen to grant him a monopoly for selling ritual garments to pilgrims. That demand was rebuffed, as was Kossai's wish for a prerogative for his sons to succeed him. The Quraysh were proud of their deal-making skills; they alternately explained their name derived from a successful caravan leader, or from *tacarassha*, meaning "to gather trade goods for sale from every direction."[13]

Kossai's descendants branched into several clans, of which the most important were the Hashimites and Omayyads. Their relationship alternated between amity and rancor; the Omayya twice challenged the Hashimites to concede to them social precedence and both occasions led to the expulsion from Mecca of the head of the Omayya.

ARAB SOCIETY

Arabs built trade routes that spanned the globe but at home did not evolve a central political authority. The heterogeneous lifestyles of Arab tribes—some nomadic, some settled—were not easy to fit into a single state. However, the Arab way of life had little need for one. The desert and the sea protected them from foreign invasions and families and tribes managed their affairs without reference to a superior authority. The only purposes for which Arabs would congregate were for worship or for trade, and conventions were held in locations across Arabia where they came together to barter, settle pending negotiations, pay debts, arrange marriages, exchange hostages, settle reparations for crimes or raise any other issue requiring arbitration or advice. Large gatherings offered opportunities for performances by entertainers, storytellers and poets, and the best ones earned lucrative and prestigious awards. In Mecca, for example, prize-winning poems were affixed to the *Kaaba*. These conventions, evolving their individual spontaneous orders, fulfilled two needs, to trade or to pay homage to religious idols. (One such market was held at Ukaz and Muhammad during his early years of preaching Islam came forward there.) Durable state structures only emerged in agricultural areas or in ports, such as Yemen or Aden. Even without overarching institutions, Arabs shared a sense their values and character set them apart from foreigners.

Conventions afforded gains from trade all round. The celebration of religious rites offered pilgrims coincidental opportunities to trade goods, and locals made a living by supplying pilgrims with provisions and other necessaries. A virtuous cycle set in once communities became aware that good infrastructure facilitated pilgrim and commercial traffic and therefore was a good investment. Mecca's business model, a symbiosis of religion and commerce, was not unique. Other towns also developed a franchise as a religious as well as a commercial center, and the fate of one of these, Najran, held out a lesson in how conspicuous success could provoke animosity and envy, and showed the path to success was fraught with peril.

NAJRAN

Najran, located at the intersection of two trade routes, was a natural trade hub where the number of visitors swelled further when Najran's Christian community there built a church attracting pilgrims. Everyone in Najran was enriched by the increase in traffic, most of all local Christians, and eventually business in Najran came under Christian control. In principle, this caused no umbrage because Arabs tolerated any religious persuasion—unless religion happened to interfere with trade. That, however, was the case here, and proved Najran's undoing. King Dhu Nawwas in neighboring Yemen was vexed that trade flows were leaking away from his own realm and believed, with some justification, that Najran's Christian shrine enhanced the city's competitive advantage. Seeking to restore a level competitive field, he demanded on pain of force Najranis raze their church. Najran's merchants understood the implications that lay in store. The church was Najran's unique selling point; without it, pilgrim traffic would contract, trade would diminish, and Christians could hardly expect to retain control over whatever commercial activity would be left. Najranis rejected Dhu Nawwas's ultimatum but paid a high price. Dhu Nawwas marched on the city, torched the church, and exterminated most of the town's Christians. The Najran massacre took place half a century before Muhammad was born, around 520, and in Mecca, anxieties about how a flourishing business community might come to an end through religious intolerance were acute. The Koran allayed such fears by condemning the attack on Najran: "Cursed be the diggers of the trench, who lighted the consuming fire and sat around to watch the faithful being put to the torture. Nor did they torture them for any reason save that they believed in God" (Sura 85:3). Mecca was only one of several pilgrim destinations in Arabia, but unlike other shrines competing for pilgrim traffic, worship at the *Kaaba* did not give precedence to any single denomination, and this proved a catalyst for an influx of pilgrims that became increasingly great. The more diverse the agglomeration of pilgrims, the longer they tarried. By Muhammad's day, the pilgrim season lasted four months. This pilgrim population needed housing, food, and daily necessities; their Meccan hosts had to ensure pilgrims were adequately provisioned, maintain public order, and set rules for performing worship. Personal security was paramount; all pilgrims were enjoined to abstain from acts of violence within a certain periphery around the *Kaaba*. This safe haven, the *haram*, became a place pilgrims could display wares for sale, and the *haram* graduated into a market. Trade followed religion.

NOTES

1. Muir, *The Life of Mahomet*, Vol. 2, 124.
2. 1 Kings IX: 26–28, 2 Chronicles VIII: 17
3. Ibn Kathir, *The Life of the Prophet Muhammad*, Vol. 3, 355.
4. Waqidi, *The Life of Muhammad*, 15.
5. Genesis XXXVII:28; Ezechiel XXVII:21–24.
6. Pliny, *Natural History*, Book 6, Chapters 28 and 32.
7. Diodorus Siculus quoted in Muir, *The Life of Mahomet*, Vol. 1, 135.
8. Herodotus, *The Histories,* Book 3, chapter 8.
9. *The Chronicles of Mecca* were edited and translated by Ferdinand Wüstenfeld.
10. Wüstenfeld, *Die Chroniken der Stadt Mekka*, Vol. 4, 30.
11. Wüstenfeld, *Die Chroniken der Stadt Mekka*, Vol. 4, 30.

12. Macoudi, *Les prairies d'or*, Vol. 3, 118.
13. Wüstenfeld, *Die Chroniken der Stadt Mekka*, Vol. 4, 25.

Chapter Three

Family Matters

Worship at the *Kaaba* was the only activity of any consequence in Mecca, and codes of conduct set for the *haram* permeated all spheres of social life. Meeting the needs of Mecca's transient but recurring pilgrim population required investment in infrastructure and provisions, incurring costs borne by Mecca's most wealthy citizens who found ways to make their investment pay, such as through a rule whereby pilgrims circling the *Kaaba* had to don garments purchased in Mecca. Civic leaders managing the *Kaaba* tended to prosper, and competition for official roles was intense. The inhabitants of Becca valley, originally a loose association of tribes, with every annual pilgrimage cycle could see how the community's standard of living rose through promoting trust and trade, and they willingly submitted to the necessity for rules that made prosperity possible. Custody of the *Kaaba* therefore brought with it the authority to set informal rules of conduct, and there was little difference between the authority of the Quraysh to impose, as guardians of the *Kaaba*, rules of conduct on pilgrims and Meccans, from that of a formal government. Mecca under leadership of the Quraysh graduated into a commonwealth.

HASHIM IBN ABD MANAF

Hashim was so influential that from him his family took their name, Hashimites. A social reformer and visionary entrepreneur, Hashim was the first to impose in Mecca an income tax (reputedly "100 Greek ducats") to pay for food imports from Syria that were distributed to the indigent and to pilgrims, a first step toward transferring responsibility for poor relief from families to the community as a whole.[1] Hashim also reformed business practices. Theretofore, anyone in Mecca unable to pay their debt was expelled from the city and abandoned to perish in the desert; Hashim rebuked his compatriots "this *itifad* has nearly destroyed you" and terminated this ghastly custom.[2] Hashim also paired caravan entrepreneurs with paupers and required them to let the latter take a stake either as investors or staff. This arrangement benefited all sections of society: anyone without the means to furnish a camel now could earn a return on investment by joining a larger undertaking, while entrepreneurs achieved greater economies of scale by pooling capital and skills. Hashim also urged merchants to change their marketing. Instead of putting merchandise on display alongside well-traveled roads and waiting for potential customers to pass, merchants ought to venture forth and seek out large markets abroad.[3] To facilitate long-distance travel Hashim negotiated safe passage agreements with Bedouin tribes, the *ilaf*, who provided for caravans on their outward-bound passage through the desert to collect goods from Bedouins on consignment, sell them at their point of destination, and pay out profits on their way back. These agreements were sufficiently important to merit mention in the Koran, which lauds the *ilaf* that conferred on the Quraysh "protection in their summer and winter journeyings."[4] The term *ilaf* deserves remark. For Masudi, *ilaf* "meant security, assurance, and safe conduct."[5] Aloys Sprenger explained the term *ilaf* has Biblical antecedents: the Book of Genesis used the term to describe the process of bringing into being a community—and in the case of the Quraysh, their identity was constituted by trade.[6] Hashim and his brothers also concluded trade treaties with the Byzantine authorities and with the rulers of Abyssinia, Persia, and Yemen; Tabari recorded they were "the first to obtain for Quraysh guarantees of immunity which allowed them to travel far and wide from the *haram*."[7] The *ilaf* conferred gains on all parties involved; Bedouins gained access to export markets, and caravans were protected from ambush. As a result, Mecca's trade expanded from the confines of Mecca's *haram* into a supra-regional zone. Safe passage helped to ensure regular food supplies, reduce security risks, and increase caravanning turnover and profits. From Hashim's time on, a Meccan caravan would set out to Abyssinia and to Yemen in the winter and to Syrian markets in the summer. Hashim showed how the *haram* could grow into larger dimensions.[8] His initiatives—improving social security, introducing taxes, encouraging trade—in many respects foreshadowed those of Muhammad. Hashim was indefatigable to the last; he died on a caravanning journey to Gaza and was buried there. His legacy was remarkable; the Quraysh within three generations had risen from the position of one of several tribes inhabiting the valley of Becca into official representatives of Mecca.

ABD AL MUTALLIB

History seemed to repeat itself when Najran's fate threatened to be visited on Mecca's thriving economy. Abraha, Yemen's ruler, who had built a Christian church in Sana, was frustrated when it transpired this attraction did not divert pilgrim traffic from Mecca. Thus Abraha demanded Meccans raze the *Kaaba* and Meccans faced two unpalatable alternatives: either surrender to Abraha and give up Mecca's distinctive franchise, or refuse and risk destruction. The son of Hashim, Abd al Mutallib, counseled to stand firm and reject the ultimatum of Abraha who thereupon assembled a formidable military force and, riding on an elephant at its head, marched on Mecca. Fate, however, intervened to favor Mecca: an epidemic decimated Abraha's army and forced his retreat. Mecca's standing as a religious center now was greater than before, as was the standing of Hashimites who had guided the city through this crisis. Mecca, a city that was agnostic and tolerated a wide range of denominations, seemed to enjoy divine protection. According to Ibn Ishaq, "when Allah turned back the Abyssinians from Mecca, and inflicted upon them his vengeance, the Arabs admired Quraysh and said: 'they are the people of Allah.'"[9]

Mecca's defense and deliverance raised the city's unique aura throughout Arabia, an event of such moment it was noted even by the historian Procopius in distant Constantinople.[10] Abd al-Mutallib did well for himself; he had sufficient means to donate gold to gild the door to the *Kaaba*, and gold was woven into his burial garment.[11] Another beneficiary of Abraha's debacle was Abd al Mutallib's associate Affan ibn Abi al As, who laid the basis to his family's fortune by plundering the supplies left behind by Abraha's routed troops and whose son, Osman ibn Affan, was one of Muhammad's earliest converts and one day would become caliph. The Year of the Elephant, as the trauma and triumph was remembered, was the year claimed as the year of the birth of Muhammad. Mecca's business model—combining religious agnosticism with promotion of trade within the *haram* and with partners abroad—now was tried and tested. Kossai, Hashim, and Abd al Mutallib at each stage of Mecca's ascent had intervened to enhance the welfare of the city. Muhammad ibn Abdullah was known to everyone in Mecca as descendant of a dynasty that had managed Mecca's economic affairs for over a century and a half. There was another, more ominous legacy of that period, however, that persisted during Mohammad's lifetime and beyond. The Omayyads and the Hashimites, two branches of Kossai's descendants, still had not settled disputes over the right to supervise devotions rendered at the *Kaaba*.

Muhammad's father and uncles were well-connected sons of a wealthy civic leader who could expect to take their place among Mecca's social elite and look forward to rewarding careers. Muhammad's father Abdullah and his uncles—Abu Talib, Abu Lahab, and Al Abbas—all followed family tradition and set up as caravanning merchants. But social pedigree was no guarantee of business success and their career trajectories diverged widely: Al Abbas became one of Mecca's plutocrats; Abu Talib defaulted on his debts; Abdullah's career was cut short when in his mid-twenties he succumbed on a caravan journey. Muhammad grew up in a family where business fortune was parceled out unequally.

Life had started well for Muhammad's father, Abdullah; in his early twenties he started a family, bought a house in Mecca's most desirable neighborhood, and he and his wife Amina bint Wahb were looking forward to the birth of their first child. But Abdullah succumbed to a fatal illness when he was only twenty-five years old and he bequeathed to his pregnant widow five camels, a flock of goats, and a housekeeper—a respectable estate, considering Abdullah's brief career, but by no means enough to let his widow and son live in comfort. Muhammad would have to pay his way in life. Amina entrusted Muhammad to Bedouin foster parents, as was standard practice because infants were thought more likely to survive in desert climes than in unsanitary cities. Muhammad's toddler years were happy. Some fifty years later, Muhammad by then a feared and formidable warlord, Muslim warriors on one of their raids captured an aged Bedouin woman who remonstrated with her captors and rebuked their insolence—she insisted on being treated with respect because she, after all, was their leader's sister. Her incredulous captors were unaccustomed to such defiance and thought it prudent to check with Muhammad what to do. Muhammad was curious what drove the shrew to her claim and asked for her to be brought to him. Once admitted to Muhammad's presence, she pulled up her sleeve and showed him bite marks on her arm that were a vestige of one of Muhammad's childhood tantrums. Muhammad broke out in laughter, had his cloak spread out as a seat for his captive, and reunited with his foster sister spent the evening sharing childhood stories. Muhammad was fond of recalling his Bedouin years.

Muhammad at the age of four was returned to Amina but did not have much time to bond with his mother. When he was six, Amina died. His grandfather Abd al Mutallib then adopted his orphan grandson and was demonstrative how much he cared about him. During worship at the *Kaaba* all other family members were seated at a respectful distance from the family's patriarch, but Muhammad, on the other hand, was singled out to sit alongside his grandfather. One imagines the octogenarian grandfather regaling the sensitive boy with stories of his distinguished ancestry, going back as far as Abraham, and telling him how his forebears had defended and promoted Mecca's unique mission. A six-year-old orphan need not be very impressionable for such heritage to leave a deep impression. Abd al-Mutallib, before he died two years later, chose as Muhammad's guardian Abu Talib.

MUHAMMAD'S BUSINESS CAREER

Two phases of Muhammad's life are richly storied: the first is the period from birth until Abu Talib adopted him at the age of eight, and the second from when he began preaching Islam at the age of forty until his death at the age of sixty-three. The intervening three decades from the age of eight to the age of forty have received much less attention, and how little is known about Muhammad's early adult life is thrown into relief by the profuse records regarding the periods that went before and after. The sparse facts conventionally agreed upon for a recitation of the span of some thirty years are as follows: Muhammad as a youth eked out a living as a shepherd; at the age of twenty-five married a wealthy businesswoman, Khadija bint Khuwaylid; and around the age of forty found his vocation as Messenger of God.

Muhammad's biographies tend to focus on his personal and spiritual formation and his professional activities have received less attention. This prioritization is not surprising. Considering Muhammad's vocation was that of a prophet rather than that of an economic reformer, biographies tend to focus on his spiritual formation rather than on how Muhammad as an adult made a living, because the import of divine revelation overshadows all other aspects of Muhammad's life and thus only incidents that portend his future vocation merit scrutiny. According to this narrative, Muhammad's dedication to religion already shone through when as a young man he took a lead role when after a fire the *Kaaba* was reconstructed; in his thirties, yearning for religious inspiration led him to withdraw for extended periods from Mecca's bustle to solitary meditation in the surrounding hills; until, at the age of forty, the angel Gabriel conveyed to him his mission as Allah's Apostle. Following this narrative, one must infer that Muhammad emigrated to Medina at the age of fifty-two with professional experience consisting of shepherding and occasional support roles in caravan expeditions. Following this scenario, although Muhammad had no practical experience of any consequence, at the age of fifty-two he seamlessly assumed day-to-day managerial responsibilities ranging from framing constitutions, to negotiating diplomatic treaties, to introducing tax and commercial codes. How Muhammad could take on so wide a range of managerial responsibilities with such narrow professional experience is left unsaid; as tacit explanation must serve the transformative effect of divine inspiration.

Even accepting this explanation, however, questions remain how the adult Muhammad earned his living before he discovered his vocation. It is not intuitive, for example, why the wealthy businesswoman Khadija, who had many suitors, would have fixed on marrying a penurious, otherworldly, unambitious shepherd, and even if she did, how such a mismatched marriage held together for twenty-four years in what Muhammad always remembered as the happiest time of his life. Another incongruous fact stands out. Muhammad in his thirties every year absented himself for several weeks to meditate in solitude, leaving behind his work, his wife and six children. It is difficult to envisage his family making ends meet unless Muhammad had a good income. Allowing for the possibility that Muhammad might have pursued a career in commerce, however, such incongruities dissolve.

Such narrative alternative may be inferred from circumstantial evidence: accordingly, Muhammad at the age of eight soon after his adoption joined his uncle Abu Talib on a caravan, and when he was about twenty-five Abu Talib approached Khadija to suggest she invest in his nephew's first caravan. Abu Talib as Muhammad's guardian was responsible for preparing his charge for a career, and it is quite implausible he would have recommended Muhammad to Khadija without beforehand having seen to his nephew's professional training. It is even less plausible Khadija, a professional investor, would have consented to funding Muhammad's venture unless he had appropriate credentials. Another testimonial to Muhammad's involvement in commerce and to the wealth he earned from it is the Koran that says Muhammad was so conspicuously involved in commerce that his detractors cited his very immersion in trade to impugn his credibility. Accordingly, his opponents averred: "How is it that this apostle eats and walks about the market-squares? Why has no angel been sent down with him to give warning? Why has no treasure been given him, no garden to provide his sustenance?"[12] Prophets of old had either been wealthy (like King David) or tended flocks (like Isaiah). Muhammad, on the other hand, spent too much time in markets to be deemed to fit the traditional mold. Another passage in the Koran attests Muhammad considered his wealth a mark of divine favor: "Did He not find you poor and enrich you?"[13] Known facts—Muhammad already in childhood took part in a caravan, married into money, and was active in commerce—suggest his exposure to commerce was anything but superficial, and imply, moreover, he likely was a successful and well-versed entrepreneur. Constructing the storyline of Muhammad's early life in this way, patterns the actions he took to create a viable economy in Medina as an extension of professional experience gained in Mecca. Muhammad, who grew up without means of consequence but came from a distinguished family, through support by his future wife Khadija bint Khuwaylid was able to set up in business: her investment constituted a turning point in Muhammad's life.

MARRIAGE TO KHADIJA BINT KHUWAYLID

Muhammad was twenty-five years old when his guardian Abu Talib recommended him as a promising investment proposal to the venture capitalist Khadija bint Khuwaylid. Muhammad, looking back, said Khadija stepped in when "others denied me," so it is possible Muhammad at the time was locked in negotiations with other investors but did not agree on terms with them. Ibn Sad and Tabari, early historians, described the couple's negotiations in detail. Khadija offered Muhammad favorable profit-sharing terms ("more than she gave other men," according to Tabari) in a caravan heading to Syria. Accounts go to some length to emphasize how lucrative was this joint venture; Ibn Sad related Muhammad "sold goods on the market and bought others for her" and Khadija "sold these for twice the normal profit, so she doubled his reward."[14] Tabari confirmed Muhammad "brought Khadija her property, which she sold for twice the price or nearly so."[15] Ibn Sad and Tabari may have exaggerated Muhammad's salary and Khadija's profits (Muhammad's first commercial venture consisted of two camels). But the outlines of the business model as such are clear: Muhammad and Khadija engaged in a two-way import and export business.

Khadija was richer, older, and also better educated than her husband—Khadija, unlike Muhammad, could write. Their professional relationship grew into a personal one, and the couple soon married. Muhammad's wife was heiress to a substantial fortune—indeed Tabari and Ibn Sad claimed she was the wealthiest woman in Mecca, with relatives who were prosperous and lived in attractive properties. Her nephew owned a house facing the *Kaaba*, and one day the caliph Muawiyah would buy Khadija's property for 100,000 dirhams and pay the same price for her nephew's house. Round figures, one suspects, are placeholders for an approximation, but are there to project the properties were expensive. Khadija's nephew must have been a man of means, because he donated the proceeds from the sale of his house to charity.

Khadija managed her wealth personally; Tabari says Khadija "used to employ men to engage in trade with her property and gave them a share in the profits, for Quraysh were trading people."[16] "Trading people," equity investors such as Khadija, were critical to funding Mecca's caravan trade. Once married to Khadija, Muhammad had ready access to funds to expand his business; there are testimonials of further caravan journeys, but his principal occupation seems to have been managing a tannery together with a partner.[17] Muhammad's financial status was transformed through marriage to Khadija. Muhammad grew up with little money of his own, but after marriage took up residence close to the *Kaaba* in Mecca's most desirable neighborhood in a home that afforded a garden and was near to Muhammad's warehouse. Muhammad adopted two children in addition to the six he fathered with Khadija, managed a leather business, and set aside sufficient means to invest in Abu Sufyan's caravans. Muhammad led the life of a successful businessman and enjoyed the trappings of wealth—he competed in horse races, donned silk garments, and could afford spending money on perfume. The couple's children intermarried with Mecca's social elite; two daughters married two sons of Abu Lahab, and Khadija's son from a previous marriage married one of Abu Lahab's daughters. Muhammad and his family were doing well. The happy marriage of Khadija and Muhammad lasted twenty-four years; the couple had six children and adopted two more. But for Khadija, who set Muhammad up in business and then asked him to marry her, his business career may never have progressed. It must have been a dreadful blow to Muhammad when in 619 Khadija died.

CONFLICT WITH ABU SUFYAN

Muhammad was around the age of forty when he envisioned the angel Gabriel bestowing on him the task of preaching submission to Islam. He conveyed to Khadija what had passed after returning from solitary meditation, and for her there could have been no doubt Muhammad's vocation would change her life as much as it would change his: Khadija came from a family deeply immersed in Mecca's inseparable nexus of commerce, religion, and politics. Only recently had she witnessed how Othman ibn al Huwayrith, a member of her family, had come to a dismal end through an audacious coup to renew Mecca's religious life. The sequence of events leading to this ignominious outcome began when Othman had negotiated an agreement with Byzantine diplomats, whereby Meccans were offered trade concessions and military protection, in exchange for converting to Christianity, and, as a key clause of the pact, acknowledging Othman as monarch of Mecca. Under the terms of this agreement, Byzantines stood to gain political influence, Meccans commercial privileges, and Othman a throne. On Abu Sufyan's advice, however, Meccans rebuffed Othman's bid and the failed pretender fled to Syria, where he made a fatal mistake by persuading his Byzantine sponsors to imprison visiting Quraysh merchants as a show of force. This attempt at breaking Meccan resistance hardened opposition against the putative Byzantine puppet; assassins were sent out who killed Othman. Othman's bid to introduce Christianity in Mecca likely took place close to the time Muhammad experienced his first visions, and his fate would have been before Khadija's eyes when she learned of her husband's plans to preach a new creed.[18]

Khadija understood the consequences of Muhammad's vocation for his family were momentous and fraught with danger, but she was resolute, unwavering, and no doubt entered her mind Muhammad would succeed. Khadija became the first adherent to Islam, and thus a couple who had everything—wealth and social standing, successful careers, and children settled in good marriages—set out to risk all. Muhammad would never forget the debt he owed Khadija. His poignant attachment to her long after she died was plain even in public when after the Battle of Badr he encountered among his prisoners two family members, his uncle Al Abbas and his son-in-law. The contrast between their treatments is striking. From his uncle Al Abbas, Muhammad exacted a maximum ransom; but when his daughter Zaynab sent him as ransom for her husband an onyx necklace that had been her wedding gift from Khadija, Muhammad was overcome with emotion at the sight of the jewelry once worn by Khadija and returned his captive and the family heirloom to Zaynab.[19]

Muhammad and Khadija moved in circles "searching for a new religion, because the current was for nought."[20] A cousin of Khadija, a certain Waraka, converted to Christianity and may have translated sections of the gospel into Arabic. Support for Muhammad within his household was unquestioning and steadfast. His slave Zayd ibn Harithah, who previously had adopted Judaism, was one of his first converts, and when Muhammad offered him freedom and an option to return to his family, he declined it. A son of Abu Talib, Ali, was another early partisan of Islam. However, Muhammad long struggled to raise awareness of Islam outside his immediate family circle. Five years into his prophetic office, Muhammad may have gathered no more than fifty adherents, dismissed by Abu Sufyan as the "weak, poor, young boys, and women" rather than those who "have years and honour." However, this small group contained the first four caliphs who one day would rule the Islamic Empire.[21] Abu Sufyan and his peers might have felt they could afford to ignore Muhammad's activities as long as his following remained small and hence inconsequential, but once his congregation grew, potential adverse implications for Mecca's business model must have become apparent. Monotheism, were it to prevail in Mecca, constituted a threat to Mecca's multidenominational pilgrim traffic, and that implication was something the business community could not be expected to condone. At that point, Abu Sufyan had no reason to fear he might not thwart Muhammad's aspirations; the backers of Othman had been incomparably more influential than Muhammad's, and a creed that appealed only to the lower classes seemed a poor business proposition and bound to fade away.

Islam, however, gathered more and more adherents as time went on and tensions escalated. Eventually, Abu Sufyan sought to come to terms with Muhammad by proposing to buy him out: Abu Sufyan offered Islam would be tolerated in Mecca, provided Islam in return tolerated polytheism. This pragmatic suggestion was perfectly sensible from Abu Sufyan's point of view, because it offered Muhammad co-existence of his creed with those already established in Mecca; were he to accept these terms, business in Mecca would go on as before. Abu Sufyan even held out another inducement that the shrewd negotiator must have expected could not fail to secure an agreement, namely an offer to Muhammad of "so much wealth that he would become the richest man in Mecca."[22] (This offer further corroborates the inference that Muhammad was known to be well versed in commercial matters—Abu Sufyan would not have proffered money to someone who did not care for any.) These proposals, however, Muhammad refused; once conciliation failed, conflict was inevitable and Abu Sufyan now switched his approach to one of confrontation. All members of the Hashimite family were subjected to a commercial boycott, perhaps with the expectation that a ban blanketing all Hashimites, not only those who were Muslims, would induce Muhammad's family to silence their intransigent relative. Once more, however, Muhammad's enemies miscalculated. The boycott lasted three years, but Muhammad had the backing of Abu Talib, head of the Hashimite clan, and family solidarity with Muhammad did not break. That support was vital, as Muhammad often suffered abuse but never a physical attack. Other Muslims, on the other hand, who could not rely on influential relatives, such as the African slave Bilal ibn Rabah, for example, had to endure extreme torture and would have succumbed had not Abu Bakr bought out his owner (in all, Abu Bakr spent almost his entire capital, some 35,000 dirhams, on freeing slaves who converted to Islam).[23] The boycott, however, devastated the Hashimites' trade and income; Ibn Kathir recorded their "markets had been cut off; no food was allowed into Mecca for them, and all their business dealings were interrupted."[24] The standoff between Muhammad and Abu Sufyan ended after Abu Talib and Khadija died in short succession and Muhammad thereby lost his main backers. The new head of the Hashimite family, Abu Lahab, refused to rally behind Muhammad who now was utterly isolated. Facing defeat and anticipating an assassination, Muhammad under cover of darkness escaped to Medina, and at that moment had given up his possessions, his career, and his contacts.

NOTES

1. Wüstenfeld, *Die Chroniken der Stadt Mekka*, Vol. 4, 35.
2. Rubin, "The Ilaf of Quraysh," 180.
3. Wüstenfeld, *Die Chroniken der Stadt Mekka*, Vol. 4, 35.
4. Koran 106:1.
5. Macoudi, *Les prairies d'or*, Vol. 3, 121.
6. Sprenger, "Über die Bedeutung der edomitischen Wörter 'Alluf' in der Bibel und des arabischen Wortes 'Ylaf' im Koran."
7. Tabari, *The History of al-Tabari*, Vol. 6, 16.
8. Ibrahim, *Merchant Capital and Islam,* 41–43.
9. Ibn Ishaq, quoted in Rubin, "The Ilaf of Quraysh," 176.
10. Caetani, *Annali dell'Islam*, Vol. 1, 124.
11. Macoudi, *Les prairies d'or*, Vol. 3, 259.
12. Koran 25:7.
13. Koran 93:6.
14. Sprenger, *Das Leben und die Lehre des Mohammad,* Vol. 1, 184–85.
15. Tabari, *The History of al-Tabari*, Vol. 6, 48.
16. Tabari, *The History of al-Tabari*, Vol. 6, 47–48.
17. Caetani noted Arab historians recorded at least five long-distance journeys during Muhammad's early years and surmised Muhammad often attended markets nearby, such as Ukaz. Caetani, *Annali dell'Islam*, 1, §153.
18. Sprenger, *Das Leben und die Lehre des Mohammad*, Vol. 1, 91.
19. Waqidi, *The Life of Muhammad*, 66.
20. Wüstenfeld, *Die Chroniken der Stadt Mekka*, Vol. 4, 55.

21. Tabari, *The History of al-Tabari*, Vol. 8, 102.
22. Tabari, *The History of al-Tabari*, Vol. 6, 106.
23. Suyuti, *History of the Khalifahs*, 23–24.
24. Ibn Kathir, *The Life of the Prophet Muhammad*, Vol. 2, 27.

Chapter Four

A Mosque, a Market, and a War

Looking back, it is odd Muhammad seems to have left Mecca without any money, whereas Abu Bakr, who escaped with him, left town with 5,000 dirhams on his person.[1] No doubt Muhammad must have run down his savings during the three years of boycott, and given his last days in Mecca were fraught with tension (he was aware there was a contract on his head), perhaps he kept valuables in the *Kaaba*'s Treasury that he could not withdraw without a rousing suspicion. But Muhammad, notwithstanding his precarious financial position and fear for his life, was punctilious in settling liabilities: Ibn Kathir recorded that Muhammad escaped but "Ali ibn Abi Talib remained in Mecca for three days and nights until he had handed back the deposits made with the Messenger of God."[2] Muhammad's principal asset at that time consisted of his home, which was taken over by a cousin. (Muhammad did not demand restitution when he returned to Mecca, to the chagrin of other emigrants to Medina who had sold their homes to Abu Sufyan before leaving Mecca in what must have been forced sales since on return to Mecca they demanded restoration of their properties.[3] Muhammad, however, refused to intervene and to be drawn on the subject.)

Muhammad and all who followed him into exile were welcomed by Medina's population, which consisted of several independent Jewish communities. Muhammad's followers, the *muhajidun*, for the most part were critically reliant on their host community's hospitality and goodwill; Abu Bakr was one of the few in possession of money or valuables. Muhammad took on executive responsibilities and demonstrated his approach to leadership from the moment he arrived in Medina. Early relations between residents and newcomers were amicable, and Muhammad regulated relations with the *ansar*, as local supporters were called, through a Constitution of Medina. This new world was egalitarian of necessity; there was no prospect of survival without reciprocal support. A shapeless group of religious sectarians graduated into a community, the *umma*, with social relations defined by religion rather than by a family or tribe, and family loyalties began to give way to an ethos of solidarity between Muslims. The immediate priority pressing on Muhammad was to locate a place where his adherents could convene, and map a path toward earning a sustainable living.

Muhammad soon took steps to build a mosque, Islam's first. Abu Bakr paid ten gold dinars for a suitable building site, although there are some traditions that claimed the owners of the land refused to accept money for a property dedicated to worship. There was little money to spend on the structure and according to Baladhuri building materials were scarce: "By the Prophet's orders, bricks were prepared and used for building the mosque. Its foundations were laid with stones; its roof was covered with palm branches; and its columns were made of trunks of trees."[4]

Medina's mosque presented a quaint appearance but it afforded a full range of social services. At the mosque everyone could mingle by day, and the homeless (who passed the time sitting on a bench called a *sofa*) by night were offered food and shelter. The mosque was where issues of common concern were discussed, important announcements made, and court proceedings took place. Abu Sufyan returned from a visit to Muhammad to report he "had never seen a king among his subjects, like Muhammad among his companions."[5] Muhammad applied whatever discretionary spending that became available to enhance the appeal of the mosque—he spared no expense, for example, on liberal use of frankincense. The budget for Muhammad's own home, on the other hand, was modest. Muhammad never aspired to building a palace or to conduct official business in a dedicated government building. Muhammad's authority derived from leadership in the mosque, and through Muhammad's precedent, the mosque was made Islam's true seat of government.

The seating protocol in the mosque projected Muhammad's status as a leader. It had been customary in Arabia for leaders to be placed at eye level with their followers, and a story was told to show how jealous were Arabs of nuances of status. Accordingly, an Arab chieftain was chided for the implied presumption of trying to rise above his peers by sitting down on a stool and had to use his advanced age as an excuse—taking place on a chair was a sign of weakness rather than of superior rank. Muhammad, too, respected conventions and took his place on a leather rug in the midst of his adherents and would lean against the trunk of a palm tree. But he made subtle changes to seating protocol once success strengthened his position; first, he raised himself above the heads of his community by sitting on a tree trunk, and later, once he had become an aspirant to lead all of Arabia, he rose to an even higher level by installing a *minbar*, a chair reached by ascending three steps.

Medina's residents had supported Muhammad's aspiration to build a mosque, but he precipitated confrontation with them when he established a second hub of communal life, a market. Medina already had four markets and there was no ostensible need for a fifth. When Muhammad set up the first Islamic market, inside a tent, the chief of the Jewish community, Kab ibn al Ashraf, brought it down by cutting its ropes. This action enraged Muhammad who searched for a new site and selected a large open area sized such that a camel's saddle placed in the center was visible from the market's perimeter. It is not clear why Muhammad now opted for a venue with much larger capacity than a tent; one reason may have been that it would be impossible to interfere with an open-air market; alternatively, he may have brought forward plans originally envisaged for a later stage. The new market Muhammad inaugurated with words to the effect: "This is your market. Do not set up sections in it and do not impose taxes on it."[6] Muhammad stipulated his market be tax free—by inference the other markets were taxed, which may explain Kab ibn al Ashraf's opposition to a market where tax exemption would divert trade from existing markets. Muhammad also stipulated rules for conduct of trade. All trade had to take place in public view; when he caught sight of a tent pitched on the market, he torched it. The Prophet's injunctions his successors followed to the letter: Umar banned a smith who set up a furnace in the market; Ali did not let traders keep their stalls in place overnight—first arrivals of the morning could place their stall wherever they wished but by dusk had to take it down. Ali gave out the following rule: "For the Moslems, the market is similar to the place of worship: he who arrives first can hold his seat all day until he leaves it."[7] A large open area, unlike a tent, could accommodate caravans; indeed one of Muhammad's companions, Abd ar Rahman, on arrival in Medina had asked for directions to the market where he soon accumulated sufficient capital from trade to set up as a caravan merchant. Long-distance trade ventures soon issued from Medina. A prominent companion, Talha, embarked on a caravan mission to Syria two years into the community's life; Abd ar Rahman, within several years of settling in Medina, led caravans of 700 camels.

RAIDS AND RANSOMS

Muhammad shortly after arriving in Medina gave instructions to embark on an activity that would constitute the main source of income for his community: *ghazis*, raids on unsuspecting parties. Raids issued from Medina almost every month; Muhammad launched over sixty *ghazis*, personally leading at least twenty-six.[8] These raids began as hit-and-run ambushes but grew into a scale that finally throughout Arabia all opposition to Islam was crushed. Notwithstanding *ghazis* made Muslims notorious and loathsome to their neighbors, Muhammad was unapologetic and declared such raids were not merely dictated by the necessity of earning an income for a community facing destitution, but *jihad* was integral to the mission of promulgating Islam. The unbridled rapacity on display during campaigns directed against caravans, mines, and settlements jars with Muhammad's declared dedication to practicing piety, and Muhammad's lack of compunction against condoning banditry seemed to accord with Pliny's characterization of Arabs as a people equally suited to business and to brigandage. Pliny, however, may not have been conscious his ostensibly disparaging remark contained a deeper insight into the peculiar mix of amity and anarchy that in most of the Middle East permeated unsettled regions, where from time immemorial anyone who strayed outside the boundaries of his community was considered an outlaw who could be ambushed with impunity. Conventions that protected trade passing through Arabia no longer bound Muhammad, who had been forced out of Mecca and become an outcast from Mecca's trade community. Muhammad through launching *ghazis* served notice he would not be content with leading a renegade community in Medina surviving on Mecca's sufferance, and to Muhammad's adversaries in Mecca, who had first boycotted his business and then banned him, *ghazis* sent a message he would retaliate by disrupting the trade from which issued Mecca's standing and wealth: Muhammad through his raids declared a war on Mecca's trade.

Muhammad's *ghazis* as such were not exceptional in Arabia, where many chieftains derived income from raiding parties. Muhammad, however, succeeded on a larger scale than other chieftains through his flair for managing logistics, setting incentives, and conducting negotiations. Muhammad's planning was deliberate and circumspect: he protected against the risk of infiltration by spies by routinely spreading misinformation about the destination of raids, and on such occasions when he deputed leadership of a raid to a lieutenant, handed out sealed instructions to be opened only after departure from Medina. Muhammad set fiscal incentives to attract recruits. In Arabia, a raid's leader had a customary entitlement to booty of a quarter of the total; Muhammad, however, reduced his share to one fifth. Incentives had the desired effect; recruits streamed to his banner. At the Battle of Badr, which took place in 624, Muhammad commanded some 300 warriors; his attack force on Khaybar four years later numbered 1,500; and in 630 at the battle of Hunayn he commanded some 12,000. The deployment of cavalry was crucial to the effectiveness of Muhammad's fighting force, and between 626 and 630 the number of horses in Muhammad's cavalry increased from 10 to 300.[9] This build up also followed from judicious setting of fiscal incentives, because the profit share of warriors supplying a horse was three times the standard rate, a measure where the early Islamic jurist Abu Yusuf explained the economic rationale at work: "The reason for allowing two shares for a horse is to encourage the use of horses in God's causes, which use, however, entails more expenses."[10] Gains from raids increased exponentially: for example, a caravan raided in 624 at Buwat brought in 2,500 camels; and Muhammad's victory at Hunayn yielded 6,000 prisoners, 24,000 camels, 40,000 sheep and goats, and 4,000 ounces of silver. Raids yielded riches for warriors, but for Muhammad, the principal objective was to acquire assets to scale up operations, such as arms, horses, as well as gold and silver bullion. Muhammad raided a mine at Buhran, and on another occasion a caravan "bearing a large quantity of silver which was the greater part of their merchandise."[11] Another caravan ambushed near Uhud brought in silver coins and vessels valued at 100,000 dirhams.[12]

Muhammad was indifferent to material gains as such; an occasion when Muhammad had captured a large number of prisoners who were to be sold as slaves provided Waqidi with a contrast between the attitude of Muhammad with that of his companions. Osman ibn Affan and Abd al Rahman bought out half of Muhammad's share and then looked to make a profit from selling their captives to third parties, but Muhammad, on the other hand, after he had disposed of half of his captives, straightaway despatched the other half to Syria in exchange for weapons and horses.[13] Muhammad used booty as a source of investment to expand his sphere of operations.

The Battle of Badr brought Muhammad his first military victory over a Meccan armed force and on that occasion he took seventy prisoners. Deliberations in Muhammad's executive counsel about what to do with them revealed divergent approaches on how to advance the cause of Islam. One of Muhammad's senior advisers, Umar ibn Chattab, proposed summary execution of all prisoners on the grounds that, if released, they would plot revenge. (Umar's forecast would prove correct.) Muhammad, however, overruled Umar. To put his prisoners to death would have forfeited a lucrative commercial opportunity in the shape of ransoms charged for their release. Thus Muhammad overruled Umar, and faced Mecca's chief negotiator, Abu Sufyan, for the first time from a position of strength. Waqidi and Tabari gave accounts of the conduct of negotiations that evinced Muhammad's bargaining skills, because the progress of negotiations showed the balance of power between Muhammad and Abu Sufyan was changing.

Muhammad's first step was to set a high benchmark for financial demands, to avoid the mistake of underpricing ransoms. Thus he opened bargaining by choosing as his first candidate for release someone unlikely to balk at a high demand for ransom, and his choice fell on a prisoner who, he explained, had "an elegant son in Mecca who has money, and he will exceed his ransom." Muhammad demanded 4,000 dirhams for this and for every other prisoner. Of course, Muhammad must have been conscious that only wealthy prisoners could raise such sums, but to pitch a high reference price still left ample room for concessions later. Abu Sufyan, for his part, also was a shrewd negotiator. When Muhammad's demand was communicated to him, his reaction was to play for time to avoid prejudicing the benchmark for subsequent ransoms because otherwise, he pointed out, "Muhammad will see how much we desire 'our prisoners' and increase the ransom against us."[14] Abu Sufyan thus rejected Muhammad's opening offer and held out for improved terms. Muhammad, however, may have anticipated Abu Sufyan might have difficulty enforcing a common stance among families anxious for the lives of their captive relatives, and his intuition was vindicated when the prisoner's son broke ranks and left Mecca under cover of night to deliver the required sum. When Abu Sufyan discovered the young man had lost his nerve and left for Medina, he was furious—he rebuked the "young and opinionated boy" who had spoiled his negotiating tactic. Muhammad then tested Abu Sufyan again, issuing a demand for the release of Abu Sufyan's own son, which, however, Abu Sufyan brushed off with the gruff remark "they can keep him as long as they like."[15] Abu Sufyan was loath to be outfoxed and instead made a counteroffer: Abu Sufyan kidnapped a Muslim and offered his release in exchange for his son. Muhammad agreed to this barter transaction that saved Abu Sufyan from losing face. Muhammad, for his part, conducted ransom negotiations unaffected by family sentiments. Among Muhammad's captives was his uncle Al Abbas whose expectations of preferential treatment he summarily dismissed. Al Abbas, a wealthy man, had lost twenty ounces of gold that had been confiscated by raiders, and which, he argued, should be credited toward his ransom payment. But Al Abbas pleaded in vain; Muhammad pointed out loss of possessions did not count toward ransoms, and moreover, as it was known Al Abbas kept substantial amounts of gold at home in Mecca he could well afford to pay his ransom. In the end, Al Abbas paid ransoms for himself as well as for three others.[16] Muhammad now could afford to make concessions. Reduced ransoms and flexible payment terms were charged for other prisoners on a case-by-case basis; for example, prisoners were offered an option to buy back their freedom by giving tuition in writing in Medina. From a protracted negotiating process, Muhammad emerged with a reputation for generosity to captives because, as Waqidi put it, "the Prophet was kind to them."[17] That generosity Muhammad could easily afford—a typical ransom for a prisoner at Badr was some forty ounces of gold.[18]

The Battle of Badr was a stark demonstration for Mecca's ruling elite that Muhammad was in command of a formidable military force, and that Medina, located to the north of Mecca, was ideally located for intercepting caravans on their way to and from Gaza. This threat Meccans realized they could not afford to sit out, and there was no alternative to running the gauntlet, because "if we stay," it was argued during consultations in Mecca, "we eat up our capital."[19] A Meccan punitive expedition set out and vanquished Muhammad in the Battle of Uhud, but fell short of its ultimate objective of overrunning Medina. A brittle stalemate prevailed for several years; Muhammad alternately raided and then retreated, but over the course of several years he steadily consolidated his power base and successively evicted or eliminated neighbors and rivals in Medina. A new phase in Muhammad's campaigning began in 628 when Muhammad commanded an expeditionary force of some 1,500 warriors to march on Khaybar, a fertile agricultural area ringed by substantial fortifications, and there broke resistance after a successful siege and assault. The conquest of Khaybar (and of adjacent settlements in Fadak and Katiba) transformed Muhammad's power base and had the collateral consequence of making Muhammad the richest man in Arabia. The conquest of Khaybar also had ramifications for Muhammad's management of community finances. Theretofore, all of Muhammad's military exploits had been hit-and-run missions that yielded one-time windfalls distributed on the spot, and there were conventions for partitioning troves of movable assets. The disposal of occupied lands surrounding Khaybar, on the other hand, posed a new challenge, namely how to treat land and the inhabitants who worked it.

Precedents set by the partition of Khaybar had far-reaching import. Muhammad set aside as his personal entitlement one fifth of Khaybar and then designated eighteen beneficiaries to share the remaining four fifths. His own share Muhammad allocated to his wives and personal favorites, and in some cases—and this would give rise to legal disputes continuing for generations—Muhammad granted an endowment subject to certain conditions, such as using agricultural yields for poor relief. In effect, concessions were granted in trust for designated beneficiaries. Muhammad's precedents in Khaybar later were applied more widely to taxation of lands in conquered countries, and, as a secondary effect, to the creation of charitable endowments, called *waqfs*.

Muhammad's position by 628 had become unassailable, and Abu Sufyan was a pragmatist who recognized he needed to seek terms. If Mecca's business model would survive only if he made concessions regarding religious practices, Abu Sufyan would be open to proposals. Muhammad, for his part, was watchful for an opportunity to reach an agreement, and such occurred when in 628 Muhammad issued from Medina to lead a train of pilgrims to Mecca. Meccans, fearing a full-scale invasion, readied troops to defend the city and blocked Muhammad's progress when he reached the border of the *haram* at Hudaybiyyah. Muhammad acquiesced to this blockade, to the surprise of his adherents who anticipated this interruption were only a momentary lull until he would command them to attack and rout their enemies, and crafted an agreement that let Abu Sufyan save face but that conceded to Muhammad the right to enter Mecca, albeit unarmed and only after a delay of one year. Many of Muhammad's partisans would have preferred him to settle his feud through battle and felt their leader had been too conciliatory, but Muhammad took the long view—he had no need to fight for a prize that was his for the taking if only he were patient. Muhammad did not want to destroy his adversaries, he aimed to win them over, and by signaling he was not vindictive Muhammad allayed lurking fears Mecca's idolaters might endure the same ordeal of Najran's Christians. A year later, Muhammad entered Mecca in a peaceful takeover, the terms of which included a general amnesty to all converts to Islam (save for a small minority). Abu Sufyan, the very foe who once had hired assassins to kill Muhammad, was appointed Muhammad's deputy in Mecca, and Abu Sufyan's son Muawiyah as Muhammad's private secretary. The tradition of Hashimite and Omayyad power sharing had been revived, and the rivalry between Hashimites and Omayyads laid to rest, it seemed. The outbreak of peace was cause for celebration. Muhammad made his way to the *Kaaba* and destroyed the idolatrous images and figures. Polytheism was banished but certain rites and practices retained, such as ritual circling around the *Kaaba*. The end of polytheism also had ramifications for doing business in Mecca; within a year, it was decreed only Muslims could worship at the *Kaaba*, which implied non-Muslims no longer had admittance to the *haram* and thus coincidentally were excluded from any trade transacted there. Market entry had become a Muslim monopoly and to stay in business in Mecca, a merchant had to convert to Islam.

Muhammad in his early sixties began to show his age. His hair had turned gray and he walked with a stoop. A sudden and short terminal illness struck him down at the age of sixty-three; its onset was marked by severe headaches that forced Muhammad to take to bed, and he deteriorated within days to the point that his uncle Al Abbas after visiting him said he "recognised death in the Messenger of God's face." Muhammad's wife, Aisha, remembered Muhammad telling her he had "been given the choice between this world and that which is with God, and he has chosen the latter," and that at that moment she knew her husband would go no further. Muhammad's terminal illness lasted fifteen days. He passed away without leaving a will and appointing a successor, which seems out of character considering he had always planned ahead and made clear what he expected his followers to do. This failure to act has nourished suspicions of meddling by interested parties who wished to claim his position and his wealth.

NOTES

1. Suyuti, *History of the Khalifahs,* 23–24.
2. Ibn Kathir, *The Life of the Prophet Muhammad,* Vol. 2, 178.
3. Ibn Ishaq, *The Life of Muhammad*, 230.
4. Baladhuri, *The Origins of the Islamic State*, Vol. 1, 30.
5. Abulfeda, *The Life of Mohammed,* 119.
6. Kister, "The Market of the Prophet," 273.
7. Baladhuri, *The Origins of the Islamic State,* Vol. 1, 463.

8. According to Macoudi, estimates vary from thirty-five to eighty-eight; Macoudi *Prairies d'Or*, Vol. 4, 145.
9. Watt, *Muhammad at Medina*, 257.
10. Abu Yusuf, *Kitab al kharaj*, 52.
11. Ibn Kathir, *The Life of the Prophet Muhammad*, Vol. 3, 2.
12. Waqidi, *The Life of Muhammad*, 99.
13. Waqidi, *The Life of Muhammad,* 257.
14. Waqidi, *The Life of Muhammad,* 65.
15. Tabari, *The History of al-Tabari*, Vol. 7, 72.
16. Tabari, *The History of al-Tabari*, Vol. 7, 72.
17. Waqidi, *The Life of Muhammad,* 65.
18. Sprenger, *Das Leben und die Lehre des Mohammad*, Vol. 3, 138.
19. Waqidi, *The Life of Muhammad,* 98.

Chapter Five

Muhammad's Household Finances

A consideration of Muhammad's approach to economic policies would be incomplete if it did not take note of his own and his family's personal finances. Across a distance of nearly 1,500 years it is infeasible to make comparisons between income levels then and now, but it is possible, however, to advance a notion how Muhammad's income developed from the time when the Koran stated in Mecca he was "walking about the market-squares"; during his early years in Medina; and after conquering Khaybar in the final phase of his life. There are known facts and figures about Arab commerce that allow drawing inferences regarding Muhammad's income. Abu Sufyan had paid a compliment to Muhammad about his riches (which, one suspects, was more heartfelt than his profession of faith). According to Waqidi, Muhammad on a campaign "had plundered much silver; four thousand measures. The plunder was gathered in front of the Prophet. Abu Sufyan ibn Harb came, and before him was the silver. He said: 'O Messenger of God, you have become the most wealthy of the Quraysh!' The Messenger of God smiled."[1] Muhammad had every reason to smile. The Italian orientalist Leone Caetani confirmed Abu Sufyan was right: Muhammad by the end of his life was the richest Arab of his time. Caetani assessed Muhammad's income following the conquest of Khaybar and calculated his annual income came to 1,500,000 gold franks.[2]

Muhammad in his youth could not possibly have imagined ever to become so rich. Muhammad's father did not leave a large estate, and as a teenager he eked out a living as a shepherd. Muhammad's first opening to establish himself as an entrepreneur occurred when he embarked on his first caravan expedition, journeying with two camels and selling merchandise on both legs of his journey. One can derive a notion of Muhammad's income at the early stages of his business career from Aloys Sprenger's estimates of the revenues from selling a camel load of leather; accordingly, a camel load of leather goods was priced at 70 dinars; a dinar weighed 4.25 grams of gold; and profit margins were 100 percent.[3] Since the means of payment in Arab commerce of the time was in gold, accordingly, the profit earned per camel might have been five ounces of gold. Inferences how such figures translate into present-day conditions are spurious. But even allowing for drastic downward revisions, it is not implausible to infer profits from caravan trade were substantial. Adding as a further defensible assumption that Muhammad over time was likely to have increased his earnings, these figures militate against the assertion Muhammad's income during his years in Mecca always was inconsequential.

Later in his career, Muhammad together with a partner managed a warehouse in leather goods, but his business must have suffered when his adversaries imposed a three-year boycott on him. When Muhammad arrived in Medina, at any rate, he was destitute and his standard of living did not improve for years. Abu Horaira said, "a fire would not be kindled in any one of his houses for one or two months; when their subsistence would be on dates and water."[4] Just how much his standard of living had dropped is thrown into relief by a comparison between the banquet served at Muhammad's wedding with Khadija in Mecca, which included wine and rich servings of meat, with the dishes at his daughter Fatima's wedding to Ali in Medina, where wedding guests were served dates and olives.[5] Muhammad's home in Medina was made of unbaked brick with leather curtains for doors, did not contain valuable furniture, and he had no room of his own. His personal possessions were few, consisting mainly of diplomatic gifts, such as a crystal goblet sent from Egypt; among his personal effects, the sole conspicuous object was a signet ring. Muhammad mended his clothes and shoes and took his meals together with his family and his slaves. His favorite dishes were meat cooked with bread; dates soaked in milk; and honey. Muhammad even at the low point of his fortunes sent food from his table to the poor camping nearby at the mosque's entrance.

However, Muhammad never complained about his reduced circumstances and did not change his spending habits when his fortunes turned up. The sole exception seems to have been expenditure on his personal appearance, since he liberally spent money on perfume and on eye make-up. One suspects this mattered because Muhammad was mindful of how he appeared in public; that same motivation would explain why he spared no expense for buying frankincense for use in the mosque. Muhammad was tolerant of flamboyance in others—his close advisers donned shirts made of silk, and his wife Aisha was partial to wearing garments that were dyed in bright red. But in general, Muhammad frowned on material ostentation. The wives of Muhammad, unlike the wives of successful warriors who often were gifted jewelry, had to sell any jewelry that came their way and donate proceeds to charity. Excessive demands for financial assistance Muhammad would dismiss without ado. One of his adherents, Abu Hadrad, on one occasion asked Muhammad (by this time secure in his position as Medina's ruler) to contribute to his dowry payment, but when Muhammad asked what amount he had in mind and heard the sum came to 200 dirhams, exclaimed: "Goodness gracious, I swear by God, if you were just picking up the money from a valley floor, you couldn't have paid more. I swear, I don't have enough to help you."[6] This restrained, almost austere lifestyle irked his wives who could not help notice their standard of living was falling behind that of their neighbors. But Muhammad inclined to a demonstratively simple standard of living and rebuked them: "Stay in your homes and do not display your finery as women used to do in the days of the *jahiliyya*."[7]

Muhammad's finances were transformed after the conquest of Khaybar.[8] When Fadak and Katiba, communities neighboring Khaybar, opted to head off an assault and voluntarily submitted to Muhammad, his personal estate was enlarged further, because in the latter takeovers no military force had been required and so in these instances he was not bound to share booty. Muhammad's annual income from crops, consisting mainly of dates and grain, now was immense. Tenants were required to pay over 50 percent of their harvests, and Muhammad's personal share enabled him to provide for the nutritional needs of some 4,000 beneficiaries.[9] Caetani, in 1907, converted Muhammad's revenue into 1,500,000 gold franks. In today's environment, that figure would be a multiple of millions of dollars. Money as a means to improve his personal standard of living, however, meant little to Muhammad; his estate included seven properties in Medina bequeathed to him by a local admirer, Muqairiq, and according to Ibn Ishaq, Muhammad "took over his property and all the alms he distributed in Medina came from it."[10] However, following the conquest of Khaybar, Muhammad by any standard was a business magnate, and his family and friends must have been aware that whoever would inherit Muhammad's estate one day would be very rich, and very powerful.

FAMILY LIFE AND FINANCES

Muhammad at the time of his death was married to eleven wives, and Muhammad's family life opens to view aspects of the economic status of women in early Islam. Khadija, Muhammad's first wife, was a venture capitalist, but as such was not unique. Hind bin Utbah, the wife of Abu Sufyan, also set up as a merchant after she and her husband had divorced. Nor was Khadija the only female entrepreneur in Muhammad's family. The wife of his great-grandfather Hashim, Selma, also was a merchant. The couple had met when Hashim, passing through Medina on business, there noticed "in the crowd of vendors and purchasers a woman of distinctive skill and beauty."[11] Thus Hashim caught sight of his future wife Selma, trading through agents; she was a divorced woman with two sons from a previous marriage. Selma accepted Hashim's marriage proposal on condition she could continue her career and she moved back to Medina after Hashim died. There are noticeable parallels between the careers of Selma and Khadija: both were women of independent means, had been previously married, and continued their career after they married. One is tempted to suspect storytellers shaped Selma's biography to suggest Hashim's marriage portended Muhammad's marriage to Khadija.

Anecdotes abound about Muhammad's domestic life from the moment he had become a public figure. Muhammad and Khadija had six children; he was a supportive father who twice adopted sons: Ali ibn Abi Talib, who became an early loyalist and married his daughter Fatima, and Zayd ibn Harithah, a slave in his household. Muhammad let Zayd choose whether he wished to return to his natural parents, but when Zayd preferred to remain with Muhammad, he adopted him. Tiffs between Muhammad's wives seem to have exasperated him—such, at least, is the inference from his advice to his wife Safiya when she asked him to stop other wives from taunting her on account of her Jewish background, and he recommended she stand her ground with words to the effect that "Aaron is my father, Moses is my uncle, and Muhammad is my husband." But there also were rows between Aisha and Muhammad, such as when Aisha called Khadija a "toothless old woman," a jealous taunt from a teenage wife resenting her husband's affections for a mature rival. Muhammad rebuked Aisha for her outburst and told her how much Khadija's support had meant to him: "She believed in me when the people disbelieved, and trusted me when they distrusted. She shared her wealth with me when others denied me."[12] That exchange is revealing. Even Aisha, his favorite wife, did not provide the emotional companionship Muhammad had found in Khadija. Nor would this expectation have been realistic. Khadija was a mature, resolute and well-educated woman, with a career of her own. Aisha, on the other hand, had been betrothed to Muhammad when she was eight years old; she remembered Muhammad gifted her toys in her early years of marriage and could hardly expect to grow up to be an equal of a husband who was over fifty years old when they married. Neither Aisha nor any other of Muhammad's later spouses ever took Khadija's place in his affections. Aisha may have sensed Muhammad mourned the loss of emotional fulfillment he had found in his first marriage, and that must have frustrated her as much as it did him and all his other wives. Very late in life, Muhammad and his wife Mariam fathered a son and he was inconsolable when the toddler died before his second birthday. It seems Muhammad, in spite of an increasing number of doting wives, often felt profoundly lonely.

It deserves remark that while Muhammad's polygamy has always excited attention, it would have been even more surprising had he stayed monogamous. Polygamy, at the time, was the norm, and indeed Muhammad traced his family lineage to Abraham, who had fathered his sons Isaac with his wife Sara and Ishmael with his concubine Hagar. The number of wives tended to correlate with social status. (King Solomon, for example, was said to have had seven hundred wives and three hundred concubines.) Thus Muhammad's marriages to eleven wives were unusual but not unique; in fact, Muhammad's injunction restricting the number of spouses to four in some cases compelled new converts to Islam to divorce supernumerary spouses. Leaving Muhammad's high-handed disregard for marital decorum aside as a private matter, the aspect of his polygamy most relevant for a consideration of Muhammad's character as a manager is not the number of his wives, but his reasons for choosing them: sex alone does not explain all of Muhammad's marital choices.

In early Islam, politics was a family affair. Muhammad's union with Khadija had taught him how marrying well would advance his career, and that lesson was not lost on him. Muhammad's marriages helped him create a cluster of interrelated families that boosted his career and in due course provided the power elite of early Islam. His first two successors, Abu Bakr and Umar, were his fathers-in-law; his third and fourth successors, Osman and Ali, were his sons-in-law.[13] Muhammad's marriages often presaged political alliances and their political intent was transparent. During the delicate phase when Muhammad was looking to ease tensions with his Meccan adversaries Abu Sufyan and Al Abbas, Muhammad married Abu Sufyan's daughter Omm Habiba and Al Abbas's sister-in-law Maimuna. His fresh in-laws took the hint. When Abu Sufyan heard his long-standing adversary had become his relative through marriage, he quoted an Arab proverb "some camels are impossible to rein back," a compliment to the vigor of a man who refused to take no for an answer.[14]

Muhammad through legal injunctions improved the status of women overall. One example was his cap on the number of wives (previously, there was none); another is that he laid down property rights for widows (again, a first); and he prohibited forcing slaves into prostitution. A fundamental reform was his proscription of a custom that inflicted appalling grief on Arab parents, the infanticide of female babies. The caliph Umar, notorious for his grim self-denial, only once was seen shedding tears in public, namely when his baby daughter touched his beard while he buried her. That this anecdote should have been attributed to Umar shows how deep was the trauma this custom inflicted on young parents.

Arabian women, unlike women in Europe of the time, were entitled to personal property. Bridal money—a payment by a husband at marriage—was vested to a wife and handed over in case of divorce or on the husband's death. Muhammad's bridal payments give an insight into his and his wives' increasing prosperity. In the early years of his exile, Muhammad paid 10 ounces of gold when he married Juwayra, and 12½ ounces when he married Zaynab. He had become a rich man by the time he married Omm Habiba, and on that occasion, possibly with a view to impressing his future father-in-law Abu Sufyan, he paid 400 ounces of gold.

Women's right to property were not curtailed after Muhammad died. In fact, his widows received pensions that were higher than the salaries of the first caliphs. After Muhammad died, his widows engaged in property transactions and often made astute investments. Muhammad's home had been modest and it seems his wives would have wished for more spacious lodgings. Such is suggested by the fact that Muhammad's wife Omm Salma once seized the opportunity of his absence from Medina to add an extension to her room, which precipitated a row when Muhammad returned. "The most unprofitable thing that eats up the wealth of the Believer," he upbraided her, "is building." After Muhammad died, however, his widows were free to enlarge their constrained quarters and became active property managers. Hafsa paid Abu Bakr 40,000 dirhams for a house next to the mosque—one suspects she moved into larger accommodations. Omm Habiba did not stay in Medina; she moved to Damascus where her brother Muawiyah was the governor and thus in a position to offer her a more comfortable home. Muawiyah also acquired two apartments in Muhammad's home, those of Safiya and of Aisha, paying 180,000 dirhams for each (a comparison of the prices paid by Hafsa for a house and by Muawiyah for an apartment shows the property market was booming). Aisha also had more room after Sauda bequeathed her her own apartment, and she sold both apartments to Muawiyah on condition of continued residence there for life.[15] Aisha was conspicuously wealthy: her pension was higher than the salary of the caliph; sold her property but continued to use it; and additionally received from Muhammad's companion Talha a stipend of 10,000 dirhams. Safiya, another widow, also lived in comfortable circumstances; she left an estate of 100,000 dirhams.

NOTES

1. Waqidi, *The Life of Muhammad*, 463.
2. Caetani, *Annali dell'Islam*, Vol. 2, No. 1, 47.
3. Sprenger, *Das Leben und die Lehre des Mohammad,* Vol. 3, 95. This price is for Khorasan, and I am assuming a dinar weighed one mithqal (i.e., 4.25 grams).
4. Abulfeda, *The Life of Mohammed*, 155.
5. Weil, *Mohammed der Prophet,* 90.
6. Ibn Kathir, *The Life of the Prophet Muhammad*, Vol. 3, 303.
7. Koran 3:29.
8. Caetani, *Annali dell'Islam*, Vol. 2, No. 1, 38–47.
9. See Caetani, whose figures were reviewed by Altheim, *Finanzgeschichte der Spätantike*, 134.

10. Ishaq, *The Life of Muhammad*, 241.
11. Wüstenfeld, *Die Chroniken der Stadt Mekka*, Vol. 4, 35.
12. Ibn Kathir, *The Life of the Prophet Muhammad*, Vol. 2, 90.
13. Aisha was a daughter of Abu Bakr, Hafsa of Umar. Osman married Muhammad's daughters Rockaya and Omm Kulthum, Ali his daughter Fatima.
14. Tabari, *The History of al-Tabari*, Vol. 8, 110; Abulfeda, *The Life of Mohammed*, 124.
15. Samhudi, *Geschichte der Stadt Medina*, 66–68.

Chapter Six

Muhammad's Executive Office

Eight years after escaping an assassin's dagger, Muhammad returned to Mecca, welcomed by the very enemies who once had tried to kill him. Clearly, Muhammad had been a shrewd negotiator and astute military campaigner with an uncommon ability to look beyond current conditions to the long term and prepare for them. But to put into effect the unification of Arabs within a single state—a goal theretofore beyond the grasp of any pretender—Muhammad in addition to his personal capabilities needed an effective executive office.

Muhammad's congregation in Medina in the beginning did not call for a large administration and he managed his administration in its early stages along informal reporting lines. Muhammad every day conferred with his closest advisers about business arising; Abu Bakr, Umar and Ali all had their homes nearby. Members of the congregation could approach Muhammad directly and raise issues in plenary sessions at the mosque. Dedicated administrative support, however, was needed to handle correspondence with other tribes, and Muhammad at first had to resort to recruiting a secretary from outside his congregation because he could not find someone among his adherents capable of reading and writing. Muhammad's congregation had very low standards of literacy; the Islamic historian Baladhuri listed the names of seventeen men capable of writing at the time Muhammad settled in Medina, and he would not have deemed this number worth noting unless it illustrated a contrast with later conditions. Standards of literacy in Muhammad's own households in Mecca and in Medina, on the other hand, were exceptionally high: Khadija and his adopted son Ali could write; so could two of his wives, Hafsa and Omm Kulthum; Aisha could not write but knew how to read. Muhammad promoted literacy—prisoners of war could attain their release if they agreed to teach writing skills—and progress must have occurred quickly because the Koran recommended using scribes to witness business transactions ("When you contract a debt for a fixed period, put it in writing. Let a scribe write it down for you with fairness.")[1] Muhammad wished staff to acquire new skills; for example, he instructed his secretary Ziyad to speak and write Hebrew. Promotion was rapid for officials with demonstrable competencies. During the conquest of Iraq, Ziyad, although even then still "but a lad with curls," as Baladhuri pointed out "presided over the division of this spoil; and was paid two dirhams a day."[2] In all, Muhammad made use of ten different scribes over the course of ten years.

Muhammad throughout his career continuously widened the reach of his address and paid attention how it should be delivered; he crafted his public image and reputation with care and employed two full-time members of staff with responsibility for projecting messages to wider constituencies, Bilal ibn Rabah and Hassan ibn Thabit. Muhammad soon after arriving in Medina appointed Bilal to the office of a *muezzin* with responsibility for summoning the congregation to the mosque. But Bilal had additional responsibilities: he also acted as Muhammad's herald, head of protocol, and private secretary. When Muhammad on important occasions proceeded through Medina, Bilal would hold a canopy over him and convey into the mosque symbols of authority, a baton and a short lance; once inside the mosque, Bilal would stand guard while Muhammad delivered a sermon. When foreign dignitaries came to Medina on official visits, Bilal's ceremonial duties included presentation of gifts. Bilal's routine duties included running errands for Muhammad and settling his personal expenses.[3] (Muhammad paid Bilal well—he retired a rich man to Damascus where his grave was still tended in the nineteenth century.)

Muhammad from an early age was acutely aware how public opinion in Arabia was shaped by poets. As a young man he had attended market days at Ukaz and there competed against storytellers and poets for the attention of crowds. Delivery of public communication was a key plank of Muhammad's management approach and he courted poets who spoke well of him: to Tumathir, a female poet who lauded him, he paid compliments; whereas Asma, a poet who ridiculed him, he moved to have assassinated. Abu Sufyan shared Muhammad's sense of the influence poets had on shaping public opinion; he offered the poet Ascha one hundred camels, were he to suppress a poem extolling Muhammad.[4] Hassan ibn Thabit was a professional poet, whose brief was to write laudatory accounts of Muhammad's deeds for circulation across Arabia. Hassan also regaled tribal leaders on official visits to Medina; one delegation wavering whether to embrace Islam was persuaded by one such encomium to convert. Muhammad accorded Hassan great respect; Hassan married a sister of Mariam, mother of a son of Muhammad, and through that marriage, Muhammad and Hassan effectively became in-laws.

That Muhammad's vision for Islam's expansion from the very start reached beyond Arabia, later was claimed by Muslim rulers who found themselves masters of an expanse bounded by the borders of China and the Atlantic. As a key piece of evidence for this claim was adduced an address Muhammad issued to foreign heads of states demanding submission to Islam. But this claim has been deemed a transparent boast put into circulation to supply retroactive legitimacy for the Islamic Empire's conquests, because no such document was ever found. Weighing circumstantial evidence, however, the claim that Muhammad might have issued correspondence to foreign heads of state was not implausible. On the contrary, since a pattern of projecting messages to an ever-widening constituency had taken shape from the earliest phases of Muhammad's career, for Muhammad to address foreign heads of state would have been a logical extension of a long-term communication strategy.

There would have been present to Muhammad's mind a precedent from his own family in that Hashim, his great-grandfather, had signed trade agreements with foreign heads of state and thereby raised the prestige of the Quraysh; according to Tabari these agreements prompted Arabs to bestow on the Quraysh the title *al-mujabbirun*, "those who make mighty." For Hashim's lineal descendant Muhammad, issuing correspondence to foreign heads of state would have accorded with his bid to speak on behalf of all Arabs. Accordingly, Muhammad wrote in his capacity as Apostle of God to the rulers of Byzantium, Persia, Yemen, Abyssinia, and Egypt, and through this correspondence gave out key messages to constituencies within Arabia as well as beyond Arabia's borders. To Arabs, Muhammad's letters signaled Hashim's mantle now was borne by him; to the world outside Arabia, Muhammad let it be known that he, rather than any other authority, was representative of a wider community. Although Muhammad's demands were rejected, nonetheless he would have booked an important result: the leading powers of the world had taken note of Muhammad and what he stood for.

This begs the question of where and how correspondence was stored, since Muhammad did not build a town hall and his home did not contain space dedicated to official business. Participation in *ghazis* was voluntary and accurate logs had to be kept to pre-empt disputes over entitlements to booty. For exploits of great moment, such as the Battle of Badr, lists of veterans were kept for centuries. Plausibly, the mosque served as depository, given the precedent whereby in Mecca important documents as well as valuables were stored in the *Kaaba*'s precincts. Muhammad also had no need for a community treasury, because public and private revenue consisted mainly of booty distributed immediately after a raid. Such booty, even when it became too large to be distributed on the day of arrival, was kept in the open rather than stored out of sight in a dedicated strong room. Such was the practice even years after Muhammad had died; Muhammad's first successor,

Abu Bakr, stored incoming revenue in his own home and relied on a female assistant to weigh incoming tributes and without affording a guard for it; Umar on receipt of tribute from Persia remarked: "No roof except the sky shall cover it till I distribute it among the people."[5] But even without the need for a government treasury, prize monies over time swelled cash in circulation and with it arose a need to provide storage space for valuables.

NOTES

1. Koran 2:282.
2. Baladhuri, *The Origins of the Islamic State*, Vol. 2, 55.
3. Matthews, *Mishcat-ul-Masabih*, Vol. 2, 36.
4. Jacob, *Altarabisches Beduinenleben*, 49.
5. Abu Yusuf, *Kitab al kharaj*, 72.

Chapter Seven

Muhammadan Taxation

Ghazis swept riches to Medina, but riches did not reach every household. Raiding was rewarding but dangerous; survivors reaped rewards, while the risks of raids showed up in an increasing number of widows, orphans, and cripples. There also were some who lacked the ability to carve out a living and stayed as poor as they had been on arrival. Poor relief theretofore was a discretionary matter for families and tribes, and Muhammad practiced personal charity by habitually sharing food from his table with the indigent. However, to mitigate poverty more had to be done, and Mohammad and his successors put poor relief on a systematic footing through introducing taxes on agriculture, commerce, and mining. Step by step, Muhammad introduced a tax system with differential rates for Muslims and for religious minorities. The highest rate of taxation, however, Muhammad applied to himself.

TAXING MUSLIMS: *ZAKAT*

For the introduction of poor relief Muhammad could look to two policy precedents. His great-grandfather Hashim was the first in Mecca who had imposed on every Meccan a levy to support destitute pilgrims, and in Medina Muhammad had before his eyes poor relief as practiced by Medina's Jewish community, called *sadaka.* The levy imposed by Hashim applied to everyone in Mecca, while *sadaka*, on the other hand, was voluntary. The Islamic variant of poor relief, called *zakat*, combined elements of both approaches. *Zakat* was a flat tax; it was assessed at 2½ percent of a taxpayer's wealth (with the exception of 20 percent in the case of mining). Over thirty Koranic verses exhort Muslims to contribute *zakat* and to consider poor relief a supreme social virtue. Anecdotes illustrated Muhammad's closest advisers strove to set an example of civic solidarity and vied with one another to donate *zakat*. Thus Umar on one occasion placed in Muhammad's hands half of his savings and was disappointed when Muhammad told him that Abu Bakr earlier had donated his savings in full.[1] Such anecdotes, one suspects, may have been intended as veiled messages to rulers not to scrimp with welfare provision.

TAXING NON-MUSLIMS: *JIZA*

On non-Muslims was imposed a separate tax, *jiza*. Non-Muslims were not allowed to bear arms but were entitled to practice their religion and they and their property were afforded defense by Muslim authorities. As such, *jiza* was protection money and, in effect, a performance-related payment. Baladhuri recorded that Muslim forces in border regions reimbursed taxes when they were forced to retreat ahead of a Byzantine incursion.[2] Tax rates for *jiza* were progressive; a standard rate applied to peasants and artisans, double rate to middle incomes, and quadruple rate to high earners (such as doctors and merchants). Some groups were exempted from tax, namely women, children, the disabled, and clerics. Religious minorities could impose communal taxes at their discretion to fund upkeep of churches or administration of their judicial system. Non-Muslims comprised the vast majority of the population once Islam grew into an empire and through *jiza* became key contributors to government income.

TAXING TRIBES ACROSS ARABIA

Tribes in Arabia that converted to Islam became liable for *zakat*. When visiting tribal emissaries complained to Muhammad about their tax rates, he told them one day the benefits of paying taxes would be plain to see: overland travel in Arabia would have become safe even for women and besides, one day Muslims would come to possess the treasures of the Persian king and then they would look back on payments as a mere pittance. Arabs once combined in a single state, such were his visitors to infer, would have more money, much more money. Muhammad pressed forward with his fiscal policy, making use of entreaties and concessions, and collection of revenue became an important instrument of Muhammadan statecraft. But flexibility was called for because collecting taxes was a delicate task. Muhammad briefed his tax collector Muadz ibn Jabal, "Deal gently with the people and be not harsh. Scare them not, but rather cheer."[3] In Bahrain, *zakat* payments were not contentious as long as these were distributed entirely within the local community, but Bahrainis balked at paying *zakat* once payments were transferred to Medina. Indeed, after Muhammad's death, tax treaties were revoked in Bahrain, Oman, and elsewhere. Some tax collectors were killed, but others, such as Muadz, became exceedingly wealthy men. Tributary tribes retained autonomy in most matters, but the prerogative of finance inspectors to audit tribal accounts gave Muhammad a lever to dispense and withhold favors, and as such, through fiscal administration Muhammad achieved what had ever been beyond the reach of armies: the integration of a pan-Arabian state.

TAXING MUHAMMAD

Muhammad's personal taxes deserve remark because he paid a tax rate much higher than that which he imposed on everyone else. Muhammad's income was divided in fixed proportions between five different groups—of which his immediate family was only one. Thus, Muhammad claimed 20 percent of all booty but his effective tax rate was 80 percent (against a standard rate of *zakat* at 2½ percent). Of course, his extraordinary income let him bear that rate with ease. But Muhammad settled most of his properties on friends and family and gave over all of his income from property rents in Medina to welfare, and the disparity between Muhammad's comparatively frugal standard of living and what he might have been able to command for his and his family's personal needs shows Muhammad applied his egalitarian social philosophy to himself as he did to everyone else. Government finances, such as they were, were managed by Muhammad; he negotiated tax and trade treaties, and dispensed monies to support the poor and equip soldiers for *jihad.*

NOTES

1. Waqidi, *The Life of Muhammad*, 486.
2. Baladhuri, *The Origins of the Islamic State*, Vol. 1, 211.
3. Muir, *The Life of Mahomet*, Vol. 4, 222.

Chapter Eight

Succession

Muhammad left no instructions who should succeed him after he died and what should happen with his property. This omission is puzzling. Conceivably, however, he expected his circle of advisers to settle these issues because in Arabia leaders traditionally were not thought to have a right to appoint a successor, an issue decided by the community at large. Muhammad's silence under the circumstances thus may have accorded with conventions. Choosing Muhammad's successor was fraught, since he had ruled in his capacity as Apostle of God and only Mohammad's secular power could be passed on, whereas his prophetic office, on the other hand, had died with him. Two challenges were commingled in the issue of succession: who should be the new leader, and also on what basis would rest his authority. In the immediate aftermath of Muhammad's death there emerged precedents for establishing political legitimacy and the right to own property.

Planning succession to Muhammad was an issue that sparked contention during his final days. According to Abdullah al Abbas, a thirteen-year-old boy present at the time, Muhammad wanted to draft a will but was prevented by his wives Aisha and Hafsa, the daughters of Abu Bakr and Umar. Accordingly, Muhammad "asked for Ali, but Aisha said, 'I wish you had asked for Abu Bakr!' Hafsa said, 'I wish you had asked for Umar!'"[1] Al Abbas did not pass on how Muhammad, weakened by his illness, responded, but did recall that Muhammad on his deathbed issued three express instructions; Al Abbas said he remembered two of them but had forgotten the third.

Succession needed to be settled promptly, if the *umma* was to survive. Medina threatened to break up into two separate communities, because within hours of Muhammad's death, there were demands that Medina's communities, *muhajirun* and *ansar*, should each elect their own leader. Muhammad's close advisers also must have been alive to the prospect that many tributaries throughout Arabia would consider Muhammad's death terminated their alliance (and tax obligations). At the moment of Muhammad's passing, Ali, husband to Muhammad's daughter Fatima and father of Muhammad's grandchildren Hussayn and Hassan, would have seemed to be Muhammad's obvious successor. Indeed Ali seems to have taken it for granted succession would fall to him, but events proved him wrong.

The sequence of events that placed Abu Bakr in power followed from a minute change to protocol when Muhammad, after he became too weak to lead prayers, had asked Abu Bakr to take his place at the mosque. This transfer of authority was only momentary, but its consequences were lasting. For once Muhammad had ceded to Abu Bakr his place in the mosque, however briefly, no rival candidate for supreme authority could produce a more compelling endorsement. Immediately after Muhammad's passing, Abu Bakr and Umar made haste to intervene in discussions to whom leadership should fall; Umar carried the day by offering homage to Abu Bakr and by his example swayed the entire assembly to acquiesce to his election, and his intervention cut short wrangling over succession and pre-empted Muhammad's polity from unraveling. Abu Bakr's accession confronted Ali with a *fait accompli*, and he was not alone in being taken by surprise by this turn of events. Abu Sufyan in Mecca, ever mindful of social pedigree, archly remarked that one would not have expected a leader to emerge from one of the less prestigious Quraysh clans. To some, the manner of Abu Bakr's accession smacked of a coup.

The first task confronting Abu Bakr was to decide what should happen with Muhammad's estate, an issue as divisive as the transfer of political authority. Abu Bakr had to determine the status of Muhammad's property—specifically, whether it had been possessed by Muhammad personally or in his capacity as leader. In the first case, Muhammad's property would go to his closest relatives; in the second case, it would devolve on his successor. When Fatima presented Abu Bakr her claim to Muhammad's properties a day after her father died, Abu Bakr asked her for proof Muhammad actually intended to leave her these. Testimonials duly supplied, consisting of statements by her husband Ali and a female slave, Abu Bakr insisted he needed to call further witnesses. Next, Abu Bakr summoned Muhammad's widow Aisha to testify, who flatly contradicted Fatima by stating she remembered Muhammad said there had never been a prophet who owned property. The implication of Aisha's account was Muhammad had been only the nominal owner of his vast land holding, and therefore his community of adherents, rather than his family, were his true heir. Basing his ruling on Aisha's testimony, Abu Bakr rejected Fatima's claim.

Ali filed an appeal. He countered Aisha's reference to Biblical prophets and likewise adduced precedent from the Bible. Muhammad had been not only a prophet, said Ali, but also a ruler. The single Biblical prophet who was an apt comparison with Muhammad was King David, and he had passed his property and throne to his son Solomon. Biblical precedent, Ali averred, contradicted Aisha's reasoning, and he implied Muhammad's property should stay in the family. Ali's argumentation escalated the dispute, because had Abu Bakr conceded Ali stood in relation to Muhammad as King Solomon had stood to King David, then Ali after succeeding to Muhammad's property could file an ulterior claim, namely to Muhammad's position as ruler. Abu Bakr could hardly have granted Ali's claim to property without jeopardizing his own position as caliph: Ali's appeal failed.

To Fatima, this decision came as a shock. She suspected Abu Bakr of bias: Aisha, after all, was his daughter, and Aisha, for her part, was known to harbor grudges against Ali. Indeed the inconsistencies in Aisha's account were glaring. First, it was odd nobody stepped forward to corroborate Aisha's testimony. Further, Aisha although she claimed Muhammad possessed no property, took no steps to move out of her marital home. Altercations and ill will festered for generations. Umar modified Abu Bakr's judgment and released the portion stemming from Muqairiq's bequest to Ali. The Omayyads, after they vanquished Ali, again confiscated the property, and the Abbasids, after defeating the Omayyads, reinstated Ali's descendants. The long drawn out property saga ended in the late eighth century with final confiscation by the caliph Al Mansur.

Ali and Fatima thus had lost their claim to power and property within days of Muhammad's death. Fatima felt duped and never again spoke to Abu Bakr, and only after she died six months later did Ali pledge allegiance to him. In fairness to Abu Bakr, however, it should be noted he did not take personal advantage of succeeding to Muhammad's property; his lifestyle, in fact, was ascetic to the point he even milked his own goats. But recriminations and allegations over manipulation of Muhammad's succession have never gone away, and contentions over a ruler's right to rule remained unresolved and resurfaced at each transition of leadership.

Abu Bakr had overcome his first challenge, but still faced many more, of which the most formidable was to demonstrate he could hold together the polity brought into being by his predecessor. Muhammad in exile at first had led a small, low-income community, and he then proceeded to put in place a framework for a society that would get bigger and richer in the long run. Muhammad had been a de facto head of state, who crafted legislation, managed finance, and commanded an army. He bequeathed to his successors a realm that encompassed a mainly rural, sparsely populated region; non-Mulims there were in the minority. Muhammad's successors proceeded to scale Islamic institutions to suit the dimensions of an empire inhabited by a multitude of peoples, religions, and urban cultures as diverse as Damascus, Jerusalem, and Alexandria; non-Muslims there were in the majority. The expansion of Islam had been rapid during the last decade of Muhammad's life, but after he died, the growth trajectory steepened.

NOTE

1. Tabari, *The History of al-Tabari*, Vol. 9, 179.

Chapter Nine

Rise of the *Rashidun Caliphs*

The first four successors of Muhammad are known by their collective title, *rashidun caliphs*, the Righteous Caliphs. The first four successors, Al Fahkri wrote, had been so close to Muhammad their subjects were moved to feel even if the Prophet no longer was present in person, in them breathed his very spirit; indeed the *rashidun* "in all things seemed more a spiritual than a worldly authority."[1] The triumphs and travails of the *rashidun* provided countless anecdotes for literary classics, such as the *Arabian Nights* or the *Meadows of Gold*, and also served as case studies for jurists and economists from Abu Yusuf to Ibn Khaldun. In the remembering, the actions they took and the words they spoke may have been embroidered, but in the telling, these memories took on a glow of nostalgia for an era that built an empire. The actual events, however, that took place during their reign hardly were the material from which historical romance could be wrought. The *rashidun* oversaw huge territorial expansion and a spectacular economic boom, but their tenure was ridden with internal conflicts that were visceral and violent. Only the first of the *rashidun* died a natural death; his three successors succumbed to assassins (which term is Arabic). An estimate of the *rashidun* divides attention between the four individuals who shaped the office of caliph: Abu Bakr as Siddiq, Umar ibn Chattab, Osman ibn Affan, and Ali ibn Abi Talib. Each *rashidun* was shaped by his individual personal history, and contended with the challenges he faced differently. From the turmoil following the death of the Prophet emerged as his first successor Abu Bakr.

ABU BAKR AS SIDDIQ

Abu Bakr (ruled 632 to 634) backed Muhammad with his money and his life. In Mecca he had run down nearly all of his savings—35,000 out of 40,000 dirhams—to ransom slaves who wished to convert to Islam. He tied the fate of his family to Muhammad when he arranged for Muhammad, a widower after the death of Khadija, to marry his daughter Aisha, and he bound his own life to that of Muhammad when together they escaped from Mecca and hid in a cave from a posse of pursuers. Abu Bakr passed on the moment when the pursuers could be heard drawing near the mouth of the cave and he gasped under his breath to Muhammad two men on their own cowering in a cave had no hope of survival, but Muhammad had the presence of mind at that moment to whisper "no, Abu Bakr, in this cave we are three: you, I, and Allah." When after a time the pursuers turned their steps away and retreated to Mecca, Muhammad and Abu Bakr crawled out of their hideaway and set out for Medina where Abu Bakr, after a time, bid for a plot of land using what meager savings he had left, and on it was built the mosque.

Abu Bakr took his duties as caliph seriously. He retired from business to devote all his energies to his official duties; was content with a comparatively modest annual salary of 6,000 dirhams; did not enlarge his house; and personally visited families fallen on hard times to see how he could help. Abu Bakr had a gift of inspiring loyalty. During the critical days Abu Bakr and Muhammad spent in hiding after escaping from Mecca, members of his household slipped out in secret from Mecca to bring them food and water, risking their own lives when rewards beckoned to anyone betraying the whereabouts of the fugitives. However, there was another side to Abu Bakr's godfatherly character—he exacted unqualified compliance to his directives and was capable of merciless vengeance in persecuting any perceived lack of loyalty. Just how grave Abu Bakr would deem any lapse became apparent from his treatment of a certain tax collector, Malik ibn Nuwayra, who was on his way to Medina to deliver his tribe's tax payments when he heard the news of Muhammad's death and thereupon turned back and reimbursed his tribesmen's taxes. Malik ibn Nuwayra may have acted on impulse—the assumption that Muhammad's death voided tributary obligations was plausible—but had no notion what ferocious backlash his insubordination would unleash: Abu Bakr had Malik ibn Nuwayra put to death.

As if to emphasize taxes were non-negotiable, payment of *zakat* became mandatory rather than voluntary. Payments for the most part were made in kind; cattle owners, for example, would pay one suckling camel for 25 camels, one calf for 30 cows, and so on. (Calculation of tax dues had the collateral benefit of promoting one of the key advances of Arab mathematicians, calculating fractions.) Although tributary revenues flowing into the caliph's coffers during Abu Bakr's short reign were comparatively modest, some 200,000 dirhams, the trajectory was steep; Bahrain's taxes doubled from one year to the next.[2] Abu Bakr had been in office for two years when he died, and his humility set an exacting standard for any successor who would rule a society that was rapidly getting richer.

UMAR IBN CHATTAB

Umar was conscious many resented his rise to the caliphate (he ruled from 634 to 644). But for the advent of Islam, Umar could never have aspired to a comparable position—his father did not belong to Mecca's upper class and his mother had been an African slave. Many shared the sentiment of Abu Sufyan, scion of Mecca's aristocracy, who let it be known it grated on him to find someone from a lowly social background rank ahead of him. Ali empathized with Umar's concerns and advised him after his election: "If you want to reach the position of your friend, your predecessor, you should personally patch your shirt, reverse your robe, repair your sandals and boots, curtail your aspirations and eat moderately."[3]

Umar took the hint and agreed to a pay cut (his salary was 5,000 dirhams, Abu Bakr's was 6,000 dirhams). The need to placate critics became more urgent with every increase of assets passing into the caliph's possession. Al Fahkri related Umar once was noticed wearing a garment woven of cloth that had been part of a tributary payment, and a member of the community confronted Umar, saying a man of his height (Umar was a very tall man) could not have had such garment tailored without having appropriated more than was his due. The anecdote showed how sensitive Umar was to criticism—he felt obliged to have his son testify he had let his father have his own share.[4] Abu Yusuf related when Umar set his eyes on booty of "pearls and diamonds, gold and silver, no eye had seen before," he broke into tears because "God does not bestow this on people without planting among them enmity and hatred."[5] Umar warned his family that "the people look at you as birds look at flesh" and threatened any infraction they committed would prompt twice the punishment inflicted on anyone else. Umar was true to his words: a son convicted of drinking alcohol he flogged in public.

Umar sensed the swelling tide of tributes flowing into Medina would inspire avarice and acrimony. Indeed already then these were considerable; according to Abu Yusuf the state holding under Umar's reign included 4,000 horses.[6] Umar resisted every temptation for enrichment: "I have no greater right on your money," he assured his subjects, "than a guardian on the property of an orphan."[7] Umar's probity was exceptional; his food ration during a famine, for example, was the same as that of every other adult. Of a time Umar's wife Umm Kulthum was gifted jewels by the Byzantine emperor's wife, he insisted she hand same over to the treasury because gifts passing between households of heads of state were public property.

Umar imposed his standards on senior officials who were required to disclose their assets before taking up appointment and account for increases in their wealth while holding office. Officials even at the highest level of government were subjected to Umar's inquisitive audits. Thus Amr ibn al As, the conqueror of Egypt, was forced to sell a residence he had acquired there on the grounds he already owned a property in Medina and did not need a second home. Umar visited a swingeing humiliation on Khalid al Walid, the army's commander–in-chief, when he was found to have spent government money on personal entertainments: Umar fired him; Khalid died a poor man.

UMAR'S REFORMS

The Islamic Empire had taken shape in an instant. Muslim hit-and-run raids on Byzantine border settlements were followed by deeper incursions, then by full-scale invasions, and within a decade of Muhammad's death a vast area had come under Muslim permanent control. During Umar's tenure were conquered Iraq, Syria, Palestine, and Egypt. Military success produced elation but on Arab society it also put immense stress. Persian or Byzantine retaliation constituted potential external threats and insurrections posed internal security risks. The Muslim armed forces were overextended; Arabs were outnumbered by their subjects but withdrawal was not an option. The only other empire assembled at similar speed, that of Alexander the Great, had dissolved at the instant of his death. If the legacy of Muhammad were not to be as fleeting as that of Alexander, Umar knew, an empire could not be ruled through arms alone: he needed to win over the empire's diverse subjects, or at the very least, give them an incentive not to conspire. Arab conquests had evinced an uncommon capability for planning military strikes, but Arabs had scarce experience in managing administrative machinery. If the successors of Muhammad were to overcome the challenge that had defeated the successors of Alexander, Umar had to build an efficacious civil administration.

Umar introduced sweeping administrative reforms. Umar daily convened his executive committee that included representation from Medina's Muslim as well as non-Muslim communities; every member of the community could freely approach him during his daily visits to the mosque. But in an expanding empire, the agenda of this central executive lengthened, as did lines of communication. Consequently, Umar installed provincial administrations and appointed salaried governors with delegated authority for raising taxes and for the judiciary. Umar also reformed the penal system; punishment until then consisted only of flogging, but henceforth convictions could lead to prison sentences. Tax evasion was made an offense and treasury and policing functions often were combined; the governor's residence in Basra kept under lock and key cash as well as prisoners.

Umar had at his disposal a single source of administrative expertise, the civil servants who had previously administered the Persian and Byzantine Empires. Working through these, Umar devised three fiscal innovations of great moment: a land tax; a public treasury; and a government pension plan.

Byzantine practices inspired the land tax *kharaj*; from Persia likely came the government treasury, the *diwan*. The first two measures, a land tax and a treasury, evinced Umar's capacity to assimilate foreign expertise, but Umar's crowning achievement was an innovation without precedent prior to the advent of Islam: the world's first government pension plan.

KHARAJ

In conquered territories, owners of land retained possession of their farms and had to pay land taxes designated as *kharaj*. The Arab term *kharaj* was an adaptation of the Byzantine term for land taxes, *chrysargion*, a portmanteau for the Greek words for gold and silver (*chrysos* and *argos*). Gold was the currency base in former Byzantine regions, silver in Persian. For the first time, taxes were levied that were not derived from the Koran. There now existed two distinct tax liabilities on non-Muslims and landowners: the personal income tax *jiza* and the land tax *kharaj*. The distinction between the two in practice was often blurred and given the diversity of territories within the empire, regional variations were inevitable. But taxpayers discovered a tax loophole. Since *jiza* and *kharaj* were imposed only on non-believers, anyone who converted to Islam could apply for exemption. Tax authorities plugged this loophole with a new tax; converts instead of paying *kharaj* had to pay *ushr*, charged, to their chagrin, at comparable rates.

Umar needed to audit how much land was liable for tax. To that end, he established land registries, but since there was no Arabic precedent for land registries and staff shortages were pressing, Umar recruited Persian, Greek, and Coptic personnel who drew up registers in their native language. Non-Muslims of necessity were promoted to upper administrative echelons where they worked closely with Muslim rulers, and Islamic statecraft performed a significant shift when non-Muslims came to be drafted to senior official positions.

THE *DIWAN*

Umar was unprepared for the swelling flood of cash flowing into the government's coffers. Abu Hurairah was fond of relating the story how long it took Umar to find his bearings when he heard the tribute from Bahrain amounted to 500,000. Umar demanded Abu Hurairah repeat what he had said to make sure he had heard correctly, and it took some time, said Abu Hurairah, until Umar grasped the import of what he had told him, because Abu Hurairah had to break down the sum into portions, slowly enumerating them one by one: "100,000 and 100,000—and I counted to five."[8] It seems, Umar still performed calculations using his fingers, which would explain why coming to terms with such staggering amounts must have been a challenge.

Muslims came to control large expanses of land through their conquests of most of the Middle East and Egypt. In the past, spoils had consisted of movable goods and these were distributed and disposed of on the spot. Now that booty consisted of conquered land, this practice was obsolete. Umar was entitled to one fifth of incoming tribute and converted his share into a permanent trust, the *sawafi*, which by the end of his reign included some 40,000 heads of cattle; the annual income of the *sawafi*, according to Yahya ibn Adam, ranged between four and seven million dirhams.[9] This income, Umar felt, was property of the people, rather than his own, and he solicited advice from his counselors on how to use it. Umar rejected the option of letting soldiers take possession of individual parcels of land. He feared soldiers who settled into farming would lose their commitment to military service, and Muhammad had warned against weakening Islam's martial culture: "The stability of my congregation rests upon the hoofs of their horses and the point of their lances, so long as they do not work the land; whenever they do that they become like the rest of men."[10] But Umar also objected on the grounds of intergenerational and social fairness: "What about the future generations of Muslims who will find that all the lands with the tenants on them are already distributed, occupied and inherited? . . . And who will care for the children and widows?"[11]

Ali and Osman suggested that if soldiers should not own land direct, the revenue accruing from land taxes ought to be shared out. Al Mughirah suggested drawing up a log of every soldier's salary because, he said, that was how the Byzantines had managed their payrolls and that approach seemed to have worked well. Umar followed that recommendation and tasked Al Mughirah with drawing up accounts to track salaries for Muslim warriors billeted abroad. Umar put government accounts on a new footing through setting up a financial clearinghouse that became the *diwan*, a term originally signifying a file or ledger, but that came to refer to government offices and treasury more widely. Several sources claimed the term *diwan* originated in Persia where, according to Ibn Khaldun, a Persian king touring his administration's fiscal office was moved by the sight of so many scribbling officials to exclaim "*diwaneh*"—Persian for crazy.[12] (Joking about tax officials was a staple of Arab humor.)

Treasuries in provinces had delegated authority to set income and spending targets, and to transfer to Medina only the surplus.[13] Umar also introduced fiscal transfers between provinces: complaints had been received from Basra that agricultural yields in that region were lower than around Kufa with corresponding implications for government spending, and consequently a portion of Kufa's annual transfer to Medina therefore was directed to Basra. Scrutiny of provincial treasuries was strict. Treasuries were located close by mosques, so it was difficult to enter undetected. The treasury chest in some cities, such as Damascus, was placed inside the courtyard of the mosque —"raised on eight columns"—out of reach of burglars and constantly in sight of the congregation.[14]

GOVERNMENT PENSION PLAN

To introduce a third fiscal innovation, the world's first government pension plan, Umar carried out a census and used this information to set a financial allowance for every member of the community. Soldiers, veterans, civilians, women, and children—everyone henceforth received an annual pension, scaled by timing of conversion, or of contribution to the promotion of Islam, or social status. At the head of the income scale were the widows of Muhammad: his favorite wife Aisha drew 12,000 dirhams and every other wife 10,000 dirhams. The second highest category were war veterans: 4,000 dirhams for participants of the Battle of Badr; 2,000 dirhams for those of important battles in Iraq and Syria; and there were discretionary bonuses for bravery. The third category comprised the original and later converts and emigrants to Medina (3,000 dirhams and 2,000 dirhams, respectively). Everyone else received the standard pension of 1,500 dirhams. Umar also introduced a child allowance; on every baby were settled 10 dinars, increasing to 100 dinars after the baby had been weaned.

However beneficent a measure, a government pension had the effect of turning citizens into salaried dependents of the state which, some feared, might entail adverse consequences, because a government benefit system could conceivably weaken incentives to earn a living through personal effort. That was the very concern of the pragmatist Abu Sufyan, who warned Umar: "If you award pensions to the people, they will live off the *diwan* and neglect business."[15] Indeed Umar became aware how welfare recipients soon adjusted their behavior to increase income, when he discovered mothers to qualify for higher benefits weaned babies prematurely; he adjusted the child benefit accordingly.

BOOMTOWN MEDINA

Muhammad had helped many of his companions prosper. Abu Bakr, Umar, Osman, and Ali were awarded substantial land grants, and Muhammad granted Az Zobayr, another close relation, as much unsettled land around Medina as he could cover on horseback in a day.[16] Az Zobayr made his fortune from investing in properties and caravans, and he became a leading business magnate when he spotted a business opportunity in Medina's rapidly swelling flood of booty: he began accepting deposits from fellow citizens and invested them in caravan ventures, and bequeathed to his son Abdallah az Zobayr one of Medina's largest estates and a social position from which he would mount a challenge for the caliphate.

Commercial euphoria infected all layers of society. The arrival of a caravan in Medina was an event of such moment that even Muhammad could not stop his congregation from precipitately leaving the mosque as they flocked to witness its entrance to the city (and, presumably, strike bargains). So pronounced was this urge that drew them away from their devotions that a stern rebuke was issued by the Koran: "Yet no sooner do they see some commerce or merriment afoot than they flock eagerly to it, leaving you standing all alone. Say: 'That which God has in store is far better than any merriment or any commerce. God is the Most Munificent Giver.'"[17]

Az Zobayr may have made more money than anyone else, but others were not far behind. Abd ar Rahman on arrival in Medina asked for the way to the market, there struck his first bargains, and soon had earned enough money to establish his own household. Abd ar Rahman, according to Ahmad ibn Hanbal, had a reputation for finding money under every rock he turned over.[18] Masudi in *The Meadows of Gold* relished enumerating the inventory of estates left by the magnates of Medina: Abd ar Rahman's estate consisted of 1,000 camels, 3,000 sheep, and 100 horses, and each of his four widows inherited 100,000 dinars.[19] Talha and Osman each left 30 million dirhams.[20] Osman in addition owned seven properties and 1,000 camels.[21] The list of possessions—slaves and houses, cash and cattle—in many other instances could go on and on. Rounded numbers imply, clearly, that figures are estimates. But to warrant such enthusiastic attention, in any event these estates must have been very big.

Bounty from conquests indeed was staggering. The raid of the Persian royal palace in Ctesiphon alone yielded 12,000 dirhams for each of the 60,000 Muslim soldiers. Umar sold off a cache of jewels captured in Hamadan and raised 4,000,000 dirhams, which irrespective of the accuracy of that figure, shows Medina's consumers commanded the spending power to buy out a Persian royal treasure.[22] Even discounting exaggerations, rewards must have been extraordinary, and they boosted consumer spending as they trickled down through all layers of society. A flood of money turned Medina into a boomtown and property prices exploded. Az Zobayr was said to have bought a plot of land for 17,000 dirhams and sold it for 1.7 million dirhams. Most likely this particular figure was claimed for rhetorical effect (or was a scribe's slip of the pen) but it brings across mark-ups were substantial. Hassan ibn Thabit sold a property to Muawiyah, and when his friends wondered why he parted from what must have been an attractive possession, he countered: "Why should I not trade a bushel of dates for a bushel of dirhams?"[23] Muawiyah acquired prestige properties and upgraded them, using burnt bricks and plaster to present a more appealing appearance. Imported marble brightened the drab facades of Mecca and Medina and mosaics were afforded for interiors. Osman's residence was made of stone and cement with doors of teak and cypress;[24] Talha, another magnate, for his Medina residence used bricks, teak, and stucco. Az Zobayr owned homes in Kufa, Fustat, and Alexandria, and in Basra built a residence that was large enough later to serve as a hotel for "merchants, bankers, and traders from Bahrain and other countries."[25]

To anyone with a flair for commerce, the swelling flood of money circulating through society offered ample opportunities to thrive, but inevitably, some benefited more than others, in fact, much more, and in Medina's boom a sense of camaraderie bred in Islam's early years of shared hardships fell away. A new plutocrat class flaunted their wealth, and changed spending patterns affected lifestyles and attitudes.

Islam had never proscribed luxury, and luxury goods—gold, silver, and silk—had already been available in Muhammad's day. Muhammad's sword had a silver knob on its handle and silver covered the lower half of its sheath. There were many who already in Muhammad's day owned jewelry; of a time Muhammad asked for voluntary donations, the women of Medina contributed "bracelets, bangles, anklets, earrings, and rings."[26] Moreover, standards of workmanship already then were high; prosthetic devices for injured warriors on occasion were wrought of gold.[27] But luxury goods, such as there were, were displayed in moderation. Muhammad, who enjoyed wearing silk when he lived in Mecca, was never again seen wearing silk in Medina, and his companions who liked to wear silk had to find excuses when he upbraided them for such indulgence (Abd ar Rahman came up with the far-fetched pretext he needed to wear silk shirts because they did not scratch, which gave him an edge in combat—one can see his reputation for bargaining skills was well deserved.) The contrast was stark between Muhammad's home, built with unburnt brick and using leather curtains for doors, and the opulent residences of Medina's nouveaux riches.

Since Muhammad had died, Medina's way of life had changed beyond recognition. The elite enjoyed a life of ease, and from that charmed circle of plutocrats riches trickled down to all layers of society. The government pension scheme and *zakat* ensured financial security for everyone, cushioned vulnerable sections of society, and boosted consumer spending. According to Samhudi, the disposable income spent on gold and silver in Medina at the time gave employment to three hundred goldsmiths. Osman had braces for his teeth made of gold wire; silver was used to make tableware; and gold and silver to embellish warriors' cuirasses. An erstwhile refugee camp had become a boomtown. The temperate ways of Muhammad's era were made to seem parochial by comparison, and there was mounting uneasiness over the direction Islam was taking. The true spirit of Islam, such was averred, was a spirit that placed submission to Allah ahead of material gratification, and conspicuous consumption alienated sections of society who found the ostentatious display of luxury goods and finery increasingly repugnant. A society that had grown rich began to debate how to deal with wealth—debates that, ultimately, escalated to civil war.

NOTES

1. Al Fahkri, *On the Systems of Government and the Moslem Dynasties*, 25.
2. Ibn Sad, cited in Sprenger, *Das Leben und die Lehre des Mohammad*, Vol. 1, 409–10; Abu Yusuf, *Kitab al kharaj*, 68.
3. Abu Yusuf, *Kitab al kharaj*, 48.
4. Al Fahkri, *On the Systems of Government and the Moslem Dynasties*, 25.
5. Abu Yusuf, *Kitab al kharaj*, 72.
6. Abu Yusuf, *Kitab al kharaj*, 73.
7. Suyuti, *History of the Khalifahs*, 139.
8. Baladhuri, *The Origins of the Islamic State*, Vol. 2, 246.
9. Kister, "Land Property and Jihad," 40.
10. Wellhausen, *The Arab Kingdom and Its Fall*, 30.
11. Abu Yusuf, *Kitab al kharaj*, 79.
12. Ibn Khaldun, *Muqaddimah*, Vol. 2, 20, and Vol. 2, 407.
13. Baladhuri, *The Origins of the Islamic State*, Vol. 2, 240–41.
14. Quoted in Le Strange, *Palestine under the Moslems*, 227.
15. Baladhuri, *The Origins of the Islamic State*, Vol. 2, 251 (wording modernized).
16. Wüstenfeld, *Die Familie el-Zubeir*, 30.
17. Koran 62:11.
18. Waqidi, *The Life of Muhammad*, 257.
19. Muir, *The Life of Mahomet*, Vol. 2, 273.
20. Sprenger, *Das Leben und die Lehre des Mohammad*, Vol. 1, 422.
21. Masudi, *The Meadows of Gold*, Vol. 4, 253.
22. Muir, *The Caliphate*, 174–75.
23. Samhudi, *Geschichte der Stadt Medina*, 148.
24. Macoudi, *Les prairies d'or*, Vol. 3, 253.
25. Macoudi, *Les prairies d'or*, Vol. 3, 253–54.
26. Waqidi, *The Life of Muhammad*, 486.
27. Tirmidhi, *Jami*, Vol. 3, 484 (Hadith no. 1770).

Chapter Ten

Decline of the *Rashidun Caliphs*

Masudi, in *The Meadows of Gold*, related many wondered how it could be Umar had had at his disposal such immense wealth when his predecessor had had so little—surely Allah had bestowed this wealth to test Umar—and by common consent Umar had passed Allah's challenge. Masudi's anecdote contained a subtext: wrapped into praise for Umar was the implied rebuke to successors who failed to emulate Umar's probity. The first two caliphs, Abu Bakr, who had struggled to protect cash flows, and Umar, who had contended with channeling a flood of riches, bequeathed an embarrassment of riches. However, the caliphates of their two successors, Osman ibn Affan and Ali ibn Abi Talib, were marred by fractious dissent because social consensus unraveled. The election of Osman ibn Affan (who ruled from 644 to 656) passed power into the hands of plutocrats. Osman ibn Affan had grown up with privileged family connections, unlike the first two caliphs who had come from families that prior to the advent of Islam could never have aspired to prominence. Osman's father, Affan, had been one of Abd al Mutallib's advisers during negotiations to avert Abraha's attack on the *Kaaba* in the Year of the Elephant and was said to have made his fortune when he plundered the spoils left behind by Abraha's retreating army.

Osman was an astute businessman known to return from a successful day of trading to boast he "made a profit of a dinar for a dinar" (doubling one's stake was a colloquial expression to say as much as "having done well").[1] He added to the family fortune by investing in caravans and for one of Muhammad's last raids "spent a huge sum, more than anyone had ever done," which according to Tabari was "enough to equip a third of the army."[2] Osman lived in a grand manner already before he came to office, conducted government policy as if he were managing a family firm, and was indifferent to the indignation his ostentation provoked. Whereas Umar had kept separate accounts for personal and official business, Osman, on the other hand, blurred the demarcation lines between private and official accounts because, he argued, the caliph was the incarnation of the government of Islam and accounting formalities did not bind him. Umar had been respected because he was tough but fair; Osman, on the other hand, was reviled for his abuse of power and nepotism.

INVESTING IN INFRASTRUCTURE

Medina was the richest city in Arabia, but paradoxically, was at risk of famine whenever crops were poor. A barren environment and lack of infrastructure combined to exacerbate the impact of droughts and epidemics. Medina's sanitary standards were inadequate; the city's population was growing rapidly, domestic lavatories were a Byzantine innovation that had yet to reach Medina, and public hygiene in the empire's rapidly expanding capital must have been abysmal. The need for improved infrastructure was acute. Umar built a canal connecting the Nile to the Red Sea and port facilities on the Arab coast, and in this way facilitated import of grain from Egypt. He also secured the supply of fresh water to Basra through a nine-mile canal connecting the city to the river Tigris. Osman improved roads and wells on the Basra/Mecca route and recruited guards to police overland travel safety. The role of government expanded, and a new driver of economic growth, central government, step by step began to overlay the Arabic tradition of self-reliance with minimal oversight by public authorities.

Umar flanked government spending on infrastructure with measures to promote private investment in agriculture. Land grants were awarded to anyone prepared to develop uncultivated land, which coincidentally modified Muhammad's ban on ownership of land by Muslims. The new class of property magnates invested in upgrading the productivity of their estate and hired foreign experts to advise on raising agricultural yields. Osman and Talha invested in irrigation projects and land reclamation around Medina; Muawiyah recruited a Greek estate manager to look after his holdings in and around Medina and there deployed 3,000 slaves on irrigation projects. But many magnates by and by sold their estates in Arabia and reinvested in properties in Syria and Iraq; those who chose to consolidate their largest landholdings in Arabia, Ali and Az Zobayr, were to become inveterate adversaries of the Omayyads.

Public spending also was channeled into upgrading mosques. Umar had enlarged the mosque in Medina, and Osman replaced the original columns in the mosque, cut from tree trunks, with new ones of stone, and he also refurbished the *Kaaba*. Muawiyah bought up properties in Mecca, including the home of Khadija that he converted into a mosque. But these gestures failed to silence critics who doubted Osman's true motives; in fact, his lavish improvements were the very reason he alienated his critics further. Muhammad's home had been demolished in the process of enlarging the mosque, which did little to win over Osman's detractors who suspected he wanted to prevent Muslims from drawing unfavorable comparisons between his own opulent residence and the modest abode that had been sufficient for Muhammad. Osman's fundamental flaw was not that he made mistakes, but worse: he did not seem to care. The *Arabian Nights* gave a candid assessment of Osman's managerial ethics (and by implication of any other ruler acting like him):

> When the tax money was placed before Osman his son came and took a dirham from it. Ziyad burst into tears and Osman asked him why. "I brought the tax money to Umar ibn al Chattab," he said, "and his son took a dirham. His father ordered that it be snatched from his hand, but when your son does the same, I don't see anyone saying anything or taking it away from him." "And where can you find another Umar?" asked Osman.[3]

There were many examples of Osman's flagrant conflicts of interest: he provoked malcontents when he granted state lands in Syria to Muawiyah; ceded the state's claim on lands conquered in North Africa to his personal favorite al Hakam; and he inflamed public opinion when he appropriated to his personal estate the Islamic Empire's prize booty, the Persian emperor's personal treasury.

Senior officials found it increasingly difficult to work for a leader who flouted procedures. The chief of the Medina Treasury, Abdullah ibn Arqam, spoke out against making payments from the public treasury to Osman's personal favorites, and when Osman scolded him for speaking out, Abdullah retorted he considered himself a servant of the people rather than of the caliph, handed in his resignation, and snubbed his master by refusing to return the keys to the treasury to Osman and instead took them to the mosque where he hung them in public view from the *minbar*. The regime's excessive extravagance made even Medina's plutocrats feel uncomfortable. When Osman bought one of Talha's properties for 700,000 dirhams and paid in ready cash, Talha was heard to say no man should have that much money in hand and distributed the proceeds in alms. Osman's support even among the elite was ebbing away; a signal that advertised ripening discontent was the frank dissent of Abu Dharr.

ABU DHARR

Financial integrity to Muhammad had been a religious obligation. He refused to attend funerals of Muslims who had neglected settling their debts before they died unless it could be shown the deceased had been insolvent, in which case Muhammad personally took on their liabilities. Indeed one of the last actions Muhammad undertook before his own demise was to settle an outstanding debt to pre-empt Allah's wrath in the afterlife. His successor Abu Bakr, from a wish to exclude even the slightest suspicion of illicit enrichment, left instructions before he died to sell his property to repay the salary he had drawn during his two years as caliph. That same sentiment that moved Abu Bakr to eschew personal enrichment for fear of incurring Allah's wrath shone through in verses he wrote with death at his elbow:

> You now own flocks but must yield them to an heir
> In time your spoils will slip from your grasp
> Wherever you go you arrive whence you came
> But once from the path that ends when you expire.[4]

Umar's rigorous sense of duty inspired many stories in the *Arabian Nights* that issued a veiled rebuke to later caliphs who abused their position to reap immense personal gains. The *Arabian Nights* have Umar on his deathbed telling his sons: "Your father has two choices—either that you should be rich and he enter hellfire, or that you should be poor and he enter Paradise. This latter matters more than that you should be rich. Rise, then; may God protect you, for it is to him that I have entrusted the matter."[5]

Ali forcefully asserted that striving for Allah's favor was incomparably more important than accumulating worldly goods and that welfare derived from Allah's beneficence rather than from wealth: "If destiny grants you a tomorrow, God will provide for your survival. Know that everything you acquire over and above your needs is only stored up by you for the use of someone else."[6] Such poignant sentiments evoked a dormant undercurrent of fatalism, and Ali sharpened that perception with his principled disdain for avarice: "The world is made of carrion and if you want to claim a part of it you must put up with the company of dogs."[7] Of course anyone who inclined to Ali's attitudes would discern in them incitements directed against the lifestyle embraced by Osman and his coterie.

Abu Dharr had impeccable credentials as a spokesman for opposition to Osman: he had been one of Muhammad's first converts, but unlike many of Muhammad's companions, never exploited his close relations with Muhammad to seek preferment. For that reason alone, his criticism of pervasive excess was all the more trenchant. Abu Dharr condoned striving for material wealth, but only up to the point it helped prepare for the afterlife, whereas plutocratic ostentation, he implied, was not only in poor taste but also profoundly irreligious. Abu Dharr reminded anyone who would listen Muhammad once told him after looking at Mount Uhud: "If I came to own a block of gold the size of this mountain, I would give it away and only keep three dinar."[8] Nobody could verify whether Muhammad actually ever said that, but what mattered was that Abu Dharr's frank but blunt assessment voiced discontent felt by many. Osman rebuffed Abu Dharr's invectives, pointing out he paid all taxes demanded by the Koran and it was not unethical to enjoy living life to the fullest. On the contrary, such was his rejoinder to Abu Dharr's dour moralizing, the Prophet never expected a Muslim to live like a prig. Muawiyah, Syria's governor in Damascus, put Abu Dharr to a test by gifting him 1,000 dinars and a day later under a pretext demanding he return the gift, hoping Abu Dharr would have squandered the money in the meantime and thus be exposed as a hypocrite. That ploy to embarrass Abu Dharr, however, rebounded. Abu Dharr was unable to return the gift, he admitted, for the simple reason he had spent the entire windfall on alms. For once, Muawiyah stood outsmarted. Abu Dharr not only did not soften his stance, but also attacked Muawiyah for building a sumptuous palace. "If you spent public money on this building," he accused Muawiyah, "you are a traitor. If you spent your own money, you are a spendthrift."[9] Abu Dharr on return to Medina would not be silenced, and finally Osman rid himself of this obdurate critic by banishing him. In the eyes of the people of Medina, who remembered how Osman's forebears had persecuted Muhammad, suspicions took shape whether Omayyad professions of piety were a veneer for avarice, and rumors spread Osman's hidden agenda was an Omayyad takeover of Islam. If Osman's lifestyle made him unpopular, his undisguised favoritism alienated many subjects, and his high-handed management style made him intolerable. For too long Osman ignored his rising unpopularity and ultimately precipitated open revolt and his overthrow: he was besieged in his own residence, and intruders assassinated Osman, who at the moment of his death splattered blood on the Koran he held in his hands.

ALI IBN ABI TALIB

Osman's successor was Ali (ruled from 656 to 661), the first caliph who came to office without prior experience in commerce. Ali had always kept aloof from the rush to accumulate riches, in fact, never concealed his disdain for considering luxury anything other than a temporary delusion. Of a time when Umar sought advice what to do with the most spectacular prize looted from the Persian king's Ctesiphon palace, a magnificent rug interwoven with gold threads and jewels, some recommended this trophy would make for an impressive display at official functions, but Ali spoke out that a good Muslim considered all worldly goods transient and recommended the carpet be cut up and sold piece by piece. It is a sign of the respect Ali commanded at the time that his advice prevailed; how splendid was the possession that at his behest was dispersed we can infer from the fact that Ali sold his share of the carpet for 20,000 dirhams. Ali imposed his austere lifestyle on his family; Waqidi wrote he once upbraided his wife Fatima for "wearing a coloured dress and kohl in her eyes,"[10] and Al Fahkri related Ali "raised a large income from his properties all of which he expended on the poor and feeble, while he and his family were content with clothes made of rough cotton cloth, and loaves of barley bread."[11]

His election held out the promise of a return to the simple but pious ways of Muhammad's era. On accession, he broke open the treasury and disbursed funds to the poor and revoked all of his predecessor's appointments.[12] However, all those who stood to lose from his shake up of the highest echelons of government were easily persuaded to support his opponents. Battle lines were drawn between a party of tradition-minded loyalists supporting Ali and the cosmopolitan mercantile class backing Muawiyah. In an ensuing civil war that once again pitted Hashimites against Omayyads, Ali was vanquished. Before narrating how that campaign progressed, preceding remarks should go into the underlying issues that precipitated war. The sore of the body politic of Islam was that there still were contentions over the nature of a caliph's right to assume authority.

THE TITLES OF THE *RASHIDUN CALIPHS*

Muhammad's right to govern derived from his prophetic office. Adherence to Islam encompassed unquestioning recognition of Muhammad's political authority and Muhammad had made clear that government authority had its fount in the mosque. Muhammad bequeathed formidable military capabilities, comprehensive fiscal arrangements, and the basics of a judiciary. His successors, on the other hand, who could not lay claim to the unimpeachable authority of divine calling, therefore faced twofold challenges: at home, to convince their subjects their governance was doing God's work; abroad, to adapt Medina's administrative machinery to fit it to the scale of a far-flung empire.

The Prophet's death opened at the head of Islam a void that was filled by the election of Abu Bakr. Election to the caliphate in principle was open to all, and candidacies underwent a two-stage process: an inner circle of leading citizens reached consensus on a suitable nominee and his election was ratified by an assembly in the mosque. The caliphate was not hereditary; Ali arguably had better claims to the caliphate than anyone else but was always passed over until all the other main contenders for the caliphate had died. But Abu Bakr's election had resolved only who should be at the helm of Islam at that particular moment, and the deeper contention on what he should base his authority was left in abeyance.

Abu Bakr projected his conception of his office through his chosen title, *caliph*, meaning successor, which asserted he governed in his capacity as executor of the will of Muhammad. It is astonishing how in the midst of tumult erupting within hours of Muhammad's death was conceived a political title that came to last longer than any other in world history: from 632 Islam's supreme political leaders would style themselves as caliphs until the title together with the Ottoman Empire disappeared in 1924. However, subtle changes to that title by succeeding *rashidun caliphs* showed changes to the way they conceived their authority. Umar eschewed adopting the title of *caliph* because, as he argued, such might encourage the inference he was appointed as deputy of Abu Bakr (rather than of Muhammad), which implied every future succession would mark an incremental remove from the authority held by Muhammad and so erode the power vested in this office. Umar preferred styling his title as *amir al-muminin* (Commander of the Faithful) and projected his authority when he walked about by carrying a whip. When the time came to elect a successor to Umar, however, the issue was still unresolved whether a caliph's authority derived from succession to Muhammad or to his immediate predecessor. The shortlist of contenders had been whittled down to two contenders, Osman and Ali, when the appointment committee posed to both candidates the identical question: whether the only precedents considered binding were those set by Muhammad, or also those set by Abu Bakr and Umar. Osman answered in the affirmative, Ali did not; Osman's response decided the contest in his favor, Ali was passed over once more. Osman and Ali projected how they conceived the nature of their office through subtle alterations to the title of *caliph*. Osman styled his office as *chalifat Allah*, implying the caliph deputed for Allah, while Ali changed the title to *chalifat rasul Allah*, restoring his office to that of a deputy of Allah's Messenger.[13]

Changes occurred to the process of electing a leader and how he styled his title. But there never was dispute, however, that political legitimacy was not conferred by power brokers or the congregation, but only by the Koran. Any incumbent of Islam's highest political office had a vital interest to settle potential disputes over what the Koran contained. Nothing could undermine a caliph's authority more than an imputed disregard or, even worse, lack of knowledge of the Koran, and Osman faced this very allegation when Kufa's governor Abdullah ibn Masud asserted Osman's version of the Koran was flawed and circulated a variant. Osman could not afford to ignore this challenge (Abdullah was a former servant of Muhammad who had memorized the entire Koran). A lapse in Osman's paramount duty as guardian of Muhammad's revelations in the eyes of the community would have been tantamount to an indictment. Osman, departing from his usual autocratic management style, appointed a committee to sift variant versions of the Koran and to agree on a conformed copy. This agreed recension he dispatched to provincial capitals and variants were destroyed. (The capacity to distribute a conformed copy of the Koran across a vast empire, is testimony how far standards of written communication in early Islamic administration had progressed; according to the *Times*, the last surviving copy of Osman's Koran was destroyed by a fire in the Damascus mosque in 1893.)[14]

The assassination of Osman threatened not only to tear apart Islamic society, but also the religion that held it together. Religion and politics were inseparably linked in the killing of a caliph that constituted one of two—equally fearsome—acts: if the caliph had violated his duties he deserved to die, else the assassins were guilty of a heinous sacrilege. Rioting in Medina made quick election of a caliph to restore law and order paramount, but the calm ensuing from Ali's election was only temporary. Osman's relative Muawiyah let it be known Ali's condemnation of Osman's assassins seemed lax, hinting that as a beneficiary of Osman's murder he may have tacitly condoned their plot. Muawiyah demonstrated the enormity of the crime that had been committed by displaying Osman's bloodied garments from the *minbar* of the Damascus mosque. In 656, hostilities erupted and the Islamic project once again tottered on the brink of disaster. But the Omayyads vanquished each standard-bearer of Arabia's aristocracy—Ali, his sons Hussayn and Hassan, and finally Abdallah az Zobayr—until at last in 691 they became undisputed claimants of the caliphate. The civil wars swept away many of the conventions that had underpinned governance and administration of the *umma.*

ALI AND MUAWIYAH

Ali had incomparably better credentials to serve as caliph than Muawiyah. Their biographies shared superficial similarities—both had served as Muhammad's private secretaries and for decades had been policy insiders. But by personality and social background, they could not have been more different. Ali's bankrupted father had given him up for adoption as a child; Ali converted to Islam as a teenager at a time when Muhammad's adherents still numbered only a handful; and his war record was exemplary. His adversary Muawiyah, on the other hand, had converted to Islam on the eve of Muhammad's triumphal return to Mecca; owed his appointment as Muhammad's secretary to his father's successful lobbying; and pursued a career in the civil service in Damascus, at a safe distance from Medina's charged political atmosphere where Ali had been embroiled in countless clashes. But the one-time war hero Ali now was past his prime; Tabari heard him described as "bald, big-bellied, and short."[15] Military campaigning suited Ali, but his supporters must have sensed their leader's time had passed when after running to ground a prominent foe, Az Zobayr, they presented him with his fallen enemy's sword, and Ali, remembering the campaigns when he and Az Zobayr had fought side by side, was stirred to the wistful exclamation: "This sword often turned the Prophet's worries into joy."[16] The memories that claimed Ali now had a stronger hold on him than prospects of a bright future, darkening the outlook for his prosecution of the war.

The civil war in the beginning went well for Ali; he gained the upper hand in battles but failed to press his advantage. Ali made a strategic mistake by assuming his enemies cared as much for preserving Islam's past as he did. When he captured Aisha, he exhibited restraint to the point of self-denial. Ali, instead of exacting vengeance from the very foe who had thwarted his claim to Muhammad's property and succession, had Aisha escorted back to Medina to live out her days in peace. Muawiyah, meanwhile, exploited Ali's conciliatory approach and played for time. Muawiyah was famous for his presence of mind and quick wit; once a commander sought to impress Muawiyah by boasting he had never given battle without in advance planning an escape route, and Muawiyah retorted he had never given battle when he thought he might need one. Ali's grit was no match for Muawiyah's guile, his campaign lost momentum, and in 661, Ali was stabbed by an assassin and succumbed to a glancing cut from the assassin's poisoned dagger. Sadness in Medina over a death unworthy of a war hero, undefeated in battle, was compounded when lingering hopes were dashed Ali's sons might avenge their father: Hussayn died in 672, presumed poisoned, and Hassan was killed in battle in 680. Medina, a city imbued with personal memories of Muhammad, was shrouded in grief. Aisha, whose youthful exuberance once had charmed Muhammad, had been widowed at the age of nineteen and nearing her end at the age of sixty-four was heard to yearn she had never been born, and from crying so many tears, they said, had gone blind.[17]

LOOKING BACK AT THE *RASHIDUN* ERA

Muhammad had promoted enterprise and set taxes to support social welfare, and he also imposed a steeply progressive tax rate on his own income to ensure that he enriched the community rather than himself. Scaling up Muhammad's public administration had been no less challenging than bringing it into being, and innovations of the *rashidun* era were catalysts for sustained economic growth: the *rashidun* hired and trained officials to staff their administration, established a judiciary, imposed new taxes, invested in infrastructure, and created the world's first government pension plan. Controversies over distribution of income grew more acrimonious when there emerged a plutocrat class with a lifestyle in opposition to Muhammad's frugal simplicity, and tensions rose once riches flooded into Medina and the caliphs no longer were seen to reconcile the twin goals of creating wealth for individuals along with welfare for all. By and by, as Muhammad's contemporaries passed away and memories of Muhammad dimmed, the glow of personal association with the Prophet no longer counted as unassailable qualification for claiming the right to govern, and once Islam had outgrown Arabia, a new generation of leaders ousted the Medina elite from office and moved the seat of government to the new center for economic growth, Damascus.

The *rashidun* transformed the Islamic economy through three key measures. The first was to convert conquered land into a government holding. In Muhammad's day the status of every citizen was that of a partner in a collective enterprise where profit shares derived from investment in *ghazis*—either by risking life and limb, contributing cavalry, or underwriting funding. That changed once all revenue passed through the caliph's hand—albeit acting as trustee. The introduction of the *diwan* and of social security plans converted the status of Muslims: ordinary citizens received recurring income from regular operations, and the managing elite paid themselves bonuses from windfalls. The caliph's financial resources became immense and every Muslim had become a ward of the state.

The second key measure was the establishment of a bureaucracy that managed finances. Creating the *diwan* was a first step in building a large cadre of government accountants who tracked income and spending, built cash reserves and managed cash flows across great distances and budget periods. Arabs dispersed across great distances, and fiscal transfers such as those between Kufa and Basra ensured Muslims were treated equitably. Within individual cities Arabs kept intact their identity, but between regional centers such as Kufa and Basra, there emerged rivalries.

The third measure was the creation of a large trade zone. Now that tax revenue no longer was transferred to royal courts in Constantinople or in Ctesiphon, monies were spent within the Islamic Empire. Improved roads helped goods flow between the new urban centers—Kufa, Basra, and Fustat—located in regions with complementary products. Spending power in these cities grew rapidly. The acquiescence to Muslim rule—no sustained outbreaks of uprisings by the empire's new subjects occurred—is a sign that the caliphs' subjects were reconciled to the new regime. The Islamic Empire contained centers manufacturing cotton (Basra, Kirman), linen (the Maghrib), silk (Azerbaijan), damask (a luxury cloth from Damascus), perfume (Persia), and an abundance of fruit and vegetables from the Levant. These individual regional economies were in a position to take advantage of comparative advantages, and Arabs applied their traditional trade expertise in a larger theater of activity. However, Islam's prosperity undermined Medina's status as capital of the empire. Muhammad's administration suited a municipal setting, but would have been inadequate to administer an empire enveloping Iraq, Syria, and Egypt. Consequently, the *rashidun* scaled up Muhammad's administration, aligned tax regimes and introduced account management systems. But the money spent in Medina had been made elsewhere: Arabia had turned from a producer into a user of wealth. Once new opportunities beckoned from integrating the economies of Iraq, Syria, Palestine, and Egypt into a single market, Arabia was no longer the economic center of gravity of the Islamic Empire.

The *rashidun* caliphs had different leadership styles: Abu Bakr was self-effacing, Umar tough, Osman autocratic, and Ali consensual. But for all their differences, they had much in common: their formative years coincided with the period of Islam's tests and tribulations in Mecca and Medina, and each had staked his career and his very life on supporting the creed that had been placed in their hands to guard and promote. The *rashidun* were venerated as elders might have been in an extended family, indeed succession was managed as it might have been in a family business. Each of the *rashidun* was either a son-in-law or father-in-law of Muhammad, and through their relationship with Muhammad they were all related to one another and also intermarried. That did not, however, make them any less competitive. Stories of internecine intrigue abound; Abu Bakr had a son who was in the number of Osman's assassins; his daughter Aisha rallied troops in battle against Ali; and another daughter, Asma, was mother to Abdallah az Zobayr, who mounted a challenge for the caliphate. Stories of such currents and crosscurrents could easily be multiplied.

The achievements of the *rashidun* were formidable: Muhammad had turned a refugee camp into a state, and that state his successors expanded into an empire. Muawiyah turned his back on conservatives in Arabia nostalgic for the way of life of Islam's early, pioneering days. Few ruling elites could have been better suited to merging hitherto separate regions into an enlarged single market than the merchant class of Mecca. Wealth generation had shifted from Arabia to the provinces bordering on the Mediterranean, and this empire needed a new framework for government and its economy a new business model. The new regime had to overhaul and scale up the framework for government and administration to match the new dimensions of the empire. With the transfer of the seat of government to Damascus, a new era began. One of the first challenges facing an empire that housed a vast single market was to create a suitable monetary regime: the single market needed a single currency.

NOTES

1. Waqidi, *The Life of Muhammad*, 190.
2. Tabari, *The History of al-Tabari*, Vol. 9, 49.
3. *Arabian Nights*, Night 63.
4. Muir, *Annals of the Early Caliphate*, 118 (I have modernized the words of the poem's translation).
5. *Arabian Nights*, Night 66.
6. Masudi, *The Meadows of Gold*, 364.
7. Caetani, *Annali dell'Islam*, Vol. 10, 455.

8. Souck-Hurgronje, *Selected Works*, 162.
9. Kremer, *Geschichte der herrschenden Ideen des Islams*, Vol. 1, 462.
10. Waqidi, *The Life of Muhammad*, 532.
11. Fakhri, *On the Systems of Government and the Moslem Dynasties*, 70.
12. Caetani, *Annali dell'Islam*, Vol. 5, 215.
13. Madelung, *The Succession to Muhammad*, 46.
14. The *Times*, January 29, 1894: "Burning of the Great Omayyad Mosque in Damascus." The Koran in question conceivably was the copy Osman had held in his hands at the moment of his assassination.
15. Tabari, *Biographies of the Prophet's Companions*, 37.
16. Wüstenfeld, *Die Familie el-Zubeir,* 33.
17. Caetani, *Annali dell'Islam*, Vol. 5, 13.

Chapter Eleven

Journey to Jerusalem

Translating the empire's capital from Arabia to Syria constituted a momentous upheaval; religious and political considerations were inextricably mingled. Traditionalists who no longer moved in the corridors of power when the capital was moved to Damascus frowned on anything that undermined the status of Mecca and Medina. But there were several reasons for the move, one of which would have been considerations of personal security. In Medina, the ruler and his household would be exposed to constant scrutiny of a large number of disaffected rivals and live in the midst of a community constantly drawing comparisons with Muhammad. Medina was a city, said Waqidi, that "could boil like a kettle" and Muawiyah would have been conscious that Umar, Osman, and Ali all had succumbed to assassins. But Damascus also was favored by the dynamics of the empire's economy. Arabia no longer was the heartland of the emerging cross-border single market, and relocating the capital to Damascus placed it at the heart of the Islamic economy that was getting larger. The Omayyad family had long-standing links to Syria; Muawiyah's father, Abu Sufyan, owned property there already before the advent of Islam.[1] Arguably, the capital could have moved to Jerusalem, but a city where merchants and officials set the tone would have been more congenial to Omayyads than one frequented by pilgrims and divines.

The start-up phase of the Islamic economy was over the moment the *diwan* earned more revenue from taxes than from raids. "Tribute is better than booty," said Umar, "for it continues, whereas spoil vanishes."[2] Fiscal priorities shifted from seeking out new sources of revenue to improving existing ones. Moreover, a new economy had taken shape beyond Arabia's borders where in provinces from Mesopotamia to Egypt new wealth was won, whereas Arabia, on the other hand, now consumed rather than produced wealth. A third issue was that the provinces recently incorporated into the

Islamic Empire had as little in common with each other as they had with Arabia, and Arab Muslims dispersed across extensive dominions now were a religious and ethnic minority in the empire they governed. The social and economic constitution of an egalitarian warrior society sprung from Medina's refugee camp was ill adapted to the demands of governing a far-flung empire.

The Omayyads had been making a living from trade for generations and to them the benefits of integrating Persian, Byzantine, and Egyptian provinces through trade were obvious. Muawiyah and his successors pursued two interdependent policies, designed to establish their credentials as devout stewards of Muhammad's legacy and to level barriers to trade within the Islamic economy. The cornerstones of Muhammad's *umma*, the mosque and the market, through two measures the Omayyads scaled up to fit an empire: they projected their vision of a multicultural Islamic society through commissioning a building program of some of the world's most spectacular mosques, and they recast the Islamic Empire as a single market through issuance of a single currency. The most significant Omayyad mosque, the Dome of the Rock in Jerusalem, was completed in 692. The Omayyad gold dinar, the first gold standard created outside Europe, appeared in its final version in 696. Several decades of sustained effort had preceded these achievements.

CIVIL WAR AGAINST ABDALLAH AZ ZOBAYR

The civil war against Ali had claimed more lives and sacrifices than *jihad* against enemies abroad, and the struggle over the direction of Islam did not die with Ali. Muawiyah anticipated contentions over the direction of caliphal authority again would burst into bloody conflict when the time would come to choose his successor. Muawiyah aimed to pre-empt civil strife by asking regional power brokers to acknowledge his son Yazid as crown prince, but this step was a miscalculation—little could provoke traditionalists more than the presumption of dynastic prerogative, and moreover, it seemed duplicitous dynastic succession was advanced on behalf of the Omayyads who had been adamant in their opposition to this very principle when the putative incumbent had been Ali. Muawiyah's bid backfired, civil war recommenced, and ended only thirty years later, in 691, after a conflict that would see Omayyads besiege Mecca and bombard the *Kaaba*.

The backlash against the Omayyads had its leader in Abdallah az Zobayr (whose father had been a casualty in the campaign against Ali). Abdallah was one of Arabia's largest landholders and his pedigree was peerless; indeed he was so closely interrelated with the *rashidun* elite he might have been considered one himself. Abdullah was related to Muhammad (his grandmother's nephew); Khadija (his father's aunt); Abu Bakr (his grandfather); and Aisha (his aunt). Moreover, his stepmother Attika had been married to the sons of Abu Bakr and Umar.[3] Abdallah, in addition to the advantages of money and connections, matched the Omayyad flair for managing public perceptions. Abdallah styled his title as *Guardian of the Kaaba* in Mecca and took up residence there, a stark contrast to Omayyads who based themselves in Damascus. Residing in Mecca had further connotations of legitimacy, since guarding the *Kaaba* had ever been the prerogative and duty of the community's leader. Abdallah also gained an even greater psychological advantage from basing himself in Mecca, because every pilgrim to Mecca would link Abdallah and the *Kaaba* and every annual round of pilgrimages would undermine Omayyad pretensions to power and burnish the merits of his own. Abdallah could afford to sit back; control over Mecca was all that Abdallah needed to evince the Omayyads had severed their roots. Abdallah was an astute tactician who avoided Ali's mistake of attacking Omayyad strongholds in Syria and Iraq, and preferred to remain in Mecca, daring the Omayyad forces to attack Islam's most sacred city.

The Omayyads to prosecute the war had to attack Abdallah's stronghold Mecca, Islam's most venerable city. This high-risk strategy called for a commander who would not flinch from offending sensitivities, and the Omayyads had such a commander in Hajjaj ibn Yusuf, who during his siege of Mecca had no qualms against bombarding the *Kaaba* and risking damage to its fabric. Finally, however, he was able to seize the city, a victory that confirmed Hajjaj's terrifying reputation of having killed more Muslims than anyone before. In Damascus, the reaction was one of relief, coupled with the realization that after bombarding the *Kaaba*, burnishing Omayyad credentials as sincere adherents of Islam was more important than ever.

THE DOME OF THE ROCK

Mirage, the French word for apparition, came into circulation in the nineteenth century, shortly after French scholars who had accompanied Napoleon on his expedition to Egypt there encountered the Koranic conception of a *miraj*. In the Koran, *miraj* refers to Muhammad's *Night Journey*, an episode where the Prophet in the course of a single night was transported to a distant temple and thence ascended to heaven. Views differed whether the *miraj* was real or imagined, but by the Omayyad era consensus settled: the temple was that in Jerusalem, the city linked to Abraham and that had transfixed the Muslim imagination from the earliest stage of Islam. When God brought into being the universe, Samhudi wrote, Mecca was created first, then Medina, then Jerusalem, and only then, a thousand years later, the rest of the world.[4] Jerusalem was the direction Muslims faced in prayer, until Muhammad after a rift with Medina's Jewish community commanded them to turn toward Mecca. Jerusalem, alongside Mecca and Medina, the Prophet deemed one of three destinations of Muslim pilgrimage.[5] However, no mosque existed to host pilgrims in Jerusalem during Muhammad's lifetime, but the Omayyads, by building there the Dome of the Rock, made the *miraj* come true.

Jerusalem had been conquered in 635, and many in Medina thought they would never see Umar again when he set forth from Medina to Jerusalem to sign the occupation settlement: they feared Umar would stay there and Medina would cede its position as capital of the Islamic Empire to Jerusalem. That fear, however, was misplaced. Umar surprised followers and foes when he entered Jerusalem not in triumph but clad in the garb of a pilgrim. Umar made a point of exhibiting restraint throughout his visit. Led through the city he had at his mercy, Umar declined the invitation to step into a Christian church because, he explained, were he to enter other Muslims would follow; to all who stood by it was clear Umar did not cross the threshold because he wished to ensure Christian sites remain inviolate. On behalf of Muslims, Umar had but one request: to clear a site for a future mosque. That concession secured and with no more business to attend to, Umar returned to Medina.

Muawiyah, on accession to the caliphate, demonstrated his intent to interpret his office in a new way through the protocol of ceremonies. Whereas hitherto all elections of caliphs had been ratified in the mosque in Medina, Muawiyah proclaimed his caliphate in Jerusalem. And as if to underscore the motivation for choosing a city that was home to communities of Christians and Jews, he proceeded to pay a visit to Gethsemane, a site venerated by Christian pilgrims. Reaching out to Christian and Jewish constituencies that vastly outnumbered the Arab Muslims who ruled them was only opportune, and to address all three religions no city was more apt than Jerusalem. Muawiyah's inauguration signaled an agenda: to demonstrate respect for the heritage of Jews and Christians and to assert Jerusalem also was a home for Muslims.

The caliph Abd al Malik (645–705) followed Muawiyah's precedent and he, too, inaugurated his caliphate in Jerusalem. Abd al Malik had grown up in Medina where his father, Marwan, belonged to Osman's inner circle and already as a youth had learned court intrigue could be lethal. Abd al Malik was a teenager at the time Osman was assassinated; possibly even present in the same building at the very moment the murder took place. The family moved to Damascus where Marwan became caliph but he, too, died suddenly and under suspicious circumstances. (Marwan died in his harem where rumor had it his wives had strangled him.) Abd al Malik apprehended raw power alone could not shield a caliph from the visceral enmities haunting the Arab elite, and what was needed was a means to broaden and deepen support for the ruler of an empire whose compass extended also over Christians and

Jews. Muhammad had visited Jerusalem on his *miraj*; Umar there had selected the site for a mosque; and Abd al Malik wove Islam into Jerusalem's religious fabric through construction of the Dome of the Rock.

The rock that gave the mosque its name was linked to the most sacred memories of Judaism and Islam. Judaic tradition held that Abraham on this very spot had offered to sacrifice his son Isaac, and Muslim legends averred Muhammad from it had ascended to heaven. The Dome of the Rock projected links between the three Abrahamic religions through visual messaging: it was situated on the very location of Solomon's Temple and replicated the ground plan of Jerusalem's Church of the Holy Sepulchre. The mosque contains 260 meters of Koranic inscriptions, such as: "He is God, the One; God the Eternal; He had not begotten nor was He begotten; and there is none comparable to Him." Prestige trophies, such as the crown of the vanquished Persian emperor Chosroes that was hung from the ceiling, asserted the caliph's authority. Moreover, as a reminder Islam also was heir to Abraham, horns of rams from Abraham's flock were on display.

No expense was spared to ensure the site made up in glamor what it lacked in natural beauty. The Dome of the Rock was built on a derelict urban site covered by debris and land reclamation alone would have been very expensive. Suyuti recorded that building costs consumed seven years' tax revenue from Egypt, and Muslims sensed Abd al Malik's ambition to show Islam surpassing the splendor of ancestral religions. The Muslim historian Mukaddasi heard from his uncle: "Abd al Malik seeing the greatness of the Church of the Holy Sepulchre and its magnificence was moved lest it should dazzle the minds of the Muslims and hence erected above the Rock, the Dome which is now seen there."[6] Even polemics against Islam only worked to enhance the location's mystique. If St. John of Damascus, for example, cast doubts on mythical accounts Abraham and Isaac had in fact ever been present in Mecca, then by inference it was all the more compelling Jerusalem must have been where Abraham had offered to sacrifice his son Isaac. The Dome of the Rock projected Abrahamic religions as a coherent whole, asserting the claim of Islam, as descendant of Judaism and Christianity, to accede to its ancestral legacy, and coincidentally reminded viewers who had made this vision possible, namely the Omayyad caliphs.

The Dome of the Rock afforded collateral policy benefits. Construction began while the civil war against Abdallah was raging, and it must have occurred to the caliph's planning staff that, were Arabia to permanently slip from control, Jerusalem might serve as a suitable alternative to Mecca as a destination for pilgrims. Pilgrimage was an important conduit for trade flows and cutting off Arabia would have had adverse economic repercussions. Therefore, to anchor Islam in a city of unequaled religious significance opened up alternative destinations for pilgrim traffic to Arabia and for the business it brought in its wake. Al Yakubi confirmed Omayyads had this option in mind: "Then Abd al Malik forbade the people of Syria to make the pilgrimage (to Mecca); because Abdallah az Zobayr was liable to seize on pilgrims and force them to pay him allegiance . . . and the people took the custom of circumambulating the Rock, as they did round the *Kaaba*."[7] A European pilgrim who visited Jerusalem at the time, a certain Arculf, observed "an immense multitude of people of different nations are used to meet in Jerusalem for the purpose of commerce."[8] Omayyads were savvy practitioners of Islamic statecraft that ever linked politics, religions, and trade, and Omayyads made an immense financial and political investment in Jerusalem, so Yakubi's testimony is not implausible. Abd al Malik may have stopped short of making Jerusalem Islam's principal spiritual home when in 691 his general Hajjaj breached the defenses of Mecca and Abdallah az Zobayr was cornered, killed, and crucified. Now, contingency plans to find an alternative to Mecca could be quietly dropped.

THE MOSQUE OF DAMASCUS

The extraordinary efforts expended by Omayyads to influence public perceptions of Islam accorded with Muhammad's statecraft. Muhammad initially disposed of a very small budget and had a very small personal staff, but through his court poet Hassan ibn Thabit he propagated messages to the wider public. The Omayyads, with an incomparably bigger budget at their disposal, crafted their image as stewards of Islam through building and improving mosques. The Dome of the Rock in Jerusalem was the most spectacular Ommayad mosque, but only one of many. In Medina, Mecca, Damascus—everywhere Muslims congregated in numbers they had before their eyes mosques luxuriating in fine materials and showcasing the highest standards of workmanship. Particular efforts were expended on building the mosque in the empire's capital, Damascus.

Damascus had been conquered in 634. However, although Muslims now were undisputed masters of the city, they did not come to an agreement with local Christians who would take control of the city's most significant building, the cathedral. The compromise reached at last seemed Solomonic: Christians and Muslims agreed to joint use of the cathedral and each denomination worshipped at opposite ends of the building, an arrangement that continued until 705 when the caliph Al Walid demolished the cathedral to make room for a mosque. (He compensated the Christian community through restoration of previously confiscated church assets.)

Damascus had the finest mosque money could buy. Mukaddasi reports Al Walid spent seven years' Syrian tax revenue on the project;[9] Ibn Jubayr reports the budget was four hundred chests of money containing 28,000 dinars each.[10] The impression created by this building was striking; Yakut reported a Byzantine envoy to Damascus was overheard, "I had told the assemblies of Byzantium that the Arabs and their power would not last; but now, when I see what they have built, I am certain their rule will be long term."[11] Indeed the Omayyad investment of effort, time and money in building mosques paid off: in all, fourteen members of the Omayyad family acceded to the caliphate.

NOTES

1. Baladhuri, *The Origins of the Islamic State*, Vol. 1, 197.
2. Muir, *Annals of the Early Caliphate*, 243.
3. Sprenger, *Das Leben und die Lehre des Mohammad*, Vol. 1, 133; Lammens, *Le califat de Yazid Ier*, 184–85.
4. Samhudi, *Geschichte der Stadt Medina*, 12.
5. Ibn Kathir, *The Life of the Prophet Muhammad*, Vol. 2, 207.
6. Quoted in Le Strange, *Palestine under the Moslems*, 118.
7. Quoted in Le Strange, *Palestine under the Moslems*, 116. Wording modernized.
8. Wright, *Early Travels in Palestine*, 1.
9. Quoted in Le Strange, *Palestine under the Moslems*, 227–29.
10. Le Strange, *Palestine under the Moslems*, 241.
11. Le Strange, *Palestine under the Moslems* 263–64. I modernized the wording of the translation.

Chapter Twelve

Islamic Gold Currency

Arabs as a rule left civil administration in conquered countries for the most part untouched. In Egypt, however, Egyptians were confronted with a drastic instance of Muslim intervention even before they knew how to spell Muhammad's name. In the aftermath of invasion, the Coptic bishop Picendi was shocked: "Arabs take away Egyptian gold coins engraved with the cross and an image of Jesus" and replace these with inscriptions with "the name of their Prophet who they refer to as their imam, and whose precepts they follow religiously. His name is Momadonus."[1] This defacement of coinage in Egypt, where Byzantine gold coins had been in circulation from time immemorial, remained an isolated act for the time being. But when Muawiyah instigated fundamental administrative reforms, efforts resumed to reform the Islamic monetary system. Muawiyah split the *diwan* into a War Office and Treasury, introduced an audit function, and expanded the police and postal services. This last service was particularly sensitive; provincial postmasters were station chiefs of internal security whose confidential reports bypassed the local governor. (Postmasters used pigeons to airmail reports; the caliph Abd al Malik gave instructions that postmasters be admitted without prior appointments, showing short response times were vital to thwarting conspiracies.) Muawiyah deputed non-Muslims to shape government policy, and gave his backing to a worldly, cosmopolitan cadre that kept professional responsibilities separate from private convictions. Uniformity of creed was not imposed on senior officials; one Omayyad tax official who later retired to a monastery, St. John of Damascus, wrote a tract, *Islam as a Heresy*, without precipitating disciplinary action. Muawiyah strengthened his personal control of the economy. He confirmed Osman's controversial awards of land to personal favorites and coincidentally derived from this measure more advantages than anyone else. Muawiyah, during his tenure as governor of Syria, had received Osman's approval to disburse revenue from state lands in Syria as he saw fit (at the time, Muawiyah had explained to Osman he needed discretionary spending authority because governing the country was so expensive), and these extensive land holdings now passed into Muawiyah's personal estate. Muawiyah thereby became a rich man in his own right.

Abd al Malik continued Omayyad practice of appointing to senior government positions Christians, such as his court poet, doctor and chief treasurer (the latter the father of St. John of Damascus). His brother, who became governor of Egypt, had a Christian tutor. Abd al Malik would have liked to improve promotion prospects for Arabs, however, and changed the official language for business from Greek to Arabic, but was pragmatic enough to hire back Greek personnel due to a staff shortage. The Belgian historian Henri Lammens has provided vivid descriptions of how the Commander of the Faithful and his non-Muslim counselors mingled socially: Abd al Malik showed off his genial relations with Christians by tolerating his court poet Aftal's banter who explained he was late for a recitation at court because, together with another Christian, the Minister of Finance Sergius, he had been enjoying a glass of wine.[2]

BYZANTINE GOLD, ARAB BULLION

In Damascus, Syrian subjects used Byzantine coins because no other were available. The benefits of a currency issued locally were obvious; it would smooth trading flows in provinces where local business communities had to be won over to the new regime, and moreover, would impress on them that Omayyads were peers of their Byzantine adversaries. However, introducing a new currency was a formidable task that impinged upon international currency arrangements that had been in place for centuries. Islamic currency reform consumed decades of administrative effort, until it came to fruition at last in 696.

The scale of this task was thrown into relief by a comparison between the monetary system of Byzantium, where a robust gold standard had been put in place centuries ago, and the rudimentary state of coinage in Arabia. Constantine, the founder of Constantinople, issued the first Byzantine gold coin, the *solidus*, and for over three hundred years his successors minted gold coins of such purity they were called *hyperper*. Byzantine coins were a tangible symbol of the stability of the empire that issued them, and accordingly Byzantine authorities knew the high price to pay in loss of prestige and diplomatic standing if the quality of the *solidus* ever came into doubt. Byzantine diplomats insisted international treaties contained a clause that gold coinage remained a Byzantine franchise, and Persians even in times of war never ventured to challenge that monopoly, a prerogative, claimed the Byzantine Procopius, that showed the Byzantine emperor was peerless:

> And yet, while the Persian king is accustomed to make silver coins as he likes, still it is not considered right either for him or for any other sovereign in the whole barbarian world to imprint his own likeness on a gold [coin], and that, too, though he has gold in his own kingdom; for they are unable to tender such a coin to those with whom they transact business, even though the parties concerned in the transactions happen to be barbarians.[3]

The disparity between Byzantine sophistication and Arab underdevelopment in monetary systems was all the more startling considering Arabs, unlike Byzantines, had gold mines in easy reach. When and how Arabs discovered gold and how useful it could be is obscure, but mining at any rate had been undertaken from times immemorial. Mentions of Arabs already in the Bible and by Greek and Roman geographers link them to gold, and the perception that gold in Arabia was pervasive and easy to find persisted into the Middle Ages.[4] Rabbi Petachia, a Bavarian visiting Baghdad in the twelfth century, had heard that "in the land of Ishmael the gold grows like herbs. In the night its brightness is seen, when a mark is made with dust or lime. They then come in the morning and gather the herbs upon which the gold is found."[5] But more likely Arabs had to dig deep to source gold; archaeologists have located some 1,000 mining sites in Arabia dating back to the *jahiliyya* with shafts sunk up to seventy meters.[6] Arabs were conversant with the extraordinary profitability of gold mining. Muhammad taxed mining profits at 20 percent (much higher than the standard *zakat* of 2½ percent). Disputes over mining rights actuated one of Islamic law's earliest cases: the sons of Bilal ibn Rabah had sold a parcel of land and the new owner after taking possession had discovered underground ore. Bilal's sons sued to annul the transaction on the grounds the sale price had not reflected the property's fair value; they won.[7]

Although mining in Arabia was very advanced, coinage was rudimentary. In Arabia, absent a government empowered to issue coins, coinage lagged by centuries that of Persia and Byzantium. Arab merchants abroad used whatever happened to be the local currency of choice, and at home valued coins the same way they would gold nuggets—by weight. "The dinars of Heraclius used to be current among the people of Mecca before Muslim times," said Baladhuri, "but it was not customary to buy and sell with them except by considering the coins as bullion."[8] Such customs remained unchanged from the days of Hashim until Umar. Bahrain's remarkable tribute passing into possession of Umar was said to have comprised 500,000 coins, but no indication was made of denominations, and Umar apportioned coins by the handful—a patently imprecise approach that shows individual denominations did not matter even in the days of the *rashidun*. Gaps in financial literacy were wide. Al Fahkri in his account of the Iraq campaign cannot resist telling a joke about a warrior who had no notion that gold was more valuable than silver; accordingly the hapless warrior asked: "Who will take this yellow stuff and give me white?" because he "thought that silver was more valuable than gold."[9] (In Arab literature, uncharitable jokes about failed traders are as conspicuous as eulogies for successful ones.)

Arabs were unprepared for the deluge of bullion that conquests swept into their hands, and those unsuspecting of sharp business practices often must have let riches slip between their fingers. But moneychangers in Medina, for their part, must have been hard pressed to provide reliable and comprehensive exchange services; volumes were immense and trained staff was lacking. Umar proposed decoupling currency from bullion, by issuing monetary tokens made of camel hide, but his advisers warned of unintended consequences: "Umar ibn al Chattab once said that he wanted to make dirhams out of camel skins, but someone said to him in that case there would be no baby camels, and he gave the idea up." Umar's conception of money, as something not necessarily based on bullion, was ahead of his time—paper money came into circulation in China some one hundred and fifty years later. But Umar on this occasion withdrew his proposal and instead introduced copper coins to ease day-to-day shopping. The absence of coinage hardly mattered for markets for daily necessities; but lack of coinage hampered trade once borders disappeared, roads were upgraded, and the flow of goods across distances quickened. Then, every time a merchant entered into a transaction with a customer in a distant location, he had to spend time and effort on valuing coins sent from abroad. But complications also were encountered by other sections of society. Analogous difficulties arose for any tax collector reconciling payments from different provinces; and pensioners suffered the inconvenience of uncertainty what the coins in their hands would be worth. Lack of a currency, in other words, added to transaction costs.

Byzantine gold coins, bearing the image of the Byzantine rulers and overt Christian iconography, continued in circulation in Syria long after the last Byzantine soldier had left there. In the 660s Muawiyah began trialing new coins, but he failed because these coins, while featuring an image of Heraclius, left out an image of the cross and "the populace did not accept it as there was no cross on it."[10] Syrians were as wary of new coins as had been Bishop Picendi in Egypt thirty years before, indeed they suspected that coins that had no religious symbols were fakes. The next iteration of coins duly reflected users' preferences. Thus in Persian regions, coins issued by Omayyad moneyers depicted Zoroastrian fire altars. Omayyads had given up attempts to launch an indigenous Islamic currency, it seemed.

When Abd al Malik acceded to the caliphate, he faced enemies on two fronts: the Byzantine emperor Justinian in the north and Abdallah az Zobayr in the south. Abd al Malik could not confront his adversary in Constantinople until he vanquished his enemy in Mecca, and he bought time by signing a truce with Justinian at the cost of an annual tribute in gold. One day, however, Byzantine diplomats would discover a clause in the treaty's fine print that would give Abd al Malik a pretext to overturn the Mediterranean trade zone's monetary order. But before that would come to pass, Abd al Malik scrupulously discharged to the last ounce his liabilities to Justinian and first turned his attention to overcoming his internal foe Abdallah az Zobayr.

Abdallah issued coins as a means to proclaim his fidelity to Islam and broke new ground when he issued coins, according to Baladhuri, "after the model of the Persian coins, with the words 'Blessing' and 'Allah' upon them."[11] This step exposed a glaring contrast between Abdallah and the Omayyads: in Arabia, Abdallah was circulating coins with inscriptions lauding Allah at a time when in Syria coins still featured the cross. Mecca not only in a spiritual sense was Islam's capital, that was obvious already, but also seat of a government that succeeded in areas where Omayyads palpably were failing. The Omayyad deputy Hajjaj ibn Yusuf countered Abdallah's lead, in that he "inquired after the procedure of the Persians in the matter of coining dirhams, and then erected a mint, and assembled men to do the stamping . . . and kept as profit whatever remained after paying the wages of the workmen and coiners."[12] These coins bore the inscription *Recite: God is One*. The significance of projecting the caliph's prestige through coins was not lost on Abd al Malik.

By 691, after Abd al Malik had rid himself of Abdallah az Zobayr, he could afford to take a more assertive stance in his dealings with Justinian. Abd al Malik complied with the terms of his contract and paid in full the tribute, but showed his hand by despatching coins that had been minted in Damascus. In Constantinople, the effect produced by the sight of gold coins issuing from a foreign mint was shock—a nominal tributary had the impudence to usurp a Byzantine prerogative that even Persia's king had never dared challenge. Byzantine authorities understood Byzantium's gold monopoly was under attack, and that were they to condone taking receipt of Islamic gold coins a precedent would have been set that would render their monopoly obsolete.

Currency wars were a novel arena of Byzantine and Muslim competition, and from either camp issued perspectives on events as they unfolded. Muslim versions from Baladhuri to Ibn Khaldun can be juxtaposed with one by the Byzantine historian Theophanes the Confessor.[13] These accounts differed in particulars, but they agreed currency competition was a reflection of religious and political controversies. Accordingly, the dispute commenced when Abd al Malik noticed his Egyptian subjects manufactured papyrus for export to Constantinople bearing the motto *Father, Son, and Holy Spirit*. This inscription he ordered substituted with the motto *God is my witness there is but one God*. This new design was brought to the attention of Justinian who filed a protest; he pointed out the predecessors of Abd al Malik had never taken umbrage at the traditional styling, and surely Abd al Malik would not wish to imply his predecessors had been at fault. Justinian's logic was unassailable, but Abd al Malik sidestepped being trapped in contradictions and did not deign to respond. Justinian thereupon stepped up pressure, and threatened that unless Abd al Malik changed his mind he would mint coins denigrating Muhammad. Such a threat Abd al Malik would not countenance, and perhaps even welcomed a pretext to escalate the dispute; in any event, Abd al Malik minted gold coins of his own and these he then dispatched to Constantinople to pay the agreed tribute. According to Theophanes, Justinian "refused to accept the minted coin that had been sent by Abd al Malik because it was of a new kind that had not been made before." For Abd al Malik, now was the moment to remind Justinian of the terms of their contract—no clause stipulated that coins necessarily had to be minted in Constantinople, and further, Abd al Malik argued "inasmuch as gold was paid by weight, the Romans did not suffer any loss from the fact that the Arabs were minting new coin."[14] What mattered, in other words, was how much gold a coin contained, not how it looked. Inarguably, Abd al Malik was in compliance with the letter of the agreement, although, as Theophanes adds, he added the provocative statement "Arabs could not suffer the Roman imprint on their own currency."[15] Considering that this is precisely what Arabs had been doing since time immemorial—Baladhuri conceded "Arabs used to get the dinars from the Greeks"[16]—this disingenuous remark was a calculated affront.

The political and religious dimension of this confrontation now in full view, the Byzantine side advanced theological argumentation to demonstrate the superiority of the *solidus*; Justinian issued coins bearing an image of Christ with the inscription *rex regnantium (king of rulers)*. The subtext was plain: if kings were ruled by Christ, then by implication someone whose authority was not derived from Christ could not be considered a true king. Abd al Malik retaliated in kind; if Byzantine coins were emphatically Christian, then his would be unequivocally Islamic. The final version of Islamic gold coins had no figurative image and featured an inscription in Arabic: "*Declare: Allah is one*!" The Byzantine monopoly to mint gold coins now was obsolete.

The Islamic gold dinar went into circulation between 691 and 696 and replaced Byzantine coinage in the Islamic realm through a combination of regulatory provisions and competitive advantages. Byzantine coins were no longer accepted in payment of taxes but there were facilities to switch them into dinars.[17] The weight of the Islamic gold dinar constituted a subtle incentive for conversion. The dinar weighed one *mithqal*, a customary Arab metric, slightly less than the *solidus* (4.25 grams rather than 4.55 grams). Thus recasting Byzantine coins as dinars yielded a larger quantity of coins. Circulation of dinars expanded further when Christian clerics, previously tax-exempt, were made to pay taxes, and since many clerics had meager income they liquidated church treasuries. Additional bullion was supplied by Arabian and Persian mines, and by treasures from Pharaonic graves in Egypt.

The Omayyad monetary system was trimetallic, that is to say, it included coins in gold, silver, and copper. Islamic coinage maintained familiar coinage conventions: the gold *dinar* took over the name of its Roman ancestor *denarius*; the silver *dirham* adapted the name of the Greek silver *drachma* and weighed precisely the same as their Sassanian predecessors.[18] Copper coins, used as small change, consisted of Byzantine coins with Arabic countermarks. The caliphal administration in Damascus supervised the gold mint, whereas silver coins were minted in several provincial capitals where designs varied and coin clipping was common.

As the monetary base expanded, so did the economy. Repercussions of the new currency rippled across the Islamic Empire and beyond, promoting intraregional as well as intercontinental trade. Islamic dinars circulated throughout Europe and were used as a means of payment in England, the Baltic, and also by the Vatican's treasury. Gold coins put purchasing power into the hand of Muslims and helped evolve a market that encompassed the realms of Islam and Christendom and introduced what the French historian Maurice Lombard called "l'âge du dinar et de la suprématie économique du monde musulman."[19]

NOTES

1. Sauvaire, "Matériaux pour servir à l'histoire de la numismatique et la métrologie musulmanes," 456–57.
2. Lammens, *Études sur le siècle des Omayyades*, 213.
3. Procopius, *History of the Wars*, Vol. 4, London, 1924, 439.
4. Genesis II:11–12; Ezechiel XXVII:22; Solomon's purchase of gold to adorn the temple: 2 Chronicles III:6. Greek and Roman authors include Agatharchides, Horace, and Strabo.
5. Petachia, *Travels of Rabbi Petachia*, 51–52.
6. Heck, "Gold Mining in Arabia," 379.
7. Baladhuri, *The Origins of the Islamic State*, Vol. 1, 28.
8. Baladhuri, *The Origins of the Islamic State*, Vol. 2, 263.
9. Fakhri, *On the Systems of Government and the Moslem Dynasties*, 79.
10. Grierson, "The Monetary Reforms of Abd al Malik," 243.
11. Baladhuri, *The Origins of the Islamic State*, Vol. 2, 266.
12. Baladhuri, *The Origins of the Islamic State*, Vol. 2, 266.
13. Sauvaire provided a comprehensive overview of Muslim sources in "Matériaux pour servir à l'histoire de la numismatique et la métrologie musulmanes."
14. *The Chronicle of Theophanes the Confessor*, 509–10.
15. *The Chronicle of Theophanes the Confessor*, 509–10.
16. Baladhuri, *The Origins of the Islamic State*, Vol. 1, 383.
17. Baladhuri, *The Origins of the Islamic State*, Vol. 1, 383.
18. Heidemann, "The Merger of Two Currency Zones in Early Islam," 100.
19. Lombard, "Les bases monétaires d'une suprématie économique," 159.

Chapter Thirteen

Bankers of Baghdad

To celebrate the Abbasids, Masudi used words that invoked renewal and glamor: "Islam, shining with new splendor, eclipsed all other nations."[1] That Islam had surpassed all peers of the time was not an empty boast. In 762, in the heartland of Mesopotamia, Abbasids founded Baghdad, a new capital of Islam that within a century became the largest city in the world. Building a capital on what had been a greenfield site projected a statement of intent: the Abbasids were determined to shed conventions and apply fresh ideas. Economic growth rippled across Mesopotamia; tenth-century Baghdad had over half a million inhabitants, Basra some 200,000.[2] (To compare, London's population in the eleventh century was below 20,000.) Few vestiges of Abbasid buildings have survived—many were torched during the Mongol invasion in the thirteenth century—but monuments to a capital of commerce and culture have endured in Arab literature. The *Arabian Nights* and authors such as Miskawaihi, Masudi, and Tanukhi gave a glimpse how all levels of society were affected by a seminal economic innovation—the emergence of a banking sector.

Several circumstances combined to bring about a new mode of funding government and business. One was that tax income alone never quite seemed to match the cost of pageantry Abbasid caliphs felt their status demanded; Abbasids had a reputation for elegance as well as for extravagance and the need to find new sources of income was perennial. But other factors also mattered. In Baghdad, trade routes overland to Asia and to the Mediterranean intersected with river traffic along the Tigris to the Indian Ocean. Baghdad's mercantile class applied traditional Arab trade expertise to acquire increasingly great riches and now explored ways to protect and increase its wealth. These two factors in isolation, however, still would not have sparked financial innovation but for combination with a third: the Abbasid caliphs staffed senior levels of their financial administration with Persian, Jewish, and Christian officials who introduced financial practices that originated in ancient Babylonia. The key innovation of Baghdad's financial markets—to charge commissions and interest—had Babylonian precedents set out in the world's oldest legal code, *Codex Hammurabi*. These factors equipped a new professional class, called *jahbads*, to put government into a position to raise loans; savers to make deposits; and businesses to finance long-distance trade. Babylonian approaches to coining money and taking deposits were blended with trade finance as practiced by Arabs, and from this confluence emerged in Baghdad a banking sector.

The transfer of power from Omayyads to Abbasids had been protracted and painful. Rising prosperity helped the Omayyads keep at bay frictions between the empire's diverse communities; no insurrection against Omayyad rule ever issued from a religious or ethnic minority. However, Omayyads had been able only to allay but never to suppress a lethal threat posed by their ancestral rivals, the Hashimites, waiting in the wings for the Omayyads to make a fatal blunder. The Abbasids, descendants of Muhammad's uncle Al Abbas, had to wait patiently for an opening to dislodge the Omayyads, but such occurred after the Omayyads lost their grip on fiscal management. The empire's tax revenues contracted, paradoxically, just as the ranks of Islam's adherents swelled, because conversion to Islam released a taxpayer from the liability for the land tax *kharaj*. Every time Islam won a convert, the treasury lost a taxpayer. This tax loophole tax officials plugged by applying a new land tax, *ushr*, but tax officials by solving a fiscal problem had only created a new one. Legal scholars found no justification for differential tax treatment of new and long-standing Muslims, to boot through taxes that in any event had never been mentioned in the Koran. The imputed infraction of Islamic principles set policymakers on a collision course with religious scholars, and disaffected taxpayers swelled the ranks of malcontents who hoped to gain from a regime change. Omayyad support ebbed away and in 750 the Abbasids staged a successful coup. (A sole Omayyad survived the purge. He fled to the opposite end of the Islamic realm, to Spain, and there a new Omayyad dynasty emerged.)

The Abbasid caliph Harun al Rashid, who exchanged embassies with rulers at opposite ends of the known world, the emperors of Germany and of China, reigned over an empire whose trade relations were truly global. We will never know whether the arresting stories in the *Arabian Nights* about Harun are based on fact or hearsay, whether, for example, Harun really excelled at playing polo and chess, and whether he, as the *Meadows of Gold* claimed, "scattered both wealth and the treasure of his justice on all his subjects."[3] But we know Harun's fame reached into Christendom where William of Tyre (writing four centuries later) noted Harun's "liberality, his unusual courtesy, and most excellent character."[4] These stories may be too good to be true—but the very fact that they circulated shows contemporaries sensed uncommon charisma and perceived a scale of opulence that surpassed anything that went before. Abbasid wealth, even discounting exaggerations, must have been substantial: Harun al Rashid reportedly bequeathed 48 million dinars. Conspicuous wealth must have been on display, for example, for the *Meadows of Gold* to record Harun's wife Umm Jafar Zubaida was "the first to be served on vessels of gold and silver enriched with precious stones,"[5] traveled in a litter wrought from ebony and silver, and dressed female pages in turbans and "in close-fitting wide-sleeved robes and wide belts which showed off their waists and their curves."[6] Such observations could only issue from a society familiar with affluence, and the *Meadows of Gold* affirmed Umm Jafar was a trendsetter who introduced "fashions which spread to the public."[7] A further clue to high disposable incomes was the proliferation of libraries and institutions of higher learning. Arab literature showed how wealth brings out the best and worst in people, and humorous anecdotes about the extremes Baghdadis went to to prevent burglary evinced the scale of wealth permeating the middle classes. For example, Baghdadis must already have had vaults, because Tanukhi told a story about an intrepid woman who trapped an intruder to her home in a strong room (a room "with an iron door") and slammed the door shut behind him to contain the hapless burglar until the police arrived. Another down-to-earth Tanukhi story is about a miser who hid his money by dropping gold coins into his toilet to throw burglars off the scent.[8] Such stories could only issue from a society where gossip revolved around money.

FISCAL REFORM

The Abbasids inherited a fiscal administration substantially unchanged from the days of Muawiyah. There were two separate government accounts, the Community Treasury and the caliph's Privy Purse. The former received the Koranic income tax *zakat*, the latter government land rents, inheritance of intestate estates, and predecessors' legacies. Each account had distinct budgetary responsibilities: the Community Treasury funded poor relief, officials' salaries, and release of slaves; the caliph, on the other hand, as spiritual head of Islam was responsible for supporting religious obligations in the wider sense, such as funding *jihad* (which included ransoming prisoners of war) and the *hajj* to Mecca. Masudi wrote Umm Jafar Zubaida donated 1.7 million dinars to build a twelve-mile aqueduct to supply water to Mecca and was a conspicuous patron who "had numerous caravanserais built at Mecca and she filled this city and the pilgrim road which bears her name with cisterns, wells and buildings which survive to this day."[9]

The Abbasid caliph Mutadid (857–902) was famous for his attention to government finances and also because—somewhat out of character for an Abbasid—he was uncommonly frugal. Mutadid had the ambition to amass ten million dinars and melt these into a gold cube that he would have put on display in his palace courtyard. However, he missed his target, if only narrowly, and when he died bequeathed nine million dinars to his son Muqtadir (895–932) who reverted to family habits and during his reign ran through seventy million dinars, leaving only half a million dinars when he died.[10] Mutadid restructured fiscal management by creating an office to supervise government expenditure and audit accounts headed by a chancellor, the *vizir*. The *vizir* needed firmness and tact to succeed at reining back government spending—anyone refusing to indulge the caliph's whims was liable to precipitate his master's ire. The *vizir* Ali ibn Isa (859–946) "was charged with parsimony, miserliness, and starving the army. He was however forced to adopt this course because he found the Sultan's expenses greatly in excess of this revenue."[11] *Vizirs* who combined accounting with diplomatic skills were remembered as statesmen rather than bureaucrats. A *vizir* was potentially more powerful than a *caliph*, and a wise ruler would appreciate the value of a sober accountant. One crown prince who swore revenge on a *vizir* who cut back his allowance thought better of it once he acceded to the throne. "The sultan needs him more," he said when reminded of his earlier threat, "than he needs me."[12]

Rivalries between Abbasid *vizirs* were as intense as those between members of the caliph's family. The orientalist Eliyahu Ashtor studied the family trees of Abbasid *vizirs* and concluded members of only four families held this office over the course of a century. Recruitment from a limited candidate pool may explain an endemic defect of Abbasid administration, namely corruption, because although *vizirs* ensured professional management of government cash flows, nobody supervised the *vizirs* who accumulated vast fortunes from "secret profits," a byword for bribes. The threat of confiscation hung over senior government appointees. Ashtor compiled a table of fines that shows confiscations in excess of one million dinars were common.[13] Harsh penalties were visited on *vizirs* following exposure; Arab histories abounded with graphic descriptions of grueling torture forcing disgraced *vizirs* to disgorge ill-gotten gains. The temptation of illicit gain coupled with the risk of confiscation instigated a vicious circle: it was only rational for a *vizir* to stash away as much money as possible to provide against confiscation that inevitably followed loss of office. The emotional stress of officials operating at the highest levels of government must have been traumatic. One *vizir* after accepting a particularly lucrative bribe broke out in tears and explained: "when a man's prosperity is of this style, what will his adversity be like?"[14]

THE FIRST GOVERNMENT LOAN

Provincial governors managed their own budgets and transferred to the center only a residual surplus. Provinces had a high degree of fiscal autonomy; they acted much like members of a federation and as such had no strong incentive to transfer funds to Baghdad. The caliph had to fund two main expenditures, the military and court life. The former was impossible to predict—wars and insurrections could break out at any time—and the latter was a constant drain. Even when the economy was booming, balancing the books was a struggle. Controlling provinces from the center was a constant challenge (hence local security chiefs were vitally important). The caliph's provincial revenues steadily eroded; the central government's tax revenue contracted by a quarter from the late eighth to late ninth century.[15]

Low cash balances forced the *vizir* to resort to creative accounting: at one point officials instead of receiving salaries in cash were issued scrips documenting payment at a later date with an option to cash these in at 50 percent of their face value. Many officials could not afford to wait for delayed settlement—and perhaps were wary settlement might be postponed again—and opted to cash in their scrips. This, in effect, amounted to a pay cut, which, however, was highly advantageous to the *vizir* who after having extinguished the government's payroll liability at a substantial discount then proceeded to credit the treasury with the full nominal amount. The *vizir* Ibn al Furat summed up his management philosophy: "governing relies on artful trickery, but when done to perfection becomes statecraft."[16] Accounting sleights of hand, however, were but a temporary remedy for structural deficits, and the treasury eventually took a step that broke new ground in managing public finance: it borrowed money from bankers.

In the mid-eighth century there appeared a new term, *jahbad*, to describe a new profession. The term was used for a government office, the *diwan al jahbad*, that managed the finances of Mutadid. One particular *jahbad* was a certain Christian by the name of Stephanos, hired by Muqtadir, and another Christian *jahbad*, Ibrahim ibn Ayyub, was recorded for 928.[17] *Jahbads* had official backing because, according to Tanukhi, if "a collector were dismissed and another appointed instead with whom the merchants had not dealt, the business of the Caliph would be at a standstill."[18] In court hierarchy the caliph's *jahbads* ranked on a par with post inspectors (that is to say, heads of internal security).

Tanukhi quoted documentation of the the first government loan advanced by two Jewish *jahbads*, Yusuf ibn Phineas and Harun ibn Amram:

> At the beginning of each month I need 30,000 dinars to pay the infantry troops within six days. I usually do not possess such sum, neither on the first nor on the second day of the month. I should like you to advance on the first day of

> each month a loan of 150,000 dirham, an amount that you will get back in the course of the month from the Ahwaz revenue; you are the collectors of the Ahwaz revenue, which will be a permanent concession to you.[19]

There was much haggling over terms (as Tanukhi phrased it, "the bankers made difficulties at first") but eventually both parties were satisfied with their bargain. In substance, this letter contained all the terms of a standard loan agreement: specifying why the borrower needs a loan, how it will be used, and when it will be repaid. The government bridged short-term cash shortages by pledging tax receipts as security, and the government's lender took charge of collecting taxes to service their advance. Moreover, this loan was not a one-off transaction, because the same *jahbads* again are mentioned in connection with another loan, this time with a sixteen-year term.[20] Lending money to government was not risk-free; in 931 the government defaulted on loans and the *jahbads* had to foreclose on crown estates.[21]

From deploying bankers as tax collectors, it was only a short step to granting them long-term concessions to act as government fiscal agents. Privatized tax collection transferred to a concessionaire the risk of reaching agreed income targets and seemed to be a solution to the caliph's chronic financial worries. Bankers and investors vied to underwrite taxes, and concessions were auctioned to the highest bidder. Ali ibn Isa opposed this practice from the outset; thus when a certain Hamid ibn Al Abbas submitted a particularly attractive bid, Ibn Isa warned "these principles might doubtless obtain a surplus for a year or two, but would introduce ruin which it might take many years to recover." However, the caliph overruled him, but soon would rue his decision. Miskawaihi gave a detailed account of the sequence of events that proved Ali ibn Isa right, when this case of misjudged privatization led to food riots in Baghdad.

Hamid had factored into his bid for tax concessions a forecast that grain prices would rise, and his business plan worked as follows: Hamid owned granaries and collected taxes from farmers in grain; thus he would warehouse grain collected from taxpayers, pay out his commitments to the government as per contract, and then sell grain into a rising market and pocket the surplus. Unfortunately, the market went against him—grain prices fell, which implied there would be a shortfall in the sums he needed to meet his commitments to the government. Hamid resorted to manipulating the market; he hoarded grain and expected lack of supply would drive up the price, which duly happened, but only further exacerbated his travails because an ensuing spike in grain prices led to shortages of bread. In Baghdad, riots broke out and warehouses were raided. Muqtadir, shocked by this turn of events, intervened with an order to "attend to the prices, and put a stop to the practice of delaying the sale of the crops, so that prices might fall." The outcome was that Hamid, who had overplayed his hand, forfeited his concession.[22] Ali ibn Isa, on the other hand, was vindicated.

SUFTAJAHS

Arab trade expertise was a key factor in evolving a fully fledged banking market in Baghdad. Pre-Islamic Arab merchants had found ways to transfer money across great distances, by the following means: they posted payment instructions that could be cashed in by a designated paying agent at a distant location. The term for these instructions was *suftajah* or *hawala*. The French term for a guarantee, *aval*, is derived from *hawala*. (A Persian variant was called *čak*, ancestor of the check—subtle differences apart, their purposes overlap.)

Suftajahs facilitated long-distance trade because merchants did not need to carry cash on their journey and so were relieved of the risk of robbery. What was needed for a working market in *suftajahs* was a network of designated paying agents in separate cities who would cash them in. Such was achieved when a merchant in, say, Baghdad, made a deposit with a local *jahbad* who would instruct a correspondent in, say, Basra, to pay out that sum to a designated beneficiary. Thus someone with an account with a *jahbad* could transfer money from Baghdad to Basra without incurring the risk of transport, and this payment system facilitated integration of an extensive trading area.[23] In principle, there was no reason why *suftajahs* could not also be used in a local market. Someone with an account with a *jahbad* could hand a *suftajah* to his grocer, and in this way even small purchases could be made without using cash. The Persian traveler Naser-e Khosraw praised the convenience of cashless shopping on a visit to Basra: "The procedure at the bazaar is as follows: you turn over whatever you have to a moneychanger and get in return a draft; then you buy whatever you need, deducting the price from the moneychanger's draft. No matter how long one might stay, one would never need anything more than a moneychanger's draft."[24] The demarcation lines between vouchers, paper money, and promissory notes were fluid. *Jahbads* charged a commission for handling *suftajahs*, usually at the rate of one dirham per dinar. In practice, the distinction between charging a commission (which was legitimate) and charging interest (which was illicit) was difficult to maintain.

Suftajahs were common before the advent of Islam and there is no reason to doubt they were in use in early Islam. The inference from a Koranic sura ascribed to Muhammad's Medinan period is that they were the subject of detailed regulation: "Believers, when you contract a debt for a fixed period, put it in writing. Let a scribe write it down for you with fairness . . . let the debtor dictate, fearing God his Lord and not diminishing the sum he owes . . .

So do not fail to put your debt in writing, be they small or large, together with the date of payment."[25] *Suftajahs* were used by Umar to pay for government spending, specifically, for food imports from Egypt to the Arabian port Al Djar. The amounts involved, it seems, must have been considerable; otherwise, Umar would have paid in cash, and also for another reason, because it came to light the volume of *suftajahs* in circulation was large enough to warrant a secondary market. Umar, on hearing *suftajahs* were traded, asked dealers to disclose how much money they had made, and when he discovered they had doubled their profits (but as ever, a rounded number signifies an approximation), he ordered them to cancel all trades. Dealers, however, found it impossible to comply with this command because too many *suftajahs* were already in circulation. In Al Djar, trading *suftajahs* continued until Osman, who deemed the practice usurious, banned it.[26] Muawiyah, on the other hand, accepted *suftajahs*, which, however, were not interest-bearing.[27] To understand how it could come about that in Baghdad interest could come to be charged, one needs to track back further than to the beginnings of Islam, to the origins of deposit-taking in ancient Babylonia.

BABYLONIAN BANKING

Coins were probably invented in the fifth century BC, but long before, the business of taking deposits existed in Babylonia in what the Belgian historian Raymond Bogaert termed "pre-monetary banking operations."[28] The Babylonian *Codex Hammurabi*, which was written around 1800 BC and is the world's oldest extant compendium of laws, included extensive rules for conduct of business, and penalties for negligence.[29] Coins were in circulation when Herodotus (ca. 500 BC) explained how Persians were thought to mint coins from bullion: "This tribute the king stores up in the following manner: he melts it down, and pours it into earthenware jars; and, after a vessel has been filled, he breaks the pottery. Whenever then there is need of money, he cuts off as much as may be required."[30]

Many financial professionals in Mesopotamia were Jewish; for example, Hajjaj ibn Yusuf employed Jewish assayers to mint early versions of Islamic dinars. The Hebrew monarchy had established a foundry linked to the temple, so there would have been Jewish assayers who were exposed to Mesopotamian minting practices during the Babylonian captivity of the Jewish people.[31] The Bible scholar Charles Torrey pointed out the Hebrew term for a professional who melted down offerings, *yoser*, comprised the Persian terms for "crucible" and "director."[32] In the course of minting coins, assayers likely took on the additional task of changing money since both activities require the same skill set, which may be the reason why the booths of moneychangers often could be found in the vicinity of religious sites.[33] Mecca's moneychangers, for example, placed their booths close to the *Kaaba*. The Babylonian term for a moneychanger, *surrupu*, migrated into Greek as *saraphes* and from there to Arabia as *sarafi*. Alexandria's moneychangers worked in the *suq al-sarf*, another term pointing to the profession's Babylonian origins, since *suqu* is an Akkadian term. In Baghdad, moneychangers were critically important to treasury officials because the Abbasid Empire had inherited from Persians and Byzantines the usage of coins of silver in the East and of gold in the West. Buoyant trade across the Abbasid Empire, combined with diverse coinage, stimulated demand for moneychangers: Ispahan in the early tenth century had some two hundred.[34]

TAKING INTEREST

The threads of the plot of how *jahbads* came to charge interest now can be pulled together. In Babylonia, even before coinage had been invented, the *Codex Hammurabi* entitled depositories to commissions; then, once coinage was invented, there emerged the profession of assayers who took on the related task of coin exchange. A tipping point for banking services in Baghdad may have occurred when *jahbads* were granted tax collection concessions on a multiyear basis, because at that juncture a recurring commission paid in regular intervals was indistinguishable from an interest payment. The borderlines between *jahbads*, merchants, and moneychangers were fluid, and a banking sector in Baghdad came into being by blending three constituents: Babylonian rules for taking deposits; Judaic assaying expertise; and Arab trade finance practices.

The benefits that would accrue to anyone who understood how to put deposits to work through lending them out were obvious (more attractive, at any rate, than hiding gold in a privy). An Arab adage set out what should be the proper academic pursuits of individual classes: "For kings the study of genealogy and histories, for warriors the study of battles and biography, and for merchants the study of writing and arithmetic."[35] Many Baghdadis must have taken this adage to heart, because financial literacy in tenth-century Baghdad was very high.

Tanukhi was conversant with the arithmetic whereby a minute miscalculation of interest payments can lead to extinguishing capital. As ever, Tanukhi wrapped his case study into an amusing anecdote. Thus a trader who had gone into debt for 4,000 dinars proposed to his debtors to repay them in ten annual instalments of 400 dinars and set out his cash flow: working with 400 dinars in capital, he will double that sum every year and pay over that profit until the debt is extinguished. His creditors suggested a tiny increase of the annual instalment, from 400 dinars to 401 dinars, but that proposal, however, met with the adamant objections by the borrower who then proceeded to demonstrate how concession of a single additional dinar would result in his inexorable ruin:

> "If I were to give one dinar more than the four hundred in the year, the four hundred dinars would by the end of nine years have disappeared and the arrears of the debt would remain where they were." We were surprised by this statement and asked him to show us how it could be true.—He replied: "Suppose I trade with these four hundred dinars for a year, and do well, the profit is four hundred dinars. Out of the total I pay 401 dinars, so that 399 remain. In the second year I trade with these, and make 798 dinars. Deduct 401, and there remain 397. At the end of the third year, the sum will be 794, deduct 401 and 393 remain. At the end of the fourth year the sum will be 786, deduct 401 and 385 remain. At the end of the fifth year the sum will be 770; deduct 401 and 369 remain. At the end of the sixth year the sum will be 738; deduct 401 and 337 remain. At the end of the seventh year the sum will be 674; deduct 401, and 273 remain. At the end of the eighth year the sum will be 546; deduct 401, and 145 remain. At the end of the ninth year the sum will be 290, which will be less by 111 than the 401 due."[36]

This anecdote demonstrated a remarkable financial sophistication. Calculating compound interest must have become a familiar mathematical technique to Islamic economists; two centuries later, al Dimashqi provided a variant anecdote that also explained the practicalities of compounding:

> A man had capital of 500 dinar, and annual income and outgoings of 500 dinar. In a given year, his expenses exceeded his income by 2 dinars and he drew these from his capital. Nine years later, he was a pauper and was sentenced to a debtor's prison. The reason was that in the first year he lost 2 dinars, in the second 4 dinars, in the third 8 dinars, in the fourth 16, in the fifth 32, in the sixth 64, in the seventh 128, in the eighth 256 and in the ninth 512 dinars.[37]

These anecdotes may be the world's oldest illustrations of the effect of compound interest.

NOTES

1. Masudi, *The Meadows of Gold*, 389.
2. Ashtor, *A Social and Economic History of the Near East in the Middle Ages*, 89.
3. Masudi, *The Meadows of Gold*, 389.
4. William of Tyre, *A History of Deeds Done Beyond the Sea*, Vol. 1, 64.
5. Masudi, *The Meadows of Gold*, 390.
6. Masudi, *The Meadows of Gold*, 391.
7. Masudi, *The Meadows of Gold*, 390.
8. Tanukhi, *The Table-Talk of a Mesopotamian Judge*, 284–86.
9. Masudi, *The Meadows of Gold*, 389-90.
10. Kremer, *Einnahmebudget des Abbasiden-Reiches*, 9.
11. Miskawaihi, *The Experiences of the Nations*, Vol. 1, 32.

12. Tanukhi, "The Table-Talk of a Mesopotamian Judge," 1929, 494–95.
13. Ashtor, *A Social and Economic History of the Near East in the Middle Ages*, 142.
14. Tanukhi, "The Table-Talk of a Mesopotamian Judge," 1930, 28.
15. Kremer, *Culturgeschichte des Orients,* Vol. 1, 271.
16. Tanukhi, "The Table-Talk of a Mesopotamian Judge," 1931, 565.
17. Fischel, "The Origin of Banking in Medieval Islam," 344.
18. Tanukhi, "The Table-Talk of a Mesopotamian Judge," 1929, 505.
19. Tanukhi, "The Table-Talk of a Mesopotamian Judge," 1929, 505.
20. Tanukhi, "The Table-Talk of a Mesopotamian Judge," 1929, 505.
21. Fischel, "The Origin of Banking in Medieval Islam," 581–82.
22. Miskawaihi, *The Experiences of the Nations*, Vol. 1, 76–82.
23. Spuler, *Iran in früh-islamischer Zeit*, 410.
24. Naser-e Khosraw, *Book of Travels*, 91.
25. Koran 2:282–84.
26. Jacob, "Die ältesten Spuren des Wechsels," 280–81.
27. Chester, "On Early Moslem Promissory Notes," xliii.
28. Bogaert, *Les origines antiques de la banque de dépôt*, 174.
29. *Codex Hammurabi,* §§ 100–126.
30. Herodotus, *Histories*, Book 3, chapter 96.
31. Torrey, "The Foundry of the Second Temple at Jerusalem."
32. Torrey, "The Evolution of a Financier in the Ancient Near East."
33. Bogaert, *Les origines antiques de la banque de dépôt*, 154.
34. Spuler, *Iran in früh-islamischer Zeit*, 410.
35. Baladhuri, *The Origins of the Islamic State*, Vol. 1, 2.
36. Tanukhi, "The Table-Talk of a Mesopotamian Judge," 1931, 188–89.
37. Ritter, "Ein arabisches Handbuch der Handelswissenschaft," 75–76.

Chapter Fourteen

Islamic Philanthropy: *Waqfs*

Muhammad was at ease with children. He let his granddaughter Omama perch on his shoulders while he prayed; when he knelt he laid her down on the ground; and he held her in his arms when again he rose.[1] A child had to do something truly naughty to make Muhammad lose his temper. One such incident occurred, however, when Muhammad's grandson Hassan spotted a date lying on the ground and unwittingly did what most toddlers do in that situation: he stuck it in his mouth. At a flash, Muhammad fingered the date out of Hassan's mouth: "Spit it out!" he scolded him. "Don't you know you are not to eat *sadaka?*"[2] No contrast could be starker than that between the Prophet, unruffled by Omama tugging his hair during prayers, and Muhammad glowering over Hassan innocently sucking something sweet. Muhammad's outburst was not in character, and we may assume Muhammad on this occasion contrived his ire to convey an unequivocal message: nobody, not even a child, had a right to take away property rightfully owned by the poor.

Property rights were taken very seriously in early Islam, and Amr ibn al As claimed the Prophet had dictated to him an entire manual on the subject.[3] That Amr al As would have liked others to believe he had inside knowledge of the Prophet's thoughts could hardly be coincidental; Amr al As's embezzlements during his tenure as Egypt's governor were egregious and such a manual would have done much to exonerate him. Amr al As, however, when challenged to produce the manual, had to admit that unfortunately he had lost it (which response did little to repair his reputation for unreliability). That Muhammad's successors deemed it credible, however, that such a dictation might exist, shows they knew how much importance Muhammad attached to defining property rights.

Providing alms was a central obligation for Muslims, and early Islamic societies from a combination of Koranic injunctions, Muhammadan precedents, and institutional learning evolved institutions dedicated to perform that express purpose, called *waqfs*. Initially, *waqfs* operated on a small scale, such as by giving over an orchard to grow food for the poor, but aims of *waqfs* proliferated and their endowments grew to substantial dimensions. *Waqfs* by the sixteenth century were capable of funding a comprehensive range of social services. In 1552, Suleyman the Magnificent's wife Roxelana endowed a *waqf* in Jerusalem with income from "26 entire villages, several shops, a covered bazaar, 2 soap plants, 11 flour mills, and 2 bathhouses, all in Palestine and Lebanon."[4] The origins of *waqfs*, however, lie in the early years of Muhammad's tenure.

Islamic society did not invent philanthropy, but innovated how philanthropy was delivered. Before the advent of Islam, care for the indigent for the most part was in the hands of their families. But alternatives existed. In ancient Rome, the state looked after the poor; after the Roman state collapsed, Christian churches succeeded to that mandate. However, charitable giving as a rule was voluntary and ad hoc. The closest precedents to *waqfs* existed in Jewish communities; Jews during their exile in Babylonia tasked their temples to manage charitable donations and from there the practice may have spread throughout Jewish communities. Samhudi reported Osman ibn Affan paid 40,000 dirhams for a well in Medina owned by a Jewish neighbor and gave it over to free use by Muslims.[5]

The purpose of a *waqf* and of *zakat* is the same, but they differ in the way they are funded. *Zakat* was levied from annual income; a *waqf*, on the other hand, consisted in vesting a fixed asset—say, an orchard—and setting aside its future income—its fruit—for predetermined beneficiaries. This difference had far-reaching consequences, because once a *waqf* had an independent source of income, it could commit to paying for recurring needs, it could even, as in the case of Roxelana's bequest, pay for public infrastructure. This was an institutional innovation of great moment, because social welfare in early Islam thus had two sources of funding: the government paid for pensions, and privately funded endowments provided charitable purposes outside the government's remit. *Waqfs* promoted social welfare in the widest sense: its origins went back to actions taken by Muhammad.

MUQAIRIQ AND MUHAMMAD

Muhammad laid the foundation of Islam's charitable sector with Judaic practices before his eyes.[6] Muqairiq, a Jewish recruit to Muhammad's army who was fatally wounded at the battle of Uhud, bequeathed to Muhammad seven properties with the dying wish he use them for the promotion of Islam. Thus passed into Muhammad's possession properties subject to constraints predetermined by the donor. A grateful Muhammad singled out Muqairiq for praise by calling him the "best of the Jews." Muqairiq had exposed Muhammad to a new concept, one that he apprehended quickly and soon adapted to his own uses. Muhammad applied the principle of tied giving after the conquest of Khaybar when he vested his companions with land grants—but stipulated how harvests were to be distributed. Umar (and others) thus came to possess large swaths of land, but with property rights constrained in a way that in practice he was a trustee rather than an owner. Some traditions claimed Umar had taken the initiative to endow a *waqf* and had received Muhammad's express permission.[7] In any event, endowments granted by Muhammad after the conquests of Khaybar were *waqfs* in all but name, and a formative moment for the evolution of *waqfs* took place through the settlement of Muhammad's estate when his successors refined the concept.

Muhammad's executor Abu Bakr, faced with the decision what to do with Muhammad's properties in Medina, Khaybar, and Fadak, looked for guidance in the Bible; given Muhammad was a prophet, he inferred his estate should be settled in the same way as that of every other prophet, and, since no prophet had ever bequeathed to his family conspicuous wealth, it followed that Muhammad's next of kin had no claim on his assets. Abu Bakr reasoned Muhammad had ruled in his capacity as Messenger of God, which implied his assets belonged to his office rather than to his person. Thus Abu Bakr established property could be held either in a personal capacity or on behalf of a third party, and this fine distinction he applied not only to passing on power but also to passing on property. Into Islamic legal thinking at that moment entered a subtle but crucial legal distinction between personal and fiduciary ownership.

Abu Bakr put this approach into practice in settling his own estate. Abu Bakr as caliph never took advantage of his official position to enrich himself, but his personal property, on the other hand, he vested in a *waqf* where he nominated his family members as beneficiaries. Abu Bakr, in other words, created a family trust fund, and anyone who wished to keep wealth in the family copied this example. His successor Umar applied the concept of fiduciary ownership to virtually all of the booty that came into his possession in his capacity as caliph. All of Egypt, recently conquered, Umar vested in a *waqf* and designated as beneficiary the *umma*. Osman refused to respect the distinction between personal and fiduciary property (and thereby precipitated his overthrow), but he, too, was conversant with the concept of vesting property for public use. When Osman defended himself against charges of embezzling public monies, he reminded his accusers of the well in Medina he had bought and given over to free use. Ali, on succeeding Osman, emulated Umar's precedent and gave over most of his personal property to support the poor.

LEGAL FRAMEWORK

Waqfs were a hybrid form of social institution, outside control by government or by private interests. The legal structure of *waqfs* was refined over time. *Waqfs* developed from embryonic charities into fully fledged entities with their own legal framework, governance structure, and endowments. To qualify as a *waqf*, a bequest had to meet three criteria: first, it had to be irrevocable, perpetual, and inalienable; second, residual assets in case of termination fell to poor relief; and third, a jurist and witnesses had to attest the vesting process had been carried out in compliance with the law.[8]

Corporate governance was designed to guard against conflicts of interest. A benefactor was prohibited from drawing personal benefits from his endowment and had to appoint a manager, the *mutawalli*, who balanced the books and managed the *waqf*. The donor determined the purposes of a *waqf*, and if unforeseen circumstances rendered the original *waqf* statutes obsolete, clarification of discretionary authority was subject to approval by a *qadi*. Court cases involving *waqfs* were frequent. Maya Shatzmiller has pointed out one court case in medieval Fez where Islamic courts discerned the fine distinction between a *waqf*'s asset base and cash flow.[9] On that occasion, a benefactor in Fez had endowed a *waqf* to maintain a local mosque with the stipulation never to permit alterations to the mosque's structure. A legal dilemma arose when a Jewish community living in quarters adjoining the mosque asked the *mutawalli* for permission to channel water to their homes from a well in the mosque's courtyard. This proposal placed the *mutawalli* in a quandary: on the one hand, he would have liked to earn an annual fee, but on the other hand, laying a canal would break down the wall to the courtyard and thereby contravene the *waqf*'s statutes. A *qadi* who was asked for a ruling approved the transaction on condition the lessees agreed not only to pay annual rent but also defray the costs of building the canal and repairing the wall. Through assigning capital costs to the lessees, the *waqf*'s asset base remained undiminished and the *mutawalli* remained compliant with the *waqf*'s statutes.

The economist Timur Kuran has pointed out that *waqfs* were not immune to corporate abuse.[10] *Mutawallis* could overcharge for their services, or worse, misappropriate funds. In another case from medieval Fez, a *mutawalli* had speculated in grain markets and squandered the entire endowment when the market went against him. The greatest risk, however, was expropriation. Judges had to be resolute and honest in equal measure to protect the integrity of *waqfs* against abuse by managers as well as by governments. The Baghdadi author Tanukhi gave a glimpse of the tensions involved in several stories about a fictional judge, Abu Hazim. In one of these stories, Abu Hazim confronts a *mutawalli* over a shortfall in a *waqf*'s accounts and it transpires the *mutawalli* has a debtor he is too timid to pursue: he is none other than the caliph Mutadid. The reader at this point empathizes with the *mutawalli*'s hesitation—who would dare risk a caliph's wrath by insisting he settle his debts? But Abu Hazim stands firm: he rebukes the *mutawalli* and threatens to fire him unless he presses his claim. The *mutawalli*, faced with the prospect of losing his job, has no option but to confront Mutadid, and Tanukhi lets his readers know into how suspenseful a situation Abu Hazim had forced the *mutawalli* to venture because the caliph, after hearing the demand for money, "was silent for a while, rapt in thought." Fortunately, tensions are resolved and there is a happy ending: Mutadid pays his arrears; the *waqf* meets its commitments; and the *mutawalli* keeps his job. Tanukhi sums up the moral of the story that "there was general gratitude to Abu Hazim for his boldness, and to Mutadid for his justice."[11] In another story, Abu Hazim prevails upon Mutadid to respect the benefactions for orphans because there "is God's law concerning those who are of age; how much more must it be observed in the case of infants?"[12] Tanukhi's stories have the ring of personal observation; indeed, Tanukhi by profession was a judge.

ASSETS UNDER MANAGEMENT

Endowing a *waqf* satisfied a donor's desire for social prestige, secured his assets from the government's grasp, and as a means to fulfill Islam's demand to support the poor. *Waqfs* were endowed by bequests; often one third of an estate was reserved for a *waqf*. *Waqfs* funded wells, roads, hospitals, and schools (and hence all forms of professional scholarship and research). Some schools could be luxurious; a fourteenth-century *madrasa* in Cairo was fitted with marble floors and Lebanon cedars for the ceiling.[13] Because *waqfs* controlled substantial wealth, by implication they constrained the state's tax base and power. In fourteenth-century Egypt, most of the Nile valley's agricultural land was vested in *waqfs*.

NOTES

1. Caetani, *Annali dell'Islam*, Vol. 5, 21–22.
2. Gil, "The Earliest *waqf* Foundations," 128.
3. Gil, "The Earliest *waqf* Foundations," 126.
4. Kuran, "The Provision of Public Goods under Islamic Law," 849.
5. Samhudi, *Geschichte der Stadt Medina*, 149.
6. Gil, "The Earliest *waqf* Foundations."
7. Krcsmárik, "Das Wakfrecht," 512.
8. Kuran, "The Provision of Public Goods under Islamic Law: Origins, Impact and Limitations of the *Waqf* System," 863.
9. Shatzmiller, "Islamic Institutions and Property Rights: The Case of the 'Public Good' *Waqf*," 65–66.
10. Kuran, *The Long Divergence*.
11. Tanukhi, "The Table-Talk of a Mesopotamian Judge," 1929, 496–97.

12. Tanukhi, “The Table-Talk of a Mesopotamian Judge,” 1929, 522.
13. Petry, “From Slaves to Benefactors,” 66.

Chapter Fifteen

Islamic Venture Capital: *Qirâds*

Muhammad was eight years old when his grandfather Abd al Mutallib died and his uncle Abu Talib became his guardian. At this stage in life, Muhammad had lost his father, his mother, and now a grandfather who had marked him by his favor. What feelings of abandonment these bereavements produced in the little boy we may only guess, but we sense what were his emotions from the single event in the aftermath of his grandfather's demise that Arab historians deemed noteworthy: Muhammad between the ages of eight and ten years set forth on his first caravan journey. This event, it seems, followed from his instigation. Accordingly, Abu Talib was on the eve of departing on a caravan venture, when his charge clung to him and did not stop pleading to let him join. Muhammad was a headstrong boy inclined to tantrums (his foster sister had bite marks to show for that), but Abu Talib may have empathized with the anxieties that actuated this particular outburst. Abu Talib was conscious Muhammad had been bereaved when his father had not returned from a caravan journey and again had been bereaved by his grandfather's recent passing, and now Abu Talib saw this orphan clinging to him and begging not to let him out of his sight. A little boy on a grueling trip across deserts would be a hindrance rather than help—Abu Talib knew that—but having just taken Muhammad into his care, nonetheless he acquiesced. Thus was Muhammad at a precocious age inducted to caravan life, the lifeblood of Mecca's economy, a business model that the Koran pronounced enjoyed divine approbation: "For the protection of the Quraysh: their protection in their summer and winter journeyings. Therefore let them worship the Lord in this House who fed them in the days of famine and shielded them from all peril."[1]

Few mentions were made of Muhammad's participation in other caravan journeys; Arab historians referred to five caravans where Muhammad took part, but these mentions are only in passing. The small number suggests perhaps these journeys occurred before he married, or caravan journeys generally were considered a routine activity that did not merit express notice. On the other hand, Muhammad was no stranger to the rigors of desert travel because even in his fifties he was sufficiently fit to lead raids. Also, caravan ventures were what first brought Muhammad to Khadija's notice, and Khadija is unlikely to have invested capital in his venture without prior evidence of Muhammad's competence. One historian, Bar Hebraeus, explained Muhammad embarked on caravan missions early in his career but later delegated that task to others; he claimed Khadija's financial backing was critical for Muhammad's career ("with the wealth of this woman, and with her camels he became a merchant, and he went up from Yathreb his city to Palestine.")[2] and later he left it to others to trade on his behalf ("and when those who cleaved to him increased in number, he himself did not go up with them to share in the profit, but he sent other men at the head of the caravans while he himself dwelt in honour in his city.")[3] Most likely, Muhammad after he married focused on managing his leather business and on trade in Mecca's market.

CARAVANS IN MUHAMMAD'S DAY

Mecca's caravans were communal undertakings. Goods needed to be prepared in time for despatch with northbound traffic in summer or with southbound traffic in winter. Caravans offered to the poor opportunities for employment, to the rich opportunities for investment. A convoy of 2,500 camels with some 300 staff would comprise a portfolio of manager/investor arrangements, and individual investors would have underwritten different ventures. Mecca's staple export was leather goods, and merchants on the return leg of their journey carried goods such as grain, wine, or cloth, and on arrival in Mecca, settled accounts with investors. Equipping, provisioning, and supervising the progress of caravans required managerial skill. A caravan through combining individual commercial ventures reduced overheads and achieved economies of scale. A caravan comprised multiple *qirâds*; Muhammad's first expedition, for example, consisted of two camels, and his investor Khadija would have invested capital in ventures of several other merchants. A senior business leader in charge of managing a caravan oversaw logistics and security, but individual merchants who joined his convoy traded on their own account.

Many individual merchants combined to launch a particular caravan, and each camel's cargo represented a substantial investment of labor and materials. The progress of a caravan depended on a wide range of professionals with differentiated skill sets, those of guides, guards, staff, managers, and investors. But managing logistics was but one aspect of the managerial challenges involved; a sophisticated legal framework defined the rights and duties of everyone involved, and most important, their share in profits and losses. The *qirâd* was a flexible yet durable business model enabling investors and entrepreneurs to pool resources and skills in pursuit of profit. Islamic law perfected the legal framework of *qirâds*, casting rules for profit shares, corporate governance, and business ethics. With the expansion of the Islamic Empire, business communities throughout the Middle East were exposed to *qirâds*.

An account by Waqidi of Mecca's caravan traveling to Badr gave a sense of the scale of investment committed to caravans:

> It was a caravan of a thousand camels. It contained significant wealth, for there was not a man or woman from the Quraysh in Mecca who had some wealth accruing, but it was sent in the caravan. Even the woman who had a paltry sum sent it. Some said that it contained 50,000 dinar, though others said there was less, it was said that much of what was in it came from the property of Said ibn al-As—Abu Ubayha—either the wealth belonged to them, or to those who borrowed against half the profits to be made, and most of the caravan belonged to them. Some said that it belonged to the Banu Makhzum who owned 20 camels and four or five thousand pieces of gold. . . . There were 10,000 gold pieces belonging to the Banu Abd Manaf in the caravan. Their merchandise was going to Gaza from Al-Sham and there were several small caravans that the Quraysh concealed in it—i.e., in the large caravan.[4]

Waqidi shows how these arrangements worked—merchants would invest their own capital as well as funds entrusted by third parties under profit-sharing agreements ("the wealth belonged to them, or to those who borrowed against half the profits to be made"). Waqidi's account estimated a caravan of 1,000 camels represented a value of some 7,000 ounces of gold (today, commensurate with several million dollars).

LEGAL FRAMEWORK OF *QIRÂDS*

The Koranic ban on usury was directed against lending but not, however, against investing. There is a distinction between a lender and an investor that is key: lenders are entitled to repayment irrespective whether the borrower has made a profit, whereas an investor, on the other hand, shares the risk of the undertaking. For this reason, investments were deemed licit. The complexity and compass of commercial ventures posed legal challenges: investors and managers needed to know what to expect of each other, above all, how to share profits and losses. Ali ibn Abi Talib determined the approach to allocating profits and losses: "Profit follows the conditions agreed upon, loss follows the capital."[5] The earliest compilation of Islamic law, the *Muwatta*, devoted a full section to defining terms and conditions of *qirâds*. Accordingly, the manager of a *qirâd* seeks to earn a profit on capital but is not liable for losses.[6] The Hanefite lawyer Marghinani confirmed *qirâds* "are authorized by the law from necessity; since many people have property who are unskilled in the art of employing it; and others, again, possess that skill without having the property:—hence there is a necessity for authorizing these contracts, in order that the interests of the rich and the poor, and of the skilful and the unskilled, may be reconciled:—moreover, people entered into such contacts in the presence of the prophet, who did not prohibit, but confirmed the same: several of the companions also, entered into these contracts."[7]

Sharakshi, a medieval Arab jurist, already had a conception of *qirâds* that in effect overlaps with that of a venture capital fund. *Qirâds*, he wrote, served an important economic purpose,

> because people have a need for this contract. For the possessor of capital may not find it possible to engage in profitable trading activity, and the person who can find it possible to engage in such activity may not possess the capital. And profit cannot be attained except by means of both of these, that is, capital and trading activity. By operating this contract, the goal of both parties is attained.[8]

Profit shares were fixed in advance. Investors and managers needed to set salary and bonus levels before commencing operations; indeterminacy was deemed usurious. Prohibitions applied to contingent profit shares, namely agreements where managers were guaranteed a particular profit, or would not receive any bonus unless a certain level had been reached. Typically, the profits were shared between managers and investors in a ratio of 1:4 to 3:4. However, this ratio was not legally binding and subject to negotiation; experienced managers could demand higher profit shares. Managers also were allowed to invest their own equity, in which case their remuneration combined salary and dividends.

There were loopholes for managerial abuse because managers were entitled to profit shares but exempt from bearing losses. Conceivably, a manager could act on account of two separate *qirâds* with profits accruing to distinct lines of business, say, one for trading in wool and another for trading in silk. Thus there was an incentive to book losses to one *qirâd* and profits to another, thereby excluding losses from bonus calculations. A case was brought before a *qadi* where investors sued a manager who exploited this loophole to maximize his bonus; the *qadi* imposed on the manager a duty to set off losses from profits and calculate his bonus on the residual balance.

Qirâds funded specific ventures, typically a caravan, and were wound up when the caravan had returned. Managers who demonstrated commercial acumen were in a strong bargaining position to negotiate attractive terms for subsequent assignments, whereas unsuccessful managers would be mindful they could not attract investors. Investors could spread their investment over several ventures, and invite other investors to underwrite particular ventures if the risk of loss was deemed too large. The *qirâd* combined advantages of portfolio management and of insurance. Non-Muslims could invest in *qirâds* but were not allowed to manage them, because *qirâds* had to comply with Islamic injunctions, for example, against trading in wine, and since investors could not monitor managers a ban on non-Muslims executives was the only way to ensure Islamic injunctions were respected.[9]

QIRÂDS IN EARLY ISLAM

Muhammad and his companions often acted as investors or investees in *qirâd*s. One prominent companion of Muhammad, Talha, did not take part in the Battle of Badr because he was on a trade mission to Syria; Abd ar Rahman within a few years of emigration to Medina assembled caravans of 700 camels; Al Abbas received Muhammad's express approval for terms of a *qirâd.*[10] Other *qirâd* investors from Muhammad's circle were Aisha, Umar, and most notably Osman.

Investable funds in Medina surged after Muhammad died and tax revenue flooded into the *diwan.* Officials were quick to exploit profit opportunities. Once Basra's treasurer Abu Musa entrusted Umar's sons Abdullah and Ubaidullah with tax proceeds for delivery to Umar in Medina, and Umar's sons spotted a business opportunity: the ready cash in their possession they used to buy goods in Basra, which they took to Medina and there sold, passing to the *diwan* the principal while keeping the profit. Umar, as they might have predicted, was critical of their behavior because he was ever wary of exposing his family to charges of nepotism. Umar questioned his sons whether Abu Musa had advanced funds to anyone else and when they responded in the negative accused them of abusing their privileged position: "He made you the loan because you are the sons of the Amir al-Muminin, so pay the principal and the profit." The sons protested that impounding their profits would be unfair because they had run a risk and would have been liable for losses. Umar was indifferent to their pleas, however, until a counselor found a viable solution to this impasse; he recommended treating the transaction as a *qirâd,* in which case, he argued, by casting the *diwan* as a notional equity partner, Umar's sons were entitled to half of the profit. This story likely was passed on to justify using public money to invest in venture capital.

Government service, however lucrative, was not the exclusive path to acquire wealth in early Islam. Muhammad's close adviser Az Zobayr, who pursued a career in commerce and never took up an official appointment, left an estate valued at 52 million dirhams. The outlines of Az Zobayr's business model can be inferred from Ibn Sad's account how his estate was settled.[11]

Accordingly, Az Zobayr at the time of his death left no cash and had liabilities of 2.2 million dirhams. His assets comprised two rural estates and an urban property portfolio consisting of eleven properties in Medina, two in Basra, one in Kufa, and one in Fustat.[12] On first blush, it seems incongruous how a magnate could have outstanding debt, but Ibn Sad's account reveals the reason: Az Zobayr managed an investment fund where he pledged his properties as security for investments in commercial ventures. Thus, his son, Abdallah, had to sell off properties. It took four years to wind up the estate, which suggests that some of these trade ventures must have been pending for several years. Abdallah was able to take advantage of a booming property market, selling 27 lots of property, and dividing the estate between Az Zobayr's four wives, nine daughters, and nine sons. The deceased had reserved one-third for Abdallah's children; the balance was divided into 864 lots valued at 40,740 dirhams per lot. Each widow and daughter received 1.1 million dirhams; each son 2.3 million dirhams.

Two facts stand out from Ibn Sad's account. First, the estate of Az Zobayr was larger than that left by Osman, which shows an entrepreneur could be richer than a caliph; second, Az Zobayr did not leave cash, which shows he was fully invested at the time of his death—Az Zobayr was a devout Muslim who had complied with the Koranic injunction that gold should not lie fallow.

As Waqidi's account showed, caravans offered commercial opportunities for small as well as large investors, female investors included; Umar's sons demonstrated public money could be used for investment purposes; and the settlement of Az Zobayr's estate showed how much money could be made from investment management. Islamic law framed a corporate structure sufficiently durable to enable investment in long-distance trade—to continue even in the midst of military hostilities during the crusades.

NOTES

1. Koran 106:1–4.
2. Bar Hebraeus, *The Chronography of Bar Hebraeus*, Vol. 1, 90–91.
3. Bar Hebraeus, *The Chronography of Bar Hebraeus*, Vol. 1, 91.
4. Waqidi, *The Life of Muhammad*, 15.
5. Udovitch, *Partnership and Profit in Early Islam*, 129.
6. Malik ibn Anas, *Muwatta*, 280.
7. Marghinani, *Hedaya*, Vol. 3, chapter 1.
8. Sharakshi quoted in Ray, "The Medieval Islamic System of Credit and Banking," 45–46.
9. For examples see Goitein, *A Mediterranean Society*, Vol. 2, chapter 7.
10. Maqdisi, *Short Biography of the Prophet Mohammed and His Ten Companions*, 77; Udovitch, *Partnership and Profit in Early Islam*, 173.
11. Sprenger, *Das Leben und die Lehre des Mohammad*, Vol. 1, 424–28.
12. Wüstenfeld, *Die Familie el-Zubeir*, 34.

Chapter Sixteen

Islamic Trade Centers: *Funduqs*

Markets were common in Arabia before the advent of Islam. But when the realm of Islam expanded and with it the resources and range of its economy, every aspect of markets was adapted: their infrastructure, taxation, and regulation. Merchants now were afforded trade centers, called *funduqs*, with discrete fiscal and legal provisions, where they mingled with merchants from foreign countries. Many *funduqs* were located in Islamic cities that were gateways to trade with Mediterranean Europe, particularly along the coastline from Syria to Egypt. The path tracking to the origins of Islamic markets leads back to the Medina of Muhammad, a city that contained four markets on the eve of his arrival, and where shortly after settling there he added a fifth.[1]

Pre-Islamic markets in Arabia tended to be transitory, taking place on certain days of the week or during certain periods during the year, say, the pilgrimage season. Local food markets took place outdoors on certain days of the week and traders dispersed once transactions had been settled; this was the pattern before Muhammad's eyes when he settled in Medina. Muhammad's first market in Medina consisted merely of a tent, but when competitors destroyed it Muhammad staked out a new place for trading and inaugurated it with this pronouncement to his adherents: "This is your market; and no tax will be assessed on it."[2] Two aspects of the new foundation had far-reaching implications for developing markets in Islam in future. The first was this market was sized such that a camel saddle placed at its center could be seen from every boundary; it was, in other words, much larger than a tent and offered scope for expansion. Moreover, Muhammad exempted the market from taxation. Muhammad would not have made an express point of tax exemption unless such would not have differentiated the new market from existing ones, and once again Muhammad used fiscal incentives as a means to promote his policies. Tax exemption created a competitive advantage because it reduced transaction costs. Muhammad took another step to make Medina more attractive to merchants, by declaring the Medina market a *haram*, that is to say, a safe haven for traders, in competition with the *haram* established in Mecca.

The Omayyads made sweeping changes to the Medina market, both to its physical structure and to how it was managed. Muawiyah erected two buildings on the hitherto open air market and Abd al Malik's successor Hisham replaced these buildings with a single, two-storied structure that had a ground floor given over as storage space, called *magazine* (the term is Arabic) and a first floor offering residential accommodation. The new building presented an attractive façade with doors imported from Damascus and afforded an office for an official who supervised market transactions, the *muhtasib*. Considering the market building covered the entire Medina market, no other building in Medina other than the mosque could have been of comparable size.

Building a permanent physical infrastructure transformed the character of trading on the Medina market. Before, the market had been accessible to all and nobody was allowed to encroach on it: Umar had prohibited a blacksmith from placing there a furnace; Ali had rebuked traders who had secured fixed locations for their booths: "For the Muslims, the market is similar to the place of worship: he who arrives first can hold his seat all day until he leaves it."[3] The conversion of Medina's market from an open-air into a walled structure with controlled access and storage marked a transition of Arab trade, because once the Omayyads had moved the market into a building, access to the market became subject to control. That restriction might have been expected to reduce competition, but in fact, had the effect of widening the circle of potential market entrants because merchants traveling from afar now knew that Medina's market afforded secure storage and accommodation. Moreover, merchants who rented storage space could remain on call in the market for extended periods and business could take place all year round, rather than, as had been the norm in pre-Islamic times, transacted on the day or during a particular period. Long-distance trade incurred lower costs through improved infrastructure, and new profit opportunities beckoned.

A second Omayyad departure from Muhammadan practice was the introduction of a tax on sales. Arguably, there was a justification for this tax because constructing and maintaining a building incurred costs. However, a tax on the market remained contentious given Muhammad's express provisions to the contrary, and merchants took their grievance to legal scholars who affirmed market taxes indeed had no Koranic justification. After the caliph Walid had died, Medinan traders instigated Islam's first tax rebellion: they tore down the building and tax freedom was restored. Medina's market then was constituted as a *waqf*.[4] (Tax rebellions in Islamic trade centers recurred; merchants felt they had the right to resist commercial levies that had no basis in the Koran.) Hadiths were adduced confirming conversion of the Medina market into a *waqf* accorded with Muhammad's wishes.[5]

HOSTING FOREIGN MERCHANTS

Mecca's prosperity had derived from hosting pilgrims and the trade they brought with them. Pre-Islamic hospitality carried over into Islam; providing financial support to travelers in need was one of the express purposes of *zakat*. The need for such support presumably arose often; numerous accounts of the time report the frightening incidence of banditry. Muhammad had wished pilgrims were housed free of charge in Mecca, and Umar, commanding a limitless budget, added free pilgrim guesthouses in Medina and Kufa, along with improving roads, water supply, and policing. The increasing traffic volume brought with it an increase in trade.

Pilgrims and merchants had been the wellspring of Mecca's pre-Islamic prosperity and Islam seamlessly continued promoting long-distance trade. The Koran enjoins Muslims to afford legal protection to non-Muslim travelers.[6] Foreign merchants, called *mustamin*, paid a 10 percent tax (matching that applied to Muslims entering Byzantine territory) and were entitled to a one-year residence permit (compared to a four-month cap for Muslims traveling in Byzantine territories). However, *mustamin* had to comply with Islamic prohibitions, such as those against usury and selling wine, and were barred from exporting military equipment (such as horses, saddles, and weapons).

The American medievalist Olivia Remie Constable has shown *funduqs* were a common feature of major trade centers in the Islamic Empire.[7] Affording built infrastructure to accommodate foreign merchants was not an innovation originating in Islam. *Funduqs* had not existed in pre-Islamic Arabia; even Mecca had none. Antecedents to *funduqs* existed in the Byzantine and Persian Empires that provided staging posts on overland routes, *khans* or *caravanserais*, containing stables, storage rooms, and accommodation. This fixed infrastructure remained in use after the Muslim conquests and the terms for hostel used in Greek and Hebrew, *pandocheion* and *punduk*, migrated into Arabic as *funduq*. Expatriate merchants rented rather than owned *funduqs*; local authorities were landlords and hence responsible for upkeep and repair. Ownership of the *funduq's* building put authorities into a position to monitor the comings and goings of merchants, and *funduqs* were a means to shelter as well as to control foreign visitors; at times they were suspected of spying and some were first jailed and then released, security precautions even foreigners did not consider unreasonable. An expatriate Greek merchant in Baghdad, a certain Patrikios, warned the caliph about security risks: "The markets are in the city," said Patrikios, "as no one can be denied access to them, the enemy can enter under the guise of someone who wishes to carry on trade."[8] An eighth-century pilgrim to Jerusalem, Willibald, was released after convincing authorities of his innocence and then given a tour of local markets by an Arab merchant keen to advertise the range of wares: "on Sunday he took them to church through the market, that they might see the shops, and whatever they seemed to take a liking to he afterwards bought for them at his own expense."[9] Travel conventions had improved by the ninth century, however, when a certain Bernard the Wise, embarking on a boat in Bari (then under Muslim rule), was issued by the local sultan a letter of safe passage. Bernard noted markets on his journey from Egypt to Palestine "in which the Christians and pagans traffic for the things necessary on the journey."[10] Bernard was impressed by the respect Muslims showed to Christians:

> The Christians and Pagans have there [in Jerusalem and Egypt] such a peace between them, that if I should go a journey, and in the journey my camel or ass which carries my baggage should die, and I should leave everything there without a guard, and go to the next town to get another, on my return I should find all my property untouched. The law of public safety is there such, that if they find in a city, or on the sea, or on the road, any man journeying by night or by day, without a letter, or some mark of a king or a prince of that land, he is immediately thrown into prison, till the time he can give a good account whether he be a spy or not.[11]

Security precautions were still in place in the fifteenth century when Johann Schiltberger, a Bavarian visiting Alexandria, noticed a strict curfew applied during times when Muslims assembled in the mosque for prayer: "It is the custom at Alexandria, that at the hour of vespers, all the Italians must be in their counting-houses, and no longer without about the city, which is strictly forbidden."[12]

The size of a *funduq* matched the scale of commerce of a particular city, and most cities did not need more than one. But in trade hubs such as Alexandria, *funduqs* specialized in particular lines of business, such as cloth, leather, or jewelry. Italy's mercantile republics vied with each other to obtain trade privileges for their individual *funduqs*. Muslim authorities soon learned to frame trade treaties to increase trade and maximize tax income. A *funduq* had joint Muslim and Christian sponsorship, and was administered by a consul nominated either by the home state or by local merchants whose appointment was subject to consent by local authorities. The consul's salary was variously paid by his home or host government, or by commissions on travelers' rents. The consul was the representative of the expatriate merchant community toward local authorities and could submit complaints direct to the sultan. Local staff often assimilated into local culture; when the Italian Lionardo Frescobaldi arrived in Alexandria he found the consul's worldly manner irksome: "He is from France and he has a Christian wife, born in Saracenland, and between them they have less than one ounce of faith."[13]

European merchants on arrival at their destination proceeded to their city's local *funduq* where they stored and disposed of their cargo. The largest *funduqs* were substantial buildings, several stories high, with an inner courtyard ringed by storage rooms on the ground floor and residential accommodation on the floor above. A *funduq* also offered invaluable informal benefits; local staff could help with negotiating customs duties and provide introductions, and merchants in *funduqs* after a day's work could share business tips. Coincidentally, merchants could keep an eye on each other, and investors at home thus had some assurance managers would not abuse their trust because any manager cheating his investors needed to fear his competitors' gossip after his return; a manager with a poor reputation was unlikely to raise funds for subsequent journeys.

NOTES

1. El-Ali: "Studies in the Topography of Medina," 86.
2. Baladhuri, *The Origins of the Islamic State*, Vol. 1, 30.
3. Baladhuri, *The Origins of the Islamic State*, Vol. 1, 463.
4. Samhudi, *Geschichte der Stadt Medina*, 120–21; El-Ali, "Studies in the Topography of Medina," 87.
5. Kister, "The Market of the Prophet," 275–76.
6. Koran 9:6, 7.
7. Constable, *Housing the Stranger*.
8. Lassner, *The Topography of Baghdad in the Early Middle Ages*, 61.
9. Wright, *Early Travels in Palestine*, 15.
10. Wright, *Early Travels in Palestine*, 26.
11. Wright, *Early Travels in Palestine*, 30.
12. Schiltberger, *The Bondage and Travels of Johann Schiltberger*, 62.
13. Frescobaldi, *A Visit to the Holy Places*, 38.

Chapter Seventeen

Law in Early Islam

Long before Muhammad found his calling as Prophet, he revealed his gift for adjudication on an occasion when Meccans were in acute need of an arbitrator. The circumstances of this event deserve telling. A fire had destroyed the structure surrounding the *Kaaba*, repairs had been completed, but disputes over who should have the honor of restoring the venerable cornerstone to its rightful place had reached an impasse—altercations over social precedence were intractable and acrimonious. Muhammad broke this deadlock: he proposed the cornerstone be conveyed to its place on a blanket held at each corner by a representative of each tribe. Muhammad's gift for adjudication already in Mecca earned respect, and after emigration to Medina he there assumed the office of a judge and presided over court proceedings. Muhammad's juridical authority was unimpeachable and when he died in Islamic jurisprudence there opened a void. Any newly constituted community likely would derive a social rulebook from examples set by its founder, and in the case of Muhammad, whose every pronouncement, no matter how casual, had the weight of divine authority, such was even more pertinent, because in the final analysis any however trivial contravention of an injunction constituted an infraction of religious obligations. Muhammad's decisions provided binding precedents for resolving disputes, and his successors would not have been able to cast laws unless these demonstrably complied with the intentions of Muhammad.

Abu Bakr, when elected caliph, in his accession speech acknowledged he owed submission to an authority greater than that of his office: "Obey me, even as I shall obey the Lord and His Apostle. Whenever I disobey them, obedience is no longer obligatory upon you."[1] Muhammad's dual leadership, secular as well as religious, empowered him in situations of uncertainty to point out the right way, the *sharia*. It came to be one of the core tasks of

Islamic jurisprudence to define the demarcation lines between those aspects of the *sharia* that were within or outside the bounds of human discretion. To do so, it was paramount to record all of Muhammad's sayings and actions to show how the Prophet had put into practice the Koran's guidance. Abu Bakr immediately after Muhammad's death ordered compiling and arranging Muhammad's dictations of the Koran that his widow Hafsa had in her possession, and he also ordered collecting an archive of the Prophet's words and deeds, the *hadith* and the *sunna*, which expanded exponentially since anyone who had ever met Muhammad was only too eager to preserve for posterity what had passed on that occasion. Countless testimonials were forthcoming, at least for half a century after Muhammad's death, but in theory for an even longer period—up until the moment the last person who had met Muhammad had died.

The endeavor to collect testimonials soon posed challenges to editors who had to determine the criteria for ranking accounts. The most authoritative accounts were deemed to be those by members of Muhammad's family. Of the seven most prolific contributors to *hadith* literature, three were wives of Muhammad, and a fourth, Abdallah ibn Abbas, was a cousin of Muhammad who had been present in his household during his final days. However, Abdallah at the time had been only thirteen years old, and an account by a teenager obviously could not be accorded the credibility of that of an adult. The greater the distance from Muhammad's death, the greater the awe his contemporaries inspired and the credulity for their stories, and it was inevitable some witnesses would have economized or embroidered their narratives. From the outset, the task of transmitting traditions blended into that of evaluating them, and analytical complexities multiplied as the number of traditions proliferated. Bukhari, a prodigious collector of *hadiths*, spent sixteen years editing a corpus of 600,000 anecdotes and whittled the number down to 7,000. Ahmad ibn Hanbal selected 30,000 out of 750,000 traditions.[2]

Hadiths could be challenged, for example, by allegations of bias or unreliability. Omayyad partisans were skeptical of traditions based on the testimony of their adversary, Ali; the converse was equally true. Reconciling inconsistent or contradictory sources was inseparable from critical evaluation and gradually the process of sifting incomplete and selective accounts evolved a distinct field of scholarship. "The first absolute requirement of knowledge," declared the legal scholar Nazzam, "is doubt."[3] The intellectual climate of early Islam fostered competing perspectives on traditions and what they meant, and in the process evolved guidelines for resolving issues in contention. Because the caliph did not have the last word on evaluating *hadiths*, the application of precedents derived from *hadiths* evolved an independent judiciary: the law would bind the caliph, not vice versa.

HADITHS AND JURISPRUDENCE

Muhammad had set the direction of Islamic jurisprudence through his pronouncement that Islam should have no priestly caste. The ramifications of that decree were far-reaching, because in the absence of priests, debates over the direction of Islam were conducted in terms that were legal rather than theological. The Prophet's guidance to officials had been to the effect they resolve issues at hand by reference to the Koran, to precedent, and, if these guides were not applicable, by applying their own judgment.[4] The process of blending *hadiths* into laws evolved diverse approaches, and the dividing line between traditionists and jurists was fluid. In Medina and in Baghdad, there emerged two distinct schools of jurisprudence (but there were others): the most prominent exponent in Medina as Malik ibn Anas (d. 796) and in Baghdad Abu Hanifa (d. 767). Malik ibn Anas issued Islam's first legal compendium, the *Muwatta*; Abu Hanifa compiled a corresponding legal corpus, the *Hedaya*. These two schools established dominance in particular regions: the Hanifites in the Levant, the Maliki in Arabia and North Africa. The Maliki and Hanifite schools had more in common than separated them, insofar as they both proceeded by drawing inferences from *hadiths*. But they differed, due to local circumstances, in how they weighed empirical facts and reasoning: in Medina, the shadow of Muhammad lingered in every street and the Medina school inclined toward rules set by precedent; in Baghdad, on the other hand, a city teeming with different ethnic and religious constituencies and home to busy commercial interests, jurists confronted a much broader range of issues. Baghdadi jurists of necessity could not defer decisions to colleagues in distant Medina, and they evolved a liberal application of analogy, reasoning, and deduction.

Islam's supreme authority, in the final analysis, was Koranic jurisprudence, and jurisprudents could make or break a caliph's hold on power. Consequently, the legal profession commanded immense authority and caliphs had a correspondingly great interest in a compliant judiciary. Judges, however, often were unyielding. Abu Hanifa was offered a government appointment and the tempting salary that came with it, but he refused: "Can I be sure that if I go into the sea my clothes will not get wet?"[5] The caliph showed his displeasure and Abu Hanifa ended his life in prison. Judges who defended their integrity were public heroes. Malik ibn Anas, for example, was whipped "on account of some legal opinions which did not correspond with the wishes of the sultans," wrote Ibn Khallikan, but noted, "from the time Malik ibn Anas received this flogging he rose higher and higher in public estimation, so that the punishment he underwent seemed as if it had been an honor conferred upon him."[6]

If venal judges could amass a fortune, principled judges often stayed poor. Tanukhi offered an engaging tale about one Baghdad judge with an income so meager he and his brother owned between them a single coat, so one brother had to stay at home whenever the other went about. But many judges must have had an eye on their career prospects when they handed down decisions, because in another Tanukhi story, praise for a judge's honesty prompts a barbed quip that that showed how far professional standards had fallen—integrity in a judge would have been taken for granted in the old days.[7] But shielding the judiciary from favoritism, rulers knew, was in everyone's own best interest. Tanukhi in a story lets a courtier complain to the caliph that a judge had refused him preferential treatment but the caliph Al Mutadid rebukes him: "Your connection with me does not affect the majesty of the law, whereon government and religion repose."[8]

FROM MOSQUE TO *MADRASA*

Muhammad had presided over court proceedings in the mosque and early judges emulated his practice. However, increasing caseloads and longer court sessions necessitated finding suitable accommodation. Courts moved into dedicated buildings, *masjids*, and links to the mosque loosened further when benefactors endowed autonomous institutions to train future professionals, *madrasas*. These training academies evolved a curriculum, examinations, and professional licenses, and they broadened research and education into disciplines such as comparative religion, mathematics, history, and geography. *Madrasas* afforded teaching facilities, libraries, accommodation, and scholarships. Successful students could graduate as master of law or as professor of legal opinions; the latter qualification required some ten years of study and success in examinations conducted through disputation in public. Students had free choice between *madrasas*; there were twenty-four in eleventh-century Baghdad.

Muhammad had presided over court proceedings in person; this became infeasible for the caliphs once Muslims settled in distant regions in numbers. Ibn Khaldun pointed out Muhammad "used to ask the men around him for advice and to consult them,"[9] and Umar tasked a standing committee of legal experts, the *mufti*, to pronounce jurisprudential principles, the *fatwa*. Umar also appointed eight salaried *qadi* to preside over courts in regional capitals. Umar set judges an annual salary (at 500 dirhams per month), requested they cease involvement in commerce, and defined a code of conduct—never to issue decisions in anger, wherever possible follow the Prophet's example, and otherwise apply their own reasoning.[10] Ibn Khaldun quoted Umar's terms of reference for *qadi*: "Use your brain about matters that perplex you and to which neither Koran nor Sunnah seem to apply. Study similar cases and evaluate the situation through analogy with those similar cases."[11]

Islamic law was based on the Koran and as such could only apply to Muslims but not, by implication, to other denominations.[12] Consequently Jews and Christians retained jurisdiction for intra-communal disputes and selected judges whose appointments were subject to ratification by Muslim authorities. Legal autonomy in some instances extended to managing distinct penal systems: the Jewish traveler Rabbi Petachia was astonished the Jews of Mosul administered even their own prison. The segregation of Islamic from non-Islamic legal systems had important pragmatic benefits. Muslims in Arabia were a majority, but that situation reversed once Islam expanded across the Middle East. Since Muslims were in the minority in the empire, the Islamic judiciary would have been crushed by the workload of cases brought by non-Muslim plaintiffs. Coexisting legal systems, on the other hand, gave Muslim jurisprudents an opportunity to observe at close quarters diverse legal traditions in practice and assimilate their expertise.

NOTES

1. Suyuti, *History of the Khalifahs*, 57–58.
2. Ibn Khaldun, *Muqaddimah*, Vol. 2, 456 and 461.
3. Kremer, *Culturgeschichte des Orients*, Vol. 1, 482.
4. Muir, *The Life of Mahomet*, Vol. 4, 223.
5. *Arabian Nights*, Night 84.
6. Ibn Khallikan, *Biographical Dictionary*, Vol. 2, 547.
7. Tanukhi, *The Table-Talk of a Mesopotamian Judge*, 128.
8. Tanukhi, *The Table-Talk of a Mesopotamian Judge*, 131–32.
9. Ibn Khaldun, *Muqaddimah*, Vol. 2, 7.
10. Tyan, *Histoire de l'organisation judiciaire en pays d'Islam*, Vol. 1, 22.
11. Ibn Khaldun, *Muqaddimah*, Vol. 1, 453–54.
12. See Goitein's discussion of Koran 5:42–52 in *Studies in Islamic History and Institutions*, 130–34.

Chapter Eighteen

From Law to Economics

There exists an economic proof that someone who pays too much tax will be inclined to reduce the amount of time spent at work. But as an intuition, however, this very notion was already expressed in a fairy tale told by Ibn Khaldun. Accordingly, in his story, a king is curious what messages a hooting owl was sending his companions. A man who understands the language of birds is commanded to render the owl's cries into words that humans can comprehend. His translation holds shocking news for the king: the owl is rejoicing, he learns, because owls soon will inhabit a thousand villages undisturbed by humans who are forced out of their homes because taxes are so high they can no longer pay them. There is a happy ending to Ibn Khaldun's fairy tale, because the king, dismayed and chastened, lightens the tax burden. Reading between the lines, the fairy tale shows how much tact was needed to persuade rulers a fair tax rate was in their own interest. Although Ibn Khaldun's fairy tale showed there was a link between excessive taxes and economic contraction, it did not, however, explain how that mechanism worked. Such was supplied by Abu Yusuf's book *Kitab al kharaj*, however, that deduced how taxes affect the economic incentives of taxpayers, and based on this analysis derived concrete policy advice. The *Kitab al kharaj* marked the economic turn of Islamic law.

Abu Yusuf (died ca. 800) inspired many anecdotes. Once a disciple of Abu Hanifa, as a student Abu Yusuf was so immersed in his studies he only realized how little money he was bringing home when his exasperated wife served him for dinner a plate of notebooks. Fortunately, Abu Hanifa dissuaded Abu Yusuf from switching careers, because Abu Yusuf after a time caught the eye of Harun al Rashid, who appointed him his Chief Justice. Abu Yusuf stated happiness depends on three things: being a Muslim; health; and "wealth, without which life cannot be completely enjoyed."[1] The career of

Abu Yusuf surpassed by far that of Abu Hanifa, who died in jail; Abu Yusuf's estate, Ibn Khallikan noted, included two hundred pairs of silk trousers.[2] Abu Yusuf in his book *Kitab al kharaj* set out how tax policies should aim to foster incentives that enable creation of wealth.

Equitable taxation had been a policy challenge of long standing. For the most part, land taxes in the empire's conquered territories applied as their benchmark Muhammad's 50 percent share of harvests in Khaybar. The caliph Osman, however aimed to extract even more, and smugly noted in a year when Egypt had delivered exceptional high taxes that "the camel has given more milk," to which Egypt's governor Amr al As retorted that the camel may have given more milk but the camel's young had died. Few officials, however, dared to be as blunt, and instead resorted to raising pressure on taxpayers. Tax officials levied a fixed quantum each year, and when harvests were poor, farmers were left with a diminished return or even shouldered tax liabilities that exceeded their entire crop. Farmers consequently abandoned their homesteads, which led to a contraction of the tax base (the very policy failure highlighted by Ibn Khaldun's fairy tale). The government retaliated with escalating coercion—Hajjaj ibn Yusuf prevented villagers from escaping by having them branded—but failed to reverse the trend. Abbasid fiscal managers were at a loss to find an effective remedy.

The *Kitab al kharaj* showed unfair outcomes resulted from an inflexible tax regime that did not take into account the annual harvest. Abu Yusuf argued that the current tax regime inevitably disadvantaged taxpayers because tax collectors had a choice between levying taxes either in cash or in kind (whereby a farmer settled tax liabilities by handing over a share of crops). Thus in years when harvests were good, tax collectors would demand a share of crops, but in years when harvests were poor, they insisted on payment in cash. Consequently, farmers anticipated the tax system would work against them, regardless of whether harvests were rich or poor: "The two alternating modes of fixed taxes, in kind or in cash, are also detrimental to the taxpayers because of the opportunities they provide for unjust distribution of the taxes and the oppression of the weak by the strong."[3] The remedy for a broken tax system, argued Abu Yusuf, consisted of switching from fixed to proportional taxes, which, as he reminded his readers, accorded with what Muhammad had practiced in Khaybar. Once farmers were assured an increase in yields would profit them, they would raise productivity. Therefore, tax rates for farmers who had invested in irrigation should drop, because farmers had no incentive to invest unless they had prospects of recouping their expenditure. Promoting infrastructure investment through preferential tax rates, Abu Yusuf concluded, would lead to an increase in tax revenue.[4]

Abu Yusuf's incentive-based approach to fiscal policy gained ground among Abbasid tax officials. Miskawaihi wrote that Ali ibn Isa was said to be "threatening terrible things if he found that any one of the subjects had been unfairly treated in the survey or any other transaction. In consequence, he said, we did not venture to make our demands very strict; and when the next year came, the revenue had gone up 30 percent, the rumour having spread that justice was being practiced, and that robbery and extortion were at an end. Hence people were encouraged to go in more for agriculture."[5]

An incentive-based approach to public finance—showing tax increases yielded diminishing returns, and tax yields rose through setting incentives for investment—was no longer contentious by the time Ibn Khaldun wrote the *Muqaddima*—where he explained that when taxpayers

> compare expenditures and taxes with their income and gain and see the little profit they make, they lose all hope. Therefore, many of them refrain from all cultural activity. The result is that the total tax revenue goes down, as (the number of) the individual assessments go down. Often, when the decrease is noticed, the amounts of individual imposts are increased. This is considered a means of compensating for the decrease. Finally, individual imposts and assessments reach their limit. It would be of no avail to increase them further. The costs of all cultural enterprises are now too high, the taxes are too heavy, and the profits anticipated fail to materialise. Thus the total revenue continues to decrease, while the amounts of individual imposts and assessments continue to increase, because it is believed that such an increase will compensate (for the drop in revenue) in the end. Finally, civilization is destroyed, because the incentive for cultural activity is gone.[6]

Ibn Khaldun spelled out there was a causal link between fiscal policies and economic incentives:

> The finances of a ruler can be increased, and his financial resources improved, only through the revenue from taxes. This can be improved only through the equitable treatment of people with property and regard for them, so that their hopes rise, and they have the incentive to start making their capital bear fruit and grow. This, in turn, increases the ruler's revenues in taxes.[7]

NOTES

1. Ibn Khallikan, *Biographical Dictionary*, Vol. 4, 279.
2. Ibn Khallikan, *Biographical Dictionary*, Vol. 4, 273.
3. Abu Yusuf, *Kitab al kharaj*, 101.
4. Abu Yusuf, *Kitab al kharaj*, 101.
5. Miskawaihi, *The Experiences of the Nations*, Vol. 1, 34.
6. Ibn Khaldun, *Muqaddimah*, Vol. 2, 90–91.
7. Ibn Khaldun, *Muqaddimah*, Vol. 2, 95–96.

Chapter Nineteen

Market Economics in Early Islam

Economics in early Islam soon evolved a practical bent. Muhammad had pronounced, "there is nothing wrong in wealth, but health is better than wealth, and cheerfulness is a blessing,"[1] and even was quoted as having issued straightforward investment advice such as "he who sells a house and does not buy another one instead is not likely to see blessing in that money."[2] The range of early Islamic economics, originating in religion and in ethics, is vast, and a list of representative Islamic economists includes Ibn Taymiyah, Al Dimashqi, and Ibn Khaldun. The following sections consider those aspects of Islamic economics that refer to the regulation of markets, in particular policies regarding price competition, fair trade, monopolies, mis-selling, and insider trading (however, the list of economists and of issues could be expanded with ease).

USURY AND FAIR TRADE

The cornerstone of Islamic economics is the Koranic distinction between usury and fair trade: "God has permitted trading and made usury unlawful."[3] The connotations of usury are mainly financial, but there are many others outside the sphere of finance; in fact, the majority of Islamic prohibitions against usury pertain to agricultural rather than financial markets. However, interest on loans is at the forefront of conceptions of usury. Muhammad underscored this ban in his Farewell Address when he singled out this very manifestation of usury: "God has decreed that there is no usury and the usury of Al Abbas is abolished."[4] That Muhammad castigated Al Abbas—his uncle—was hardly coincidental.

Muhammad was nearing the end of his life when he delivered his Farewell Address and memories of past events must have sharpened his censure of Al Abbas, a prominent banker in Mecca who had intervened at a key juncture of Muhammad's life. The occasion was when Abu Talib had defaulted on a loan from Al Abbas (his own brother) and no longer was able to provide for his family; then Abu Talib gave up his son Ali for adoption, and Muhammad, at that moment of crisis, reciprocated the generosity his erstwhile guardian Abu Talib had shown of a time when he as an orphan had been in need of a guardian. Once, Abu Talib had adopted Muhammad; now, Muhammad adopted Ali. Muhammad's intervention in aid of Abu Talib, and his and Ali's subsequent illustrious ascent, were a compelling illustration of the Koranic exhortation: "Those that preserve themselves from their own greed will surely prosper. If you give a generous loan to God, He will pay you back twofold and will forgive you."[5] Looking back, Muhammad and Ali had lived through extreme hardship and had emerged triumphant. No contrast could be more stark than that between the reversal of fortunes of Al Abbas, who had humiliated his own brother and had long prevaricated before he converted to the creed propagated by his nephew, and that of Muhammad and Ali, who through the victory of Islam had been exalted as Al Abbas was humbled.

Defaults were an acute social problem in the Middle East where penalties on defaulters were harsh. Defaulters in the Old Testament suffered enslavement; in the New Testament they were imprisoned.[6] Pre-Islamic Mecca imposed extreme penalties on defaulters, who were made liable for twice the principal, and if they failed to extinguish their liability were evicted from Mecca and abandoned to their fate in the desert. The Koran's exhortation to provide succor to defaulters constituted a direct opposite to pre-Islamic conventions.

To comply with Islamic prohibitions against usury, two parties in a transaction must exchange goods that are exactly equivalent. Strict equivalence was required in exchanges involving six commodities: silver and gold (which were means of payment), wheat, barley, dates, and salt (which were daily necessities). An example illustrates how the ban was applied. On one occasion, Muhammad's widow Zaynab swapped dates from her estate in Khaybar for an identical quantity of dates in Medina. Umar, however, forced Zaynab to cancel the sale although she had not made a profit on the transaction, because, as he pointed out, the price did not factor in the hidden cost of transport between Khaybar and Medina.[7] Umar's ruling shows nominal equivalence alone, as such, did not fulfill compliance with the ban on illicit gain; in addition, strict adherence to Koranic requirements required full disclosure of prices charged for each link in a value chain. This logic was applied wherever raw materials were traded for finished products—such as flour against bread, milk against cheese, or olives against oil.

The Islamic concept of usury extends beyond strictures against taking interest on loans. Usury is present in any transaction that extracts excessive advantage from a customer or denies a fair share to a business partner. There were pre-Islamic antecedents for *riba*, the Koranic term for usury. The Talmud banned gains deemed excessive (the term is *ribbit*), and pre-Islamic Meccans had clear notions of the distinction between illicit and licit trade—they refused to accept donations to the *Kaaba* earned from "prostitution, usury, or by wronging any man."[8]

The Koran, while prohibiting usury, approves trade that is fair. Usury, by implication, incurs divine wrath; licit trade, on the other hand, enjoys divine approbation. Muhammad pronounced "honest merchants will be raised up on the Day of Resurrection with the Prophets, the true, and the martyrs."[9] Islamic conceptions of fair trade had countless ramifications; here, those of concern are those for price regulation, consumer protection, and competition policy. In respect to price regulation, for example, Muhammad overturned economic conventions that had been in place from Babylonian times.

PRICE REGULATION FROM BABYLONIAN TIMES UNTIL MUHAMMAD

When, in early Islam, price controls were lifted, no less an authority than Muhammad's personal intervention was adduced to justify what constituted an economic innovation of great moment. Preliminary remarks on traditions of price regulation in Middle Eastern markets are necessary to show just how fundamental was this upheaval. Government authorities from the very inception of markets in the Middle East prescribed prices, and government price controls were undisputed. The economist Karl Polanyi pointed out prices in the Middle East traditionally "took the form of equivalencies established by authority of custom, statute or proclamation."[10] Price controls were subject to legislation, and prices were set by governments or by priests who oversaw exchanges situated near temples. The Babylonian *Codex Hammurabi* imposed penalties on anyone who dared deviate from government prices.[11] Judaic price policies applied throughout the entire economic value chain: they capped food prices and profit margins (one sixth of price); required vendors to sell direct to consumers rather than through intermediaries; banned cornering a market by buying up produce of neighboring farmers; and forbade exports even if higher prices were offered abroad. Infractions were deemed breaches of laws against usury.[12] Consequently, the authority to set prices conferred considerable power and prestige. For example, Jews in the late Roman Empire achieved a significant enhancement of communal autonomy when they were granted the right to set their own prices (in 396).[13]

There was a sphere of trade where price controls never took effect, however, namely cross-border trade, which, in contrast with domestic markets, by its nature was beyond the reach of government control. Governments tried to bring long-distance trade under control through different approaches: in Israel, King Solomon, wishing to buy gold, declared long-distance trade a royal monopoly and built bridgeheads on the Red Sea coast; in Egypt, the pharaohs allowed only priests to import cedars for their palaces. Long-distance traders, however, who camped outside of fixed settlements, were a category of entrepreneurs beyond the perimeter of government control, and while traders within a city's walls had to comply with prices predetermined and supervised by market overseers, long-distance traders customarily transacted business through bargaining. Ancient Greeks began desegregating local and cross-border markets; Greeks had conducted trade in foreign imports outside of city limits, in *emporia*, but gradually gave permission for trade to take place in the town center, the *agora*. The Greek verb *agorazein*, for "going to the agora" took on another meaning, of buying. Aristotle and Plato laid down the duties of Greek market supervisors, such as preventing vendors from cheating, investigating customer complaints, and the like.[14] But the benefits of price competition eluded Aristotle and Plato. Nor were free markets advanced by the Byzantine Empire: terms of market entry, salaries, quality of goods, and sale prices—all were prescribed.

Long-distance trade when Islam came into being differed from local trade in two respects: local trade in staple goods was subject to price controls, and long-distance trade met demand for luxury goods where fixed prices could not be enforced. Accordingly, profit differentials between local and long-distance markets must have been substantial. The benefits of deregulated pricing may have been intuitive to Arab traders, because they were accustomed to setting prices without government intervention and to earning profits through taking risks. Mesopotamian markets originated in Babylonia; the Arab word for market, *suq*, is rooted in Akkadian. But with the advent of Islam, Arabs, whose business culture was shaped by trade, risk, and bargaining, took price setting out of the hand of government and placed it in the hand of the market.[15] This radical break with commercial practice, Islamic economists explained, was instigated at the behest of Muhammad.

"PRICES ARE IN THE HAND OF GOD"

Arab traders were taken by surprise when Muhammad abandoned price regulation. Abu Yusuf collated three accounts of unfolding events; one of these follows: "Prices rose in the time of the Prophet, and the people came to him asking that a price-limit be fixed which the people could afford, but he said: low and high prices are from God and we are not allowed to go beyond His judgment."[16] According to Abu Yusuf, Muhammad enjoined leaving prices to invisible forces: "Prices, high or low," the Prophet stated, "are in the hand of God."[17] The hanifite *Mishcat* quoted a slightly different version of Muhammad's words: "God is the maker of rates, and is the giver and curtailer of sustenance."[18]

Muhammad's decision was highly contentious and—a very unusual occurrence—there were complaints. Several testimonies report Muhammad's adherents lodged protests and asked him to abate increases in the price of food. According to Ibn Taymiyah, appeals were filed twice, but Muhammad was unbending and adamant he would not intervene in prices unless he had authority from Allah ("I would rather invoke God."),[19] and after in vain seeking divine approbation to set prices, stated rises and falls of prices were beyond man's control. Setting prices, Muhammad asserted, was neither in his, nor for that matter in the gift of any other single human authority, and he would contravene God's will were he to fix what God wished to vary ("Oh no," he corrected someone asserting prices were made by man, "God raises and lowers.")[20]

These *hadiths* do not state at what point in time Muhammad derestricted prices in Medina, but in any event Muhammad's approach had already germinated when he was still in Mecca. According to another *hadith*, merchants in the market in Mecca accosted Muhammad and inquired whether his prophetic powers included the ability for business forecasts. Meccan traders asked Muhammad: "Does your Lord not tell you when prices will drop or rise, so you can gain in trade?"[21] It was in reaction to this approach, according to Aloys Sprenger, that Muhammad thereupon received the following Koranic revelation:

> Say: I have not the power to acquire benefits or to avert evil from myself, except by the will of God. Had I possessed knowledge of what is hidden, I would have availed myself of much that is good and no harm would have touched me. But I am no more than one who gives warning and good news to true believers.[22]

Muhammad's endorsement of price deregulation in Medina derived from his conception of his prophetic office, developed during his years of adversity in Mecca.

COMPETITION POLICY

When merchants are free to set prices the way they compete changes. They may raise prices (to increase profits on each sale) or alternatively reduce prices (to expand market share at the expense of competitors). Islamic jurists provided legal opinions on either competitive strategy. Raising prices to maximize profits, asserted Malik ibn Anas, was legitimate, and he adduced in support a *hadith* where Muhammad auctioned goods to the highest bidder. Ibn Taymiyah likewise affirmed that it was ethical to raise prices: "Therefore if people are selling their goods in a fitting manner, causing no injury, and the current price happens to rise either because of the scarcity of an article or on account of increased demand, then this is a matter for God. To compel people to sell at a particular rate would be unjustified coercion."[23] But controversy surrounded the alternative approach, to reduce prices to undercut competitors. Merchants complained to Umar a trader was offering raisins at a lower price than his competitors, which prompted Umar to revoke his trading license. That sanction, however, was not Umar's last word on the matter; Umar on reflection reinstated the trader and assured him: "You are free to sell where and how you wish."[24]

Some incidents consequential to the introduction of free pricing made for amusing anecdotes. According to Baladhuri, there was an entrepreneur in Basra who operated the city's single bathhouse and could not help boasting about his extraordinary profits to his brother. However, he soon had to rue having taken his brother into his confidence because his brother shared out this confidential information and the monopolist soon faced competitors. Several entrepreneurs were quick to ask the governor's permission to open new baths, with predictable second round effects: Basrans soon had a choice between eight bathhouses, and the original monopolist to his chagrin found his profits had evaporated. "May Allah cut off from him His mercy!" he cursed his brother—and Baladhuri's moral of the story is that, in truth, the boasting entrepreneur should have blamed himself for giving away his trade secret. Coincidentally, this story gives a glimpse of market frameworks of the time: the government regulated market access (bathhouses required a governor's license) but did not intervene in price competition. From this anecdote we may infer the rapid rise in living standards, and ready access to capital in Islam's young cities (eight bath houses entered into competition). Moreover, Baladhuri's list of investors shows women owned three out of eight baths, which demonstrated women at the time were significant entrepreneurs.

Price competition has ramifications for policies regarding monopolies and insider trading. On first sight it may appear startling that monopolies, a phenomenon usually associated with advanced modern economies, should have been a concern in Muhammad's era. However, rules for setting prices are allied to rules for competition, and Muhammad combined injunctions against government intervention in price setting with proscriptions of monopolies: "whoever monopolises," he said, "is a sinner."[25] Monopolistic practice, in the widest sense, consists of any abuse of a strong commercial position to distort prices—and in markets with food supply lines as precarious as those of medieval Arabia, every famine offered the temptation to extract huge profits from desperate buyers willing to pay any price to stave off starvation. Squeezing up prices through hoarding had been a well-known practice in pre-Islamic Arabia; the term for it was *ihtikar*, which Umar, quoting Muhammad, condemned in harsh terms: "whoever monopolises the food of the Muslims, may God entangle in misfortune in his body, and ruin in his property."[26] Driving up prices above competitive levels effectively constituted a religious wrong: "Whoever keeps back grain forty days, in order to increase its price, is both a forsaker of God, and is forsaken of God."[27]

Competition economics in Islam also prohibited other forms of exploiting market power, for example, by favoring certain competitors and bypassing others. Ibn Taymiyah not only exposed these practices as monopolistic but also held government responsible in such cases to intervene and provide redress:

> A more serious matter than this is where certain people have a monopoly of particular commodities, such that foodstuffs or other goods are sold only to them and then retailed by them, any would-be competitor being restrained either harshly, by imposition, or by some gentler means less open to abuse. In this situation prices must be controlled so that the monopolists sell only for value and buy people's goods only for fair value.[28]

Oligopolies (by the same token as monopolies) earn extraordinary profits through conspiring with their peers against the orderly flow of business. Ibn Taymiyah had a clear conception of the workings of collusion and why such conspiracies are harmful:

> When a group who buy or sell a certain type of commodity conspire to depreciate what they buy and so buy for less than the customary fair price while promoting what they sell above the customary price, and to malign what they buy . . . they will have conspired to wrong people so that they would have to sell their goods (for less) and to buy for more than the fair price.[29]

Ibn Taymiyah evolved a rationale for the ban on monopolies: whereas Umar had asserted monopolists are irreligious but did not explain why, Ibn Taymiyah, on the other hand, not only identified the impact of monopolies—distortion of prices—but also added a nuanced analysis of the harm caused by monopolies that consists in forcing customers to overpay.

Insider trading is usually mentioned in the context of financial markets, but the infraction as such is ancient: it consists of taking advantage of privileged information ahead of an imminent change in market conditions and is culpable because it interferes with competition. Insider trading was another instance of market abuse that already early Islamic economists identified. Such occurred in pre-Islamic Arabia, where traders with advance intelligence of a caravan's arrival were wont to intercept its progress and conclude transactions before the caravan reached the city. Muhammad legislated against such ploys, called *talaqqi*, and forbade "stopping a caravan on their way to the city and telling them that prices there are low, with the design of purchasing their goods themselves at the lowest possible price."[30] The rationale for this ban once again Ibn Taymiyah supplied; Muhammad "made the proscription," according to Ibn Taymiyah, "to avoid injury to the seller, who is cheated into selling below the fair price."[31] There were other examples of Ibn Taymiyah's preoccupation with fair pricing, such as, for example, when Muhammad banned brokers who overcharge customers ("on account of the danger of price inflation"),[32] but they all underscored that early Islamic economists considered the integrity of price competition as of fundamental importance to fair markets.

MARKET SUPERVISION

Supervisors whose responsibility it was to maintain orderly markets existed long before the advent of Islam. The remits of professional market overseers—in Greek and Judaic markets, for example, the *agoranomos* and the *hashban*—were broadly overlapping: they set rules for business conduct, investigated complaints, and imposed penalties. Judaic market regulation differed in one important particular from Greek and Roman practice, however, in that it was cast by the Talmud and as such was a religious obligation. Overseers also existed in pre-Islamic Arabian markets, called *muhtasib*, who granted trading licenses, inspected weights and measures, and pursued delinquent debtors. In Medina, Muhammad personally appointed the *muhtasib*, as later he did in Mecca. (It deserves remark that Medina's first Islamic *muhtasib* was a woman. In fact, in Middle Eastern markets traders often were female. When Herodotus visited Egypt, for example, he was surprised how frequently he encountered in markets female vendors.)[33] Muhammad underscored how important he considered the office of *muhtasib* by personally conferring the appointment; Umar confirmed Muhammad's appointments, and so the significant status of the office of the *muhtasib* was established from an early stage of Islam. It was customary for *muhtasibs* in important trade centers to be appointed by the caliph because, as Ibn Khaldun explained, market supervision was a "religious office."[34]

The principal public institution in Islamic cities, other than the mosque, were markets, and *muhtasibs* assumed many responsibilities associated with municipal administration. A *muhtasib* could order demolition of buildings deemed unsafe; demand removal of obstructions from public thoroughfares; and fine drunkards or prostitutes. The *muhtasib* would review complaints regarding unreasonable working conditions, including those of slaves, and had the authority to intervene on their behalf. In effect, *muhtasibs* shaped the public sphere of Islamic cities more widely—they were responsible for public order, health, and safety.

ABU AL FADL AL DIMASHQI

Abu al Fadl al Dimashqi, of whom we only know he lived in Damascus (hence his name), was the author of *The Beauty of Commerce*, a summary of Islamic economic knowledge (including ancient Greek sources) written in the twelfth century.[35] His book perhaps is a compilation of sources rather than an original composition; however, it contains passages where Al Dimashqi warned his readers to beware the inherent fickleness of commercial success, and there one hears an author's personal voice: "the poorest man of all is one so rich he thinks he will ever be secure from poverty."[36]

Al Dimashqi showed how society takes shape through economic activity. Accordingly, trade is the wellspring of society. Because man cannot master all skills necessary for survival, he specializes in certain skills and offers his products in exchange against others. Division of labor and the need to exchange products bring into being cities that facilitate trade, which, in turn, begets wealth. Because goods have different values and are in demand at different times, a need arises for money—which, again, is another catalyst for promoting trade.

Because trade, more than any other endeavor, creates welfare, Al Dimashqi ranks traders ahead of all other professions. All wealth, for Al Dimashqi, constitutes a social virtue: if inherited, it signals good breeding; if self-made, ambition and acumen; if the result of sheer luck, good fortune. Traders need a broad set of skills because trade conditions are inherently unstable: they need to exploit price fluctuations; to anticipate the direction of prices; to know when to stand back from investing and when to take risks. Early Islamic economists often used business cases to illustrate analysis. Al Dimashqi provided a case study that in the manner of business manuals illustrated the components of well-crafted financial management. Accordingly, the caliph Al Mamun issued instructions to regional governors how to conduct business in food markets:

> The Commander of the Faithful is expecting a good harvest and grain prices to drop. Sell all grain storages as quickly as possible, on any market and at any price, and report back on sales volume and timing with specification of quality, market prices, trade location, names of counterparties, and how much was paid in cash and how much in instalments. Remember, the Commander of the Faithful will scrutinise your report and is waiting for news—God willing.[37]

IBN KHALDUN

Ibn Khaldun's contributions to the theory of pricing and the economic rationale of commercial profit deserve mention. Ibn Khaldun explained three components enter into prices: costs of production, taxes, and profits. To show

how production costs affect the price of output, Ibn Khaldun referred to Muslims in Spain who

> had to treat the fields and tracts of land, in order to improve the plants and agriculture there. This treatment required expensive labor (products) and materials, such as fertilizer and other things that had to be procured. Thus, their agricultural activities required considerable expenditures. They calculated these expenditures in fixing their prices.[38]

The second component, taxes, enters into prices because

> customs duties raise the sales (prices), because small businessmen and merchants include all their expenses, even their personal requirements, in the price of their stock and merchandise. Thus, customs duties enter into the sales price.[39]

The wellspring of economic activity, however, stems from the final component of prices, profit:

> Commerce means the attempt to make a profit by increasing capital, through buying goods at a low price and selling them at a high price. . . . The attempt to make such a profit may be undertaken by storing goods and holding them until the market has fluctuated from low prices to high prices. This will bring a large profit. Or, the merchant may transport his goods to another country where they are more in demand than in his own, where he bought them . . . an old merchant said to a person who wanted to find out the truth about commerce: "I shall give it to you in two words: buy cheap and sell dear. There is commerce for you."[40]

Ibn Khaldun's approach was consistent with that of generations of Islamic economists inspired by the example of Muhammad whose endorsement of commercial pursuit was never questioned: "Whoever desires the world and its riches in a lawful manner, in order to withhold himself from begging, or to provide a livelihood for his family, or to be kind to his neighbors, will appear before God in the Last Day with his face as bright as a full moon."[41]

NOTES

1. Tabari, *Biographies of the Prophet's Companions*, 153.
2. Tabari, *Biographies of the Prophet's Companions*, 114.
3. Koran 2:275.
4. Ibn Ishaq, *The Life of Muhammad*, 651.
5. Koran 64:17.
6. Matthew 5:26.
7. Amedroz, "The Hisba Jurisdiction in the Ahkam al-Sultaniyya of Mawardi," 306.
8. Tabari, *The History of al-Tabari*, Vol. 6, 57.
9. Matthews, *Mishcat-ul-Masabih*, Vol. 2, 8.

10. Polanyi, *Trade and Markets in the Early Empires*, 20.
11. Rodinson, "Préface," XLI.
12. Bloch, *Das mosaisch-talmudische Polizeirecht*, 38.
13. Rodinson, "Préface," LXIII.
14. Chalmeta provided references in *El señor del zoco en España*, 257–58. (Aristotle: *Politics*, VI, 5. Plato: *Laws* VI/764, VIII/849, IX/881, XI/917).
15. Rodinson, "Préface," lix.
16. Abu Yusuf, *Kitab al kharaj*, 102.
17. Abu Yusuf, *Kitab al kharaj*, 101.
18. Matthews, *Mishcat-ul-Masabih*, Vol. 2, 29–30.
19. Ibn Taymiyah, *Public Duties in Islam*, 50.
20. Ibn Taymiyah, *Public Duties in Islam*, 50.
21. Cited in Sprenger, *Das Leben und die Lehre des Mohammad*, Vol. 2, 348.
22. Koran 7:188.
23. Ibn Taymiyah, *Public Duties in Islam*, 35.
24. Ibn Taymiyah, *Public Duties in Islam*, 47.
25. Matthews, *Mishcat-ul-Masabih*, Vol. 2, 29.
26. Matthews, *Mishcat-ul-Masabih*, Vol. 2, 30.
27. Hughes, *Dictionary of Islam*, 197.
28. Ibn Taymiyah, *Public Duties in Islam*, 36.
29. Ibn Taymiyah, *Public Duties in Islam*, 37.
30. Quoted in Essid, 156.
31. Ibn Taymiyah, *Public Duties in Islam*, 56.
32. Ibn Taymiyah, *Public Duties in Islam*, 56.
33. Herodotus, *Histories*, Book II, chapter 36.
34. Ibn Khaldun, *Muqaddimah*, Vol. 1, 462.
35. Translation by Helmut Ritter "Ein arabisches Handbuch der Handelswissenschaft."
36. Ritter, "Ein arabisches Handbuch der Handelswissenschaft," 80.
37. Ritter, "Ein arabisches Handbuch der Handelswissenschaft," 67.
38. Ibn Khaldun, *Muqaddimah*, Vol. 2, 278.
39. Ibn Khaldun, *Muqaddimah*, Vol. 2, 293.
40. Ibn Khaldun, *Muqaddimah*, Vol. 2, 336–37.
41. Quoted in Hughes, *Dictionary of Islam*, 544–45.

Chapter Twenty

Muslim Merchants Abroad

Caliphs often engaged in trade promotion. Harun al Rashid's extravagant gifts to Charlemagne (which included an elephant, a tent, and a water-clock) showcased sample goods fit to whet a prospective customer's appetite. Trade diplomacy directed at Western Europe, however, did not lead to establishment of a physical presence of Muslim traders there, whereas in Asian and Byzantine realms, on the other hand, the Muslim presence was conspicuous already at an early stage of the Islamic Empire. Constantinople's first mosque, for example, was recorded in 717.[1] The nature of trade between Islamic economies and Western Europe is thrown into relief by a contrast with the commercial presence of Arab traders in China, India, and in the realm of Byzantium.

Arab trade links to Asia were in place prior to the advent of the Islamic Empire, and the *rashidun* caliphs promoted trade by building two ports on either flank of Arabia, Al Djar and Basra. Al Djar on the Red Sea was a gateway for trade with Egypt, but boats from Asia also docked there; Basra was founded on the shores of what Arabs called the Chinese Sea (today's city has moved from the original location). Investment in infrastructure was complemented by commercial diplomacy. Umar in 637 instigated a maritime mission to Asia, and Osman around 650 sent an embassy to the Chinese emperor. Harun al Rashid sent gifts also to the emperor of China and these would have been as glamorous as those to the emperor in Germany.

Although the size of the population of Arab enclaves in Asia is unknown, they clearly were permanent and large. Masudi estimated the tenth-century Arab population south of Mumbai at some 10,000, a rounded figure that signifies a large community in a general sense, but some Muslim communities in China and India in any event were of a size that warranted maintaining their own judiciary.[2] Relations between expatriate enclaves and local communities at times were fractious. Chinese annals reported riots involving expatriate Arabs and Persians in 758, and again that in 878 thousands of foreigners—Muslims, Jews, and Christians—were victims of civil unrest.[3] Government authorities would not have afforded protection unless the size of communities and the scale of benefits from intercontinental trade had been substantial. The high regard of Arab merchants for Chinese authorities comes across from the pages of memoirs left by a ninth-century Arab trader named Soleyman, which contained a story where an Arab ivory merchant was forced to sell his wares to a Chinese official below market price and filed a complaint that reached the Chinese emperor. Accordingly, the official responsible was exposed and the emperor scolded him: "Do you want him to return saying 'I have been wronged in China, I have been robbed?'" (The official is demoted to superintendent of a graveyard to impress on him he is unfit to deal with the living.)[4] Muslim merchants were prosperous trade financiers. The fourteenth-century traveler Ibn Battuta encountered Muslim trading communities in Sumatra and China, and he wrote of that in Calcutta: "The greatest part of the Muhammadan merchants of this place are so wealthy, that one of them can purchase the whole freightage of such vessels as put in here; and fit out others like them."[5]

Several aspects of Arab commerce in Asia deserve remark: authorities intervened against recurring tensions between expatriate and local communities; expatriate communities were granted judicial autonomy; and government safeguarded intercontinental trade. There would be parallels in trade centers in the Islamic Empire and in Constantinople.

MUSLIM TRADE WITH BYZANTIUM

The advent of Islam did not sever long-standing commercial relations between Arabs and Byzantines. Few facts could illustrate better that political or religious antagonisms had little bearing on trade links than that one of the most important areas of Byzantine commercial activity in the Islamic Empire was in building mosques. The practice of hiring Byzantine builders to work on sacred sites in Arabia predated Islam. The *Chronicles of Mecca* attested Meccans in 605 hired a Byzantine carpenter to help restore the structure of the *Kaaba* after it had been damaged by a fire. On that occasion, Meccans had bought the cargo of a Byzantine boat shipwrecked on the Arab coast carrying building material intended for a church in Abyssinia, and they hired a Byzantine Christian traveling on board to install a new roof for the *Kaaba*; he was the first of many to work there.[6] (Muhammad at the time was thirty-five years old and his prophetic career had not yet begun.)

Muhammad in Medina specified the mosque's ground plan, which, as the French historian Jean Sauvaget has pointed out, was representative of that of many houses of worship in the Hellenist Orient; for example, the ordering of colonnades and lack of an apsis were analogous to contemporaneous synagogues and Coptic churches.[7] Omayyad mosques scaled up dimensions and added flamboyant decoration to walls and roofs but otherwise conformed to traditional building blueprints. There were several rounds of Omayyad improvements to the appearance of Mecca's *Kaaba*, each surpassing the glamour of the one that went before—Abd al Malik gilded ceilings, added silver chains between columns, and hung golden crowns;[8] his son Walid gilded the roof and doors, and added columns of marble;[9] the caliph Mutawakkil "plated its wall and ceiling with gold—which act was unprecedented—and clothed its pillars with silk."[10] Abd al Malik deployed Byzantine craftsmen also for projects in Mecca and for a new mosque in Ramlah.[11] Some eighty Greeks and Copts worked on enlarging the Medina mosque and decorated it with imported Byzantine mosaics. There were even claims the Byzantine emperor supported building works in Medina with money; the claim seems implausible (a slip of a scribe's pen?) but shows that Byzantine collaboration as such was not controversial.[12] Ziyad ibn Abihi built a mosque in Kufa, using marble columns from Byzantine buildings in the area, and decorated it with Byzantine mosaics.[13]

It is startling so many master builders of mosques seem to have been Christian rather than Muslim, and one might speculate what were the reasons. Byzantine builders may have been conspicuous on Islamic construction sites because architectural skills were generic, and perhaps Christians dominated the building trade at that time because sons followed their fathers into a profession and particular professions were in the hands of certain communities. Critics of hiring Byzantines to work on such projects were few—after all, Muhammad had not objected to Byzantines working at the *Kaaba*. In any event, Omayyad caliphs had no reservation against hiring expatriate Christians nor had Byzantine emperors any against releasing them, and building projects were the continuing subject of correspondence between the courts of the caliphs and the emperors. Before work commenced on the Damascus mosque, "many embassies," according to Ibn Jubayr, "went from one Sovereign to the other."[14] Byzantine influence on the Damascus mosque was pervasive; the mosque showcased technological advances, such as a water clock called *mikaniyyah* (derived from the Greek *mechane*).[15] Mosaics were dazzling, indeed the Arab term for mosaic, *fusaifusa*, may have been an import from the Greek term *psephos*.[16] In Damascus, a cosmopolitan city with a Christian majority, the presence of Byzantine artisans and the liberal display of Byzantine workmanship could hardly upset sensitivities; on the contrary, blending non-Muslim with Muslim tastes was a policy than which few could be more expressive of the ruling elite's desire to overcome barriers between conquerors and subjects.

Relations with Byzantines at official level and through private middlemen continued during the Abbasid era. Some members of the expatriate Byzantine business community in Baghdad frequented the caliph's court; a certain Patrikios borrowed money from the caliph, invested in a mill, and continued drawing income after returning to Byzantine lands.[17] Arab histories celebrated the pomp and pageantry of the occasion surrounding the visit in 917 of a Byzantine delegation to the caliph Muqtadir. Al Khatib reported Baghdad was full of "people who had come sight-seeing, and every shop and high balcony had been let for a price of many dirhams."[18] The emissaries were kept in waiting for four months until the caliph at last admitted them and displayed his treasures of curtains, rugs, jewelry, elephants, lions, and his prize bauble, a bird wrought of 50,000 ounces of silver. In keeping with the sumptuous character of his hospitality, the departing delegation received a generous farewell present.

The subject of negotiations of that particular embassy was treatment of prisoners of war, and such negotiations were conducted also through private channels. Ali ibn Isa enjoined senior Christian clerics, the Patriarch in Antioch and the Catholicos in Jerusalem (head of the Nestorian church), to intervene on behalf of Muslim prisoners of war by suggesting they threaten the Byzantine emperor with excommunication unless he improved prison conditions; both clerics were cooperative and the outcome desired was duly achieved.[19] The business sector, too, helped prisoners of war. One Muslim merchant paid for upkeep of a Christian church in Baghdad in return for a Byzantine monk's commitment to donate blankets to captive Muslims.[20]

MUSLIMS IN CONSTANTINOPLE

Constantinople was the capital of an empire dominated by politics rather than trade, and only gradually opened her gates to permanent expatriate settlers. The existence of a mosque in Constantinople is documented for the eighth and for the ninth century.[21] Syrians were the first foreign merchant community granted settlement rights in Constantinople, a concession widened by the tenth century to include Muslims, Venetians, and Russians, who had residence permits for up to three months.[22] The overriding considerations for admitting Muslims to Constantinople seem to have been diplomatic and religious rather than commercial.

Byzantine and Fatimid rulers in 1027 signed the first of several reciprocal commitments to protect rights of religious minorities. The Fatimids agreed to restore the Church of the Holy Sepulchre in Jerusalem while Constantine VIII granted protection to the mosque in Constantinople. Riots in 1044 targeted Arabs as well as other foreigners and inflicted damage on the mosque, and the Byzantine emperor Constantine Monomachos restored the mosque at his own expense. Saladin, after conquering Jerusalem, continued the policy of reciprocal protection of religious institutions by appointing Greek clerics to administer the city's Christian sites and thereby restored precedence of Orthodox over Catholics, and Isaac II Angelus reciprocated the gesture by having built a new mosque in Constantinople that was staffed with several *muezzins* to which Saladin donated a *minbar*. The mosque was located in a commercial area given over to Muslim merchants and at the official opening ceremony the local Muslim merchant community was in attendance.[23]

Italian merchants torched that mosque in 1203, but it was restored after Byzantines reclaimed Constantinople in 1261.[24] A Muslim traveler in the late thirteenth century described the Constantinople *funduq* for Muslims and Jews:

> There is a place, which is large like [the one with] two floors in Damascus, [and] is surrounded by a wall with a gate which may be shut and opened, specially designated as a lodging for the Muslims; likewise there is another place for lodging the Jews. Every night these gates are closed, along with the other gates of the city.[25]

This description of how the Muslim *funduq* in Constantinople looked and how it was managed accords with those of Muslim *funduqs* in Asia. Also, Byzantine intervention against fractious local rioters parallels that of governments in Asia. A different story unfolded, on the other hand, in Western Europe.

In Asia and in Constantinople, Arab outposts prospered as self-governing communities within clear boundaries. But whereas in Asia and in Byzantium, strong domestic authorities guarded law and order and robust host institutions smoothed trade flows, in Europe, on the other hand, local authorities were feeble. In any event, trade potential in Europe was meager. Arabs could buy silk in China and steel in India, but a country such as France offered few objects of value beyond church treasuries. For an Arab outpost in Europe, the business case rested on piracy rather than on trade. The process leading to the discovery that trade was more rewarding than rapine was arduous, protracted, and in some instances failed utterly. One notable failure was an Arab settlement established on the French coast near St. Tropez around 890.

Arabs were formidable raiders, striking deep into Switzerland and driving wealthy citizens living on Lake Geneva to retreat to Neuchatel. The extreme point of Arab raids was Lake Constance where, around 950, the abbot of St. Gall monastery rallied his monks to counterattack and imprison a raiding party; their Arab captives went on hunger strike and starved to death. That defeat marked the beginning of a counterattack on Arabs in Switzerland and France. Arabs were driven out of Grenoble valley in the mid-960s, and the Arab base camp, that never numbered more than a few hundred inhabitants, in spite of secure supply lines to Muslim Spain and North Africa was finally overrun in 975.

ARAB TRADE WITH WESTERN EUROPE

Western European economies, at that time, languished. Trade dwindled; coinage contracted. Europe's economies collapsed with the Roman Empire; cities were depopulated, farmlands abandoned, roads and bridges neglected. The remains of Rome's empire were fought over by diverse contestants: Muslims claimed Portugal and most of Spain; Byzantines held Sicily and Southern Italy; and France and Germany suffered invasions by Arabs, Huns, and Goths. A new order began to take shape when the Carolingian dynasty marshaled robust defenses against invaders, beating back a Muslim invasion of France in 732, and after firming their grip on power went on the offensive.

Peace, however, did not sow seeds of prosperity. Neither Byzantine nor Carolingian emperors found a way to resuscitate European trade. Charlemagne, for example, had to abandon his efforts to create a mint in Aachen, and the Carolingian Empire afforded a lower standard of living than her Roman predecessor. But while trade flows within Europe slowed to a trickle, in the Mediterranean new markets emerged. Across the Mediterranean, the bipolar hegemony of Muslim Arabs and Byzantine Christians no longer patterned relations once new multipolar political constellations emerged within the realms of Islam and of Christendom. Opportunities beckoned to convert the shared sea into a vast emporium through official accords with Islamic rulers established across the length of North Africa's coastline.

NOTES

1. Hergenröther, *Photius: Patriarch von Constantinople*, Vol. 2, 599.
2. Bretschneider, *On the Knowledge Possessed by the Ancient Chinese of the Arabs and Arabian Colonies and Other Western Countries Mentioned in Chinese Books*, 8–10.
3. Reinaud, *Relation des voyages faits par les Arabes et les Persans dans l'Inde et à la Chine*, Vol. 1, 64.
4. Reinaud, *Relation des voyages faits par le s Arabes et les Persans dans l'Inde et à la Chine*, Vol. 1, 106.
5. Ibn Battuta, *Travels of Ibn Battuta in Asia and Africa*, 172.
6. Wüstenfeld, *Die Chroniken der Stadt Mekka*, Vol. 4, 84.
7. Sauvaget, *La mosquée omeyyade de Médine*, 184–85.
8. Wüstenfeld, *Die Chroniken der Stadt Mekka*, Vol. 4, 144.
9. Wüstenfeld, *Die Chroniken der Stadt Mekka*, Vol. 4, 151; Baladhuri, *The Origins of the Islamic State*, Vol. 1, 75–76.
10. Baladhuri, *The Origins of the Islamic State*, Vol. 1, 76.
11. Wüstenfeld, *Die Chroniken der Stadt Mekka*, Vol. 4, 147.
12. Samhudi, *Geschichte der Stadt Medina*, 73. Sauvaget, in *La mosquée omeyyade de Médine*, provided a comprehensive critique of sources, 10–39.
13. Lammens, *Études sur le siècle des Omayyades*, 118.

14. Le Strange, *Palestine under the Moslems*, 241.
15. Le Strange, *Palestine under the Moslems*, 250.
16. Le Strange, *Palestine under the Moslems*, 230.
17. Lassner, *The Topography of Baghdad in the Early Middle Ages*, 75–76.
18. Le Strange, *Palestine under the Moslems*, 38.
19. Tanukhi, *The Table-Talk of a Mesopotamian Judge*, 32–33.
20. Tanukhi, *The Table-Talk of a Mesopotamian Judge*, 35–36.
21. Hergenröther, *Photius: Patriarch von Constantinople*, Vol. 2, 599.
22. Lopez, "Silk Industry in the Byzantine Empire," 30.
23. *Receuil des historiens des croisades*, Vol. 4: 470–72; 508–9; Lopez, "Silk Industry in the Byzantine Empire," 31.
24. Reinert, "Muslim Presence in Constantinople."
25. Al Jazari, quoted in Constable, *Housing the Stranger*, 150.

Chapter Twenty-One

Shifting Alliances

Byzantine borders blocked Islam's advance to the north and diverted the surge of Muslim armies across North Africa, Sicily, and Spain. However, although Abbasids ruled Baghdad, Baghdad no longer was the sole capital of the Islamic realm. A lone survivor of the Omayyad dynasty had fled to the extreme frontier of the Islamic dominion and in Spanish Cordoba, after a time, a rival caliphate was established. Hashimites and Omayyads who once vied for social precedence in Mecca, a city with a population of less than 20,000, now contested supremacy over the lands bordering the Mediterranean. Moreover, independent dynasties emerged all along the North African coast (one of which claimed descent from Muhammad's daughter Fatima and proceeded to establish a third caliphate, in Cairo). Leading powers on either side of denominational divides were watchful of external enemies but also looked over their shoulders at internal rivals. New power centers in Western and Southern Europe eroded Byzantine and Abbasid supremacy, and within Christendom and Islam, political unity fractured and religious harmony dissolved. Christendom split along regional lines into Catholics and Orthodox. But the Islamic world, too, underwent momentous changes, and the realm of Islam sundered when rival caliphates arose in Egypt and Spain. The loss of political cohesion within Islam and Christendom made it expedient to forge alliances across denominational divides. Carolingian diplomats pursued a three-pronged strategy: befriending Baghdad to outflank Byzantium; signing truces with Muslim rulers in North Africa; and fomenting insurrections in neighboring Spain. In 765, the Carolingian Pippin sent a diplomatic delegation to Baghdad, his son Charlemagne another in 801. Harun al Rashid and his successor Al Mamun reciprocated with embassies to Germany. Harun's and Charlemagne's good relations were common knowledge; William of Tyre reported there were "frequent envoys who went back and forth between them."[1] Eginhard, Charlemagne's court biographer, reports Harun sent as gifts "silken stuffs, spices, and other rich products of Eastern lands." A few years before he had sent an elephant, at Charlemagne's request.[2]

Charlemagne signed truces with the Aghlabid dynasty ruling North Africa, but relations with Spain, on the other hand, were tense. The Omayyad land-based invasion into France had failed and so the navy was strengthened; shipyards sprang up in Tarragona, Seville, and several other Spanish ports. Seaborne raids on French cities were frequent and hostilities persisted. Carolingian diplomats thought it opportune to nurture ties with the enemies of the ruler in Cordoba and in 777 Charlemagne entertained rival emirs in Paderborn and held out prospects of supporting insurrections. But these efforts at destabilizing Spain's domestic balance of power never produced tangible results, and once a military stalemate had stabilized Charlemagne in 810 and 816 settled for truces.

The Byzantine emperor until then had been considered sole heir to Rome's emperors and his position as the highest political authority in Christendom was undisputed. But the Vatican sundered her allegiance with the emperors in Constantinople following unresolved theological disputes between clerics in East and West, and a new dynamic in international diplomacy began to make itself felt once Charlemagne was anointed as heir to Roman emperors. Theological controversies between Orthodox and Catholics spilled over into politics when Charlemagne acquired wider responsibilities together with his new title, specifically, to guard the interests of pilgrims to Jerusalem. Until then, only the Byzantine emperor had spoken on behalf of Christendom, but now a Holy Roman emperor wished to underscore the point that Jerusalem mattered to more than one Christian denomination. Harun and Charlemagne had overlapping interests; when Charlemagne asked Harun al Rashid to grant safe passage to pilgrims to Jerusalem, the caliph would have found it expedient to grant concessions—it was in his interest to strengthen a rival of the emperor in Constantinople and build goodwill with a monarch harrying Omayyads in Spain. Charlemagne's embassy to Baghdad included Christian as well as Jewish emissaries; Al Mamun's delegation to Aachen comprised Muslims and Christians. The economy of Charlemagne's empire, however, such as it was, hardly was a peer for those of the Abbasid, Omayyad, and Byzantine Empires. Whereas in the Eastern Mediterranean war never got in the way of cross-border business, in the Western Mediterranean governments never discovered a means to promote commerce. In the absence of strong governments, it fell to private initiative to stimulate latent economic potential.

ITALY'S MARITIME REPUBLICS

Venice, Genoa, and Florence were famed centers of Italian Renaissance culture and commerce. Howevcr, these cities, in common with other notable Italian mercantile republics —Pisa and Amalfi should be added to the list—lacked pedigree. Venice and Amalfi emerged from the rubble of the wrecked Roman Empire when marauding Huns drove Italians to abandon their homes and run for their lives. The first Venetians were refugees who escaped to marshes and lagoons on the northern Adriatic coastline; Amalfitans on Italy's southern coast facing Sicily hid at the foot of cliffs so precipitous a traveler passing overhead would not guess their presence. Amalfi and Venice came into being as refugee camps threatened by instant extermination if raiders would chance to find them. Bogs and cliffs secured survival, but the living they afforded was meager. Unlike Rome, Ravenna, or Milan—cities already famed in Roman times—Italy's maritime republics had origins that were inauspicious and altogether unheroic.

Amalfi and Venice survived the Huns, and they gladly submitted to Byzantine rule when Byzantine armies restored order in Italy. The borders of three empires—Byzantine, Carolingian, Islamic—ran through Italy, and Amalfi and Venice were situated on political fault lines: Amalfi faced Muslim Sicily, and Carolingian dominions engulfed Venice. But their Byzantine master in Constantinople, for all his power, was too far away ever to guarantee meaningful defense against a serious strike. Their security remained brittle in a country where political powers were locked in contention over political hegemony. But Amalfi and Venice overcame the threat of destruction through a means of protection more effective than any army could offer: instead of fighting the enemy, they invited him to trade.

AMALFI

Most harbors lining the coasts from the Pyrenees to the tip of Italy had suffered raids by Arab pirates who plundered property, torched homes, and kidnapped anyone young and healthy enough to be sold into slavery. Marseille, Nice, Genoa, Pisa, and even Rome's harbor Ostia suffered depredations. The list could go on. But Amalfi, a tiny city on the coast opposite Sicily and an easy target once Muslims based themselves there, was left unmolested, and for this reason: Amalfi came to exploit piracy as a business opportunity and partnered with Arabs in piratical forays that had the audacity to make a target even of Rome. The Vatican in vain pleaded with Amalfitans to break with their Arab brothers-in-arms, at first offering tax-exemption, then threatening excommunication, and at last promising an annual tribute. But the Vatican's offers fell on deaf ears, because Arabs offered Amalfi better terms. Arabs reciprocated the favor of Amalfi's safe harbor. They granted Amalfitans safe passage to Arab ports, and gave Amalfitans advance warnings of a raid on neighboring Salento.[3] Eventually both parties lit upon an important discovery—windfalls from piracy were less rewarding than regular profits earned over time through trade. Trade traveled in both directions: Amalfitans exported grain, timber, and slaves; they imported spices, frankincense, and textiles.

Amalfitan trade received a significant boost in 966 from a peace treaty between the Byzantine emperor and Egypt's ruling Fatimid dynasty. Amalfi, a Byzantine subject well regarded by Islamic authorities, seized the moment to expand her franchise and opened a trade outpost in Cairo. This commercial colony soon was populated in significant numbers. In 996, riots in Cairo precipitated by fears of a Byzantine attack claimed some two hundred casualties. But the police quelled disturbances, which shows the government valued the taxes that expatriate merchants paid into the government's treasury. Amalfi's approach to business conferred benefits to everyone involved. For Islamic luxury products, the most important customer was the Vatican that had demand for products such as frankincense and oriental weaves to add luster to rituals and dignitaries. Amalfi by the late tenth century had carved out a position as a valued business partner for caliphs, emperors, and popes, with outposts at opposite ends of the Mediterranean.

Amalfi prospered by linking Arab, Byzantine, and Italian trade, and with patrons in Rome, Constantinople, and Cairo, Amalfi's commercial position seemed impregnable. Her entrepreneurs, mindful of the need to create goodwill, endowed hospitals in Jerusalem, and in Constantinople, and made donations to churches in Rome. But Amalfi's prosperity ebbed away through a combination of geopolitical changes, government intervention, and competition from new entrants into the market.

Amalfi's autonomy—Byzantine rule was notional—came to an end after Normans supplanted Muslim rule over Sicily and expanded their dominions in southern Italy. The Norman Robert Guiscard in 1073 imposed his rule on Amalfi and converted Amalfi's most lucrative line of business, exporting grain, into a state-run monopoly.[4] Robert Guiscard inadvertently dealt a decisive blow to Amalfi's commerce when in 1082 he launched an attack on Byzantium. Amalfi's merchants in Constantinople were discredited and the emperor imposed on them punitive, even humiliating tariffs. Taxes on Amalfitans in Constantinople henceforth were paid over to a competitor who had backed the Byzantine war effort, Venice. As Amalfi subsidized Venice, Amalfi's business costs increased as those of Venice declined; Amalfi's franchise gradually eroded and slipped into Venetian hands.

VENICE

The Byzantine emperor in 1082 granted Venice a further competitive advantage, a license to tradc throughout the Byzantine realm, in reward for siding with him against Normans (which decision, however, had not been entirely altruistic; Venetians had acted in their best interests following Robert Guiscard's attacks on Venetian trading posts). These fiscal and commercial concessions made Venice the most important trade hub in the Mediterranean. The scale of this achievement is thrown into relief by comparison with the city's humble beginnings. Venice at first was a mere Byzantine bridgehead on the northern tip of the Adriatic engulfed by potential enemies beyond the city's immediate outskirts. This precarious position Venice turned to advantage. The emperor in Constantinople to forestall the loss of Venetian allegiance proffered commercial privileges throughout the Byzantine Empire to help the city prosper; putative conquerors, for their part, knew the moment Venice passed into possession of another ruler she would forfeit her trade privileges. It was apparent Venice either would revert to a worthless backwater ringed by lagoons and marshes lacking fertile hinterland, or become a gateway for trade between the Byzantine and Carolingian Empires. Venetian independence was secured by free trade.

Venice's ascent to a leading position in Mediterranean trade occurred in stages. Venice in practice was autonomous; Byzantine ratification of the election of leaders was a formality. Venice linked sealanes to Byzantine and Saracen ports of the Mediterranean to land routes into Italy and across the Alps. In 840, Venetians were granted the right of unhindered travel throughout the Carolingian realm, and Venetians with every successive generation grew richer and more self-confident. The staple of Venetian trade was the merchandise that realized the highest prices in international markets, slaves, and arms. The pope lamented the greed of Venetian slave traders, the emperor censored Venetians for selling arms and timber to Byzantium's enemies. But trade embargoes were ineffectual, as Venetians complied with the letter but not the spirit of Byzantine injunctions.

Venetian shippers strayed on either side of the borderline between trade and piracy; in 827 a raiding party burgled a church in Alexandria and absconded with a prestigious relic, the body of St. Mark, that they translated to their cathedral San Marco. This pious roguery signaled Venetian aspirations to rival Alexandria, the Mediterranean's premier commercial center, and when their Byzantine overlord rebuked them for docking in Alexandria in contempt of a trade embargo, Venetians had the temerity to claim they had been blown there by a storm. They hardly expected to be believed, but however dubious and distasteful were Venetian trade practices, Byzantines looked the other way.

By the end of the tenth century, Venetians had separate trade treaties with Byzantine, Carolingian, and Islamic authorities; Venetians indiscriminately traded with allies, enemies, and countries at war against each other. In 992, Venice contracted to supply warships to the Byzantine emperor and in return extracted trade concessions. A clause in the contract stipulated ships be leased at market rates, a fateful precedent, as transpired when the crusades created increasingly large demand for transport to Palestine. Byzantines, for their part, were wary Venetians might exploit concessionary tariffs and act as shippers for third parties, and so they inserted a clause into the treaty that banned Venetians from shipping merchandise on behalf of Amalfitans, Lombards, and other merchants. The Byzantine emperor henceforth would have to pay for Venetian support if he needed it. The balance of power was shifting in Venice's favor, and at last, in 1082, Byzantium awarded Venetians concessions to trade throughout the empire: Venice had achieved mastery over Mediterranean trade routes.

Venetians by now settled in Constantinople in the thousands and other Italians followed them, in particular Genoans and Pisans. Each community there was assigned individual docks and warehouses, and each had to negotiate their particular tariffs. Setting differential tariffs was a means for the Byzantine administration to bestow patronage on favored partners. Thus Genoans paid tariffs at a rate of 10 percent, Pisans of 4 percent, but for Venetians the tariff was nil. Merchant communities lobbied for tax concessions, and if expedient, relied on intimidation and extortion to secure their aims. The Byzantine government faced manifest blackmail by her subjects: Pisans and Genoans negotiated fiscal concessions in return for a commitment to stop crusaders in transit to Palestine from raiding Byzantine cities, and Venetians felt no compunction against raiding Byzantine cities on the Greek coast to force the emperor to revoke tariff increases. The boundaries began to blur between commerce and blackmail; trust broke down between Greek hosts and Italian guests.

But tensions between expatriate Italians flared also. In 1162, Pisans with Venetian aid assaulted and raided Genoese warehouses, and damages assessed at 30,000 hyperper led to war on Italian soil between Pisa and Genoa. In 1171, when Venetians once again set fire to Genoan warehouses, the Byzantine emperor Manuel had the entire Venetian community arrested and confiscated their property. Recriminations flew; Venetians alleged the Byzantine emperor had lured them into attacking the Genoese colony to give him a pretext for reprisals. Venetians adduced circumstantial evidence—some 10,000 Venetians were jailed—suggesting the emperor's plans were laid long before, because the wave of arrests across the entire Byzantine Empire was carried out in a single day.

Venice sought redress through force. Within four months, a fleet issued from Venice, funded through a compulsory loan on every Venetian household. That attack force, however, achieved little; the ill-fated Venetian commander, shortly after returning to Venice from an inconclusive campaign, was assassinated. Venice then resorted to another threat, to enter into alliance with the arch foe of Byzantium, the Norman kings of Sicily. Byzantines at last relented and promised restitution plus financial compensation (750 kilograms of gold), but this reconciliation was but a stay of the calamity that lay ahead. In 1182, Manuel's successor accused Venetians of conspiracy and let loose mobs that torched Venetian churches, ransacked Venetians' homes, and sold inhabitants into slavery. William of Tyre provided a graphic description of the mayhem committed by Greeks:

> Monks and priests called in footpads and brigands to carry on the slaughter under promise of reward. Accompanied by these miscreants, they sought out the most secluded retreats and the inmost apartments of homes, that none who were hiding there might escape death. When such were discovered, they were dragged out with violence and handed over to the executioners, who, that they might not work without pay, were given the price of blood for the murder of these wretched victims.[5]

The scale of this atrocity against Constantinople's expatriate population—estimated at some 60,000—was immense; forty-four ships escaped with refugees, and many who were left behind were sold into slavery, of which some 4,000 slaves were later ransomed. Genoese assessed damages on this occasion at 228,000 hyperpers.[6] Escaping Venetians retaliated in kind:

> They sailed along the shores of the Hellespont . . . took by force all the cities and fortresses along both shores, and put all the inhabitants to the sword. They made their way also into all the monasteries along both shores and on the small islands scattered throughout the sea. Here, in retaliation for the blood of their brethren, they slew all those pseudo-monks and sacrilegious priests and burned the monasteries together with the refugees who had fled thither. From those places they are said to have carried off an immense amount of gold and silver, with jewels and silken stuffs in large quantities, and therewith repaid themselves many times for the loss of their property and the destruction of their goods. For, in addition to the vast wealth of the monasteries and the countless treasures which had been accumulating there for a long time, the citizens of Constantinople had deposited in these hold places for safekeeping immense quantities of gold and other treasures.[7]

Byzantium at that moment had become a rogue state: the Byzantine emperor, premier guardian of international order in the Mediterranean, had contrived to exterminate his own subjects and seize their property. Byzantium's contempt for the rule of law, however, was not unique at this time. With the first crusade at the beginning of the century, unbridled greed had become the undisguised driving force of government policies. The crusades shaped the evolution of trade in the Mediterranean, but the commercial ramifications of the crusades cannot be understood without a consideration of how entrepreneurs theretofore had transformed how business was conducted. Convoys issuing from Italy's mercantile republics had a corporate structure that however innovative in the context of Europe, was one that was akin to that of caravans departing from Mecca.

COMMENDA

The business case for a convoy was essentially the same as that of a caravan: investors had to put up the funds to equip a ship and agree how they would share profits with managers. Such firms were called *commenda*, and although terms and conditions varied from case to case, the underlying business case was unchanging: to build and equip a ship for a voyage required planning over a long period; another long period went by until that ship returned; until, at last, the *commenda* was wound up and investors were paid out. Legal agreements had to be drafted with care to forestall disputes. The oldest documentation of a *commenda* has come down to us from Venice in 976, wherein the investor—a wealthy widow by the name of Hualderada—specified how much she would invest and on what terms.[8]

Commenda contracts brought investors together "*ad risicum et fortunam*" and thus was introduced into European commerce a new term, risk. The failure rate must have been daunting, considering risks included shipwreck, piracy, and the absence of legal recourse in cases of commercial disputes in foreign jurisdictions. Of necessity, profits had to be commensurate with the risks. The return on capital on transporting pilgrims to Palestine could be as high as 100 percent, and even higher for transporting high-value goods of little bulk such as pepper. Spice traders dominated shipping; the generic term for a ship's load, *cargo*, is derived from units of weight of pepper, *carghi*. But *commendas* could be adapted to a wide range of purposes and to any scale. King Louis IX relied on *commenda* contracts to raise 1,800 ships for a crusade. For that venture, two Genoese admirals formed a company for a two-year term, leasing ships from ship owners who in turn formed syndicates to share the risks.[9] The commercial structure of this crusade in effect was that of a privateering company with profits contingent *ad consuetudinem cursi* (whence the term *corsair*).[10]

As in Mecca, where the civic calendar revolved around departure dates of caravans, in Italy's maritime cities seafaring shaped annual business cycles. Ships sailed in convoys as a precaution against pirate attacks, and consequently there evolved fixed departure dates each year, which in turn required local suppliers to adapt their production cycle. A wide range of specialist craftsmen found employment in building ships, but the most innovative impact of seafaring on employment originated from its commercial aspects. Professionals were needed who were able to cast agreements in writing and to calculate profit shares. In tenth-century Venice, very few merchants were capable even of providing signatures, so literacy and numeracy were highly prized skills.[11]

Shippers and investors had to exercise judgment of risks and returns—shippers would ask for attractive bonus arrangements, and investors would seek to spread their risks. Exact terms were negotiated on a case-by-case basis, but typically a *commenda*'s manager would claim between a quarter and a third of profits, and investors between them would share the balance in proportion to their commitment. Investors were drawn from all sections of society—patricians, judges, priests, and craftsmen.[12] The greater the number of investors in *commendas*, the greater the demand for expertise in financial mathematics and accounting—and the more promising the career prospects for bright practitioners. Scribes who stood by to provide the requisite expertise were forerunners of accountants, bankers, and lawyers.

The principal parties in a *commenda*, investors and managers, had to settle on terms that balanced their particular objectives. An investor would be wary of committing too much capital to a single venture and opt to spread investments across as many ventures as possible, whereas managers, for their part, would aim to attract as much investment as possible to afford a bigger ship. Such deliberations and negotiations between parties honed an understanding how to evolve creative solutions to commercial challenges. Once investors began to spread risk among several ventures, it was only a short step to evolve an insurance market.

Most aspects of corporate governance are intuitive—investors need assurance they are putting capital into good hands, managers wish to be rewarded for their efforts. But there were many antecedents for the *commenda*. Prescriptions for sharing risks and returns from commercial investments already feature in the world's oldest law code, the *Codex Hammurabi* of 1700 BC.[13] Judaic and Byzantine societies also previously evolved broadly similar models for establishing firms. But it is implausible that the stirring of corporate creativity in Italy at this moment could have occurred for any reason other than through exposure to commercial conventions of Islamic markets. Not only are there obvious similarities with the Arab *qirâd*—which met analogous needs of combining an investor's capital with a manager's skill. But further, the *qirâd* emerged as the standard for incorporating businesses throughout the Levant; so frequent were *qirâds* in the Jewish business community that the thirteenth-century Jewish jurist Moses Maimonides in Cairo was asked by his coreligionists to pronounce a ruling whether they could continue trading through *qirâds* alongside gentiles (the answer was yes). One might speculate what was the reason the *qirâd* had become the dominant template for corporate governance within the Islamic Empire; one possible explanation is that the *qirâd* had the most attractive incentive structure (one difference with the Judaic version of a firm, for example, was that there managers were held personally liable for losses, which was not the case under the terms of a *qirâd*). But another, more intuitive explanation may be that minorities copied practices of commercial elites because they accounted for the most significant volume of business within the Islamic Empire, and European merchants visiting Islamic trade centers copied that template when they returned to their home communities. It would be difficult otherwise to explain why *commendas* proliferated in those communities in Italy that were most closely linked to Islamic commerce.

NOTES

1. William of Tyre, *A History of Deeds Done Beyond the Sea*, Vol. 1, 64.
2. Eginhard quoted in William of Tyre, *A History of Deeds Done Beyond the Sea*, Vol. 1, 64.
3. Heyd, *Geschichte des Levantehandels im Mittelalter*, Vol. 1, 110.
4. Citarella, "Patterns in Medieval Trade," 543.
5. William of Tyre, *A History of Deeds Done Beyond the Sea*, Vol. 2, 465.
6. Heyd, *Geschichte des Levantehandels im Mittelalter*, Vol. 1, 245.
7. William of Tyre, *A History of Deeds Done Beyond the Sea*, Vol. 2, 466.
8. Silberschmidt, *Die Commenda in ihrer frühesten Entwicklung*, 38.
9. Byrne, *Genoese Shipping in the Twelfth and Thirteenth Centuries*, 19.
10. Byrne, *Genoese Shipping in the Twelfth and Thirteenth Centuries*, 62.
11. Heynen, *Entstehung des Kapitalismus in Venedig*, 81.
12. Silberschmidt, *Die Commenda in ihrer frühesten Entwicklung*, 82.
13. Codex Hammurabi: § 104–108.

Chapter Twenty-Two

Tax Havens in the Holy Land

Venetians treated the crusades as a business proposition and committed some 200 ships already to the first crusade. The considerations motivating this commitment were mercenary: the crusades offered business prospects beyond chartering ships to transport warriors and weaponry, and even greater profits beckoned from taking an active part in conquests. The reward for supporting a siege of a particular city was negotiated on a case-by-case basis, but business conventions emerged. As a standard rate for supporting a siege, Venetians demanded control of one third of the conquered city; licenses there to operate bakeries and bathhouses; and tax exemption of all commercial income. But the price could be higher if the target city contained valuable manufacturing facilities. For Tripolis, a city renowned for its silk industry, Venetians negotiated overall control of the city. Venetians took care to preserve the city's principal earning asset after the city had been conquered, and while Tripolis was to pass from Muslim to Christian rule and back again, the city's 4,000 silk looms continued spinning regardless of who happened to be the political master of the moment.[1] For the siege of Tyre, Venetians lent 100,000 bezants and recouped their investment after the city's fall through rents on properties in the quarter that came under their control. The soldiery participated in generous bonus schemes; the windfall for every participant in the campaign leading to the conquest of Caesarea consisted of cash plus two pounds of pepper. Italy's mercantile republics in their quest for market shares and commercial concessions competed against each other. In 1099, the Venetian fleet's first armed encounter on its way to Palestine was against a rival Pisan convoy that it defeated and spared on condition it turn back to Italy; Venetians had no inclination to let a business rival set foot in Palestine.

Tax concessions to the business community were lucrative and observers could not fail to notice these came at the expense of pilgrims. William of

Tyre was a contemporary witness of developments in the crusader states who quoted from a Venetian tax treaty with the King of Jerusalem that suggested the only category of Europeans in his kingdom subject to tax was pilgrims—such, at least, is the startling inference from his account:

> The Venetians need pay no tax whatever, whether according to custom or for any reason whatsoever, either on entering, staying, buying, selling, either while remaining there or on departing. For no reason whatever need they pay any tax excepting only when they come or go, carrying pilgrims with their own vessels.[2]

Palestine had become host to offshore trade centers for Italian mercantile republics that used them as a base for trade across denominational barriers. Commercial accords between Muslims and Christians across the Mediterranean had many precedents. In tenth-century Syria, Muslim rulers of Aleppo acknowledged the Byzantine emperor as their sovereign, deputed tax collection to Byzantine officials, and entered into reciprocal commitments protecting merchants traveling in either realm. In Tunisia, Muslim rulers paid an annual levy to Normans to ensure protection of Muslim shippers. In the crusader states, expatriate merchants from Europe likewise nurtured trade links with Muslims, and it became increasingly difficult to discern whether commerce served the interest of crusaders or vice versa. So conspicuous was the reluctance of crusaders to jeopardize commercial flows, Godfrey of Bouillon was suspected of shirking military confrontation to avoid disturbing the flow of commerce.[3] Ibn Jubayr, a Muslim traveler crossing from Syria into Palestine, was astonished that commerce went unmolested during a period of intense military conflict between Saladin and crusaders:

> One of the astonishing things that is talked of is that though the fires of discord burn between the two parties, Muslim and Christian, two armies of them may meet and dispose themselves in battle array, and yet Muslim and Christian travelers will come and go between them without interference. . . . The caravans passed successively from Egypt to Damascus, going through the lands of the Franks without impediment from them. In the same way the Muslims continuously journeyed from Damascus to Acre (through Frankish territory), and likewise not one of the Christian merchants was hindered (in Muslim territories).[4]

SHIFTS IN TRADE FLOWS

Muslim trade with Asia was thought to be the fount of immense riches. The Italian pilgrim Giorgio Gucci reported what he heard from other travelers: "Mecca they say is a big city and borders on India, and there collect at the said time merchants from India with great quantities of merchandise, that is, spices; and they give and take and in three days they are through with everything and start for home. It is an ordinary thing in those three days to sell and buy merchandise for two million florins."[5] Trade from Asia heading toward the Mediterranean had a choice of two routes: landfall could occur at Basra and proceed through Syria, alternatively, dock in Egypt's Red Sea harbor Aydhab and proceed via Cairo to ports in the Nile delta, Alexandria and Damietta. By the second half of the eleventh century, imports from Asia began to bypass the crusader states and reach the Mediterranean via Egypt, and as a consequence, Italian trade communities in Palestine were losing market share in trade with Asia. It could not have escaped their notice that the competitive advantage of routing trade via Egypt was because there the costs of doing business were lower.

TRADE TARIFFS IN EGYPT

A merchant's biggest cost component likely was tariffs. Between Egypt's Red Sea port Aydhab and Alexandria, few stopovers intervened, fewer, at any rate, than between Basra and the Levantine coastline. But even so, tariffs were onerous. An initial 10 percent tariff was charged on disembarkation in Aydhab, and again at each stage of the journey within Egypt—in Cairo, Rosetta, and finally on arrival in Alexandria.[6] European merchants in Alexandria paid levies at corresponding levels: they paid import taxes ranging up to 20 percent on arrival, and customs duties on departure, usually 10 percent.[7] The hidden components contained in market prices stunned medieval travelers; one medieval visitor, Piloti, estimated taxes doubled prices. (He was probably right.)[8] Military planners in the crusader states must have been conscious that diverting Egyptian trade tariffs from Muslim into crusader coffers would drain the former and enrich the latter—the case for mounting an attack on Egypt became increasingly strong.

Between 1178 and 1183, crusaders launched several naval assaults on forts in the Red Sea and endeavored to take them over. These bridgeheads constituted a dual threat, to pilgrim routes to Mecca and to commercial traffic between Asia and Egypt's Red Sea harbor Aydhab.[9] Ibn al Athir described the shock when crusaders mounted attacks that had no conceivable link to the original crusader objective of securing access to Christian sites in Palestine: "They took plunder and seized whatever Muslim ships they found and the merchants on board. They surprised the people in those regions, taking them quite unawares. They had never any experience of a Frank in that sea, neither as merchant or soldier."[10] A Muslim counterattack overwhelmed the expeditionary forces and crusaders taken captive were executed. But hostilities escalated further when Reginald of Chatillon, master of the crusader fort Krak, in 1187 ambushed a Muslim caravan, "making goods, animals and weapons his booty."[11] Chatillon's violation of safe passage for commercial traffic triggered Saladin's campaign that ended with the Muslim capture of Jerusalem.

BYZANTINES AND SALADIN

Saladin pursued a twin track policy toward his Christian adversaries: he went on the attack in Palestine and in parallel pursued diplomatic initiatives with Byzantium. Saladin's interests overlapped with those of the emperor Isaac II Angelos: both contended with crusader expansionism and also had to be watchful of internal rivals. Saladin had to be as watchful of Abbasid caliphs in Baghdad as Isaac II of Norman kings in Sicily. Byzantine diplomats suggested a pact: if Saladin would acknowledge Isaac II as his overlord, he in return would acknowledge Saladin as legitimate ruler of Egypt. This accord was never concluded, however, because once Saladin in 1187 conquered Jerusalem he no longer had a need for it. But there were diplomatic understandings between Saladin and Isaac II regarding commercial and religious policies: in Jerusalem, Saladin deputed orthodox clerics to take over responsibility for maintaining Christian religious sites, while in Constantinople, Isaac II afforded Muslims a new mosque and trading privileges.[12]

TAKEOVER OF CONSTANTINOPLE IN 1204

Many years lapsed before Europeans marshaled resources to mount a new campaign in Palestine. In 1203, at last, a crusader strike force issued from Venice with the ostensible aim of restoring Jerusalem to crusader rule. But military planners were divided whether to postpone an attack on Jerusalem in favor of first cutting off Saladin's supply lines to Palestine through an attack on Egypt. This diversionary plan of attack had much to recommend it from a commercial point of view, because Egypt was the gateway to trade with Asia. No records were kept of what passed during planning sessions, but whatever were the arguments, the outcome was the decision to sail for Egypt rather than Palestine. However, once at sea, the fleet again changed course, and now the new destination was Constantinople. What could explain this new decision was a puzzle. There were rumors to the effect Venetians had been bribed to divert the task force; allegations of duplicity were nourished by alleged sightings of Egyptian envoys in Venice during the crusade's planning period and further supported when Venetians shortly after landing in Constantinople received confirmation of new trade privileges in Egypt.[13] Venetians, however, gave out a different explanation, which was that they intended only to collect on outstanding debts in Constantinople before continuing the journey; the stay in Constantinople would be short. Whatever the true reasons—disputed to this day—the crusader fleet that anchored in Constantinople never advanced further; instead, the crusader task force in 1204 looted Constantinople and there installed a puppet emperor. Venetians never proffered a pretext for the plundering of Constantinople and never concealed the overriding objective of there extracting as much money as possible. The sack of Constantinople—executed in a campaign ostensibly instigated to liberate Jerusalem—was so egregious in enormity the Vatican excommunicated all participants. This humiliation, however, the Venetians shrugged off; the Venetian leader of the invasion, Enrico Dandolo, has a grave in Constantinople's basilica Hagia Sophia.

Venetians enlarged their quarter in the city and henceforth occupied three eighths of Constantinople's area. (The Venetian quarter was comparable to stakes in cities in Palestine where Venetians customarily occupied a third of any city they had helped conquer.) The ruler of Venice styled his title "*dominator quartae partis et dimidiae totius imperii Romaniae*," that is to say, "ruler of three eighths of the entire Roman Empire," which had some justification in fact, because Venice assumed control over the islands in the Aegean and over Crete.[14] Islamic diplomatic correspondence duly addressed the Venetian doge as "*gubernator Christianorum*," ruler of Christians.[15] Venetians also acquired a share of three eighths of Byzantium's tax revenues, a useful measure allowing Venetians to monitor trade activities of competing trade communities. It was even considered to relocate the city's leader, the Doge, to Constantinople, but this option Venetians after some deliberation rejected.

Venetians stripped Byzantium of her assets—they pillaged the capital, dismembered her provinces, and enthroned a puppet emperor to govern what was left. Furniture looted from Constantinople palaces was sold to Muslims who used it to decorate their own residences.[16] In 1240, the most spectacular acquisition occurred when Venetians sold to the French King Louis IX what was regarded as one of the most venerable relics of Christendom, the Crown of Thorns, said to have been worn by Jesus at his crucifixion. The sequence of transactions that led to this acquisition was complex: the Byzantine emperor Baldwin II had pledged the relic as a security for borrowings from the Knights Templar and had defaulted on his loan (the exact amount is not recorded, but it must have been a very large sum, since a contemporary French account too discreet to reveal a figure stated it was "*immensa pecunie quantitate*");[17] the Templars passed possession of the forfeited security to Venetians; Venetians translated the relic to Venice; and King Louis IX bought out their interest and had the relic brought to Paris where he created for it a church built expressly for that purpose, the Sainte Chapelle (the relic today is in the treasury of the cathedral Notre Dame de Paris).[18] Cities that wished to rival Venice similarly acquired relics as a means to enhance the prestige of their cathedrals. For example, Amalfitans translated from Constantinople to Amalfi the remains of St. Andrew; from Palestine, Genoans took the *sacro cantino*, the chalice allegedly used at Jesus's Last Supper, to dignify Genoa's cathedral; and in due course the Sicilian admiral George of Antioch would bring to Palermo the remains of Saint Theodore he had robbed from Corinth.

NOTES

1. Heyd, *Geschichte des Levantehandels im Mittelalter*, Vol. 1, 197.
2. William of Tyre, *A History of Deeds Done Beyond the Sea*, Vol. 1, 554.
3. It was alleged, "pacem firmissimam cum Ascalonitis atque Damascenis gratia commertiorum habuit." Quoted in Heyd, *Geschichte des Levantehandels im Mittelalter*, Vol. 1, 190.
4. Ibn Jubayr, *The Travels of Ibn Jubayr*, 300–301.
5. Gucci, *A Visit to the Holy Places*, 144.
6. Heyd, *Geschichte des Levantehandels im Mittelalter,* Vol. 2, 448. Note, Heyd's sources are for the fifteenth century.
7. Heyd, *Geschichte des Levantehandels im Mittelalter*, Vol. 2, 449.
8. Heyd, *Geschichte des Levantehandels im Mittelalter*, Vol. 2, 450.
9. Around 1430, over 40 Indian and Chinese ships docked in Aydhab. Heyd, *Geschichte des Levantehandels im Mittelalter*, Vol. 2, 445.
10. Ibn al Athir, *The Chronicle of Ibn al-Athir for the Crusading Period*, Vol. 2, 289.
11. Ibn al Athir, *The Chronicle of Ibn al-Athir for the Crusading Period*, Vol. 2, 316.
12. Hergenröther, *Photius*, Vol. 2, 599.
13. Heyd, *Geschichte des Levantehandels im Mittelalter*, Vol. 1, 443–44.
14. Heyd, *Geschichte des Levantehandels im Mittelalter*, Vol. 1, 317.
15. Heyd, *Geschichte des Levantehandels im Mittelalter*, Vol. 1, 443.
16. *Receuil des historiens des croisades*, Vol. 5, 154.
17. Delisle, *Les opérations financières des Templiers*, 17.
18. Tafel, *Urkunden zur Älteren Handels-und Staatsgeschichte der Republik Venedig*, Vol. 2, 346.

Chapter Twenty-Three

The Economic Consequences of Saladin

The conquests of Jerusalem by Saladin and of Constantinople by Venetians and crusaders created two distinct spheres of military dominance in East and West. Trade between these two blocks, consequently, might have dwindled. Indeed, Pope Innocent III following the fall of Jerusalem called for an embargo on trade with Saracens, but Venetians pointed out to the Vatican's emissaries their own economy would be the first to suffer and refused to comply.[1] Given prospects of a successful full-scale crusader invasion of Palestine were remote, one might have expected Venetians and their Italian peers to reverse the pattern of Mediterranean seafaring after the collapse of the Roman Empire when Arab pirates raided Italian coastlines, and now lose all compunction against ravaging and plundering the wealthy cities that looked out on the Eastern Mediterranean. Such was not the preferred Venetian policy, however, which must have come as a surprise to King Louis IX when he mooted the prospect of mounting another crusade and asked Venetians to name their terms for supplying ships: Venetians rebuffed his advances on the grounds they would not wish to jeopardize their trade presence in Alexandria and other cities where they maintained *funduqs*. That at this critical moment, when the Mediterranean trade zone could have disintegrated into anarchy, it instead embarked on a new phase of commercial expansion was due to policy decisions taken by the ruler who had taken command of Islamic statecraft, Saladin.

Jerusalem's conquest had not disposed of military threats; it must have been clear to Saladin crusaders were on the defensive and might counterattack Egypt to compensate for reversals in Palestine. Saladin was never averse to defusing potential conflicts through diplomacy—his negotiations with Byzantium to explore opportunities to contain crusaders in Palestine evinced his flexibility—and on this occasion lit upon the same policy that Italians once had used to ward off Arab pirates: instead of fighting the enemy, he invited them to trade. Saladin in Egypt introduced reforms that affected every sphere of society, including the judiciary, higher education, and funding of public services. In Cairo, a prison built by the deposed Fatimid regime was torn down and made room for a *madrasa* teaching law; the educational monopoly of the university founded by Fatimids, Al Azhar, was broken by *madrasas* teaching diverse jurisprudential traditions. Educational institutions were endowed with farms, shops, and *funduqs*.[2] Since commercial properties rather than government subsidies funded higher education, citizens enjoyed improved public services without paying higher taxes. The Muslim traveler Ibn Jubayr was impressed by Alexandrians' wealth and high standard of living: "As for the people in this city, they live in the height of ease and comfort. No tax is exacted from them and no revenues accrue to the Sultan himself save the *awqaf*, which are tied and devoted by his order to [charitable] purposes, and the tribute of the Jews and Christians."[3]

The sphere where Saladin's reforms had their greatest impact, however, was the economy, where his measures had ramifications for domestic and global trade. Saladin actively encouraged Europeans to establish *funduqs* in Alexandria and elsewhere in Egypt, an approach that generated wealth and had the collateral benefit of weakening the temptation to invade the country. Saladin's policy of affording Europeans a larger stake in the Egyptian economy was controversial in policy circles, and he had to defend himself against a remonstrating caliph who had difficulty seeing what good would come from opening up business opportunities to enemies. Saladin, however, offered cogent arguments in defense of his approach, specifically, he pointed out trade was beneficial if for no other reason than for giving access to military supplies. In a letter to the caliph, he pointed out his business partners from Europe "without exception supply the very arms they used to fight us, and seek our good-will by offering us riches and choice manufactures. I have established good relations with all of them and even though they were reluctant, signed peace treaties on advantageous terms."[4]

In Egypt, the presence of foreign merchants was of long standing. Amalfi's *funduq*, for example, had been licensed in the tenth century. The Persian traveler Naser-e Khosraw passing through Cairo in the eleventh century noticed there a Christian who was "one of the most propertied men in Egypt, who was said to possess untold ships, wealth, and property,"[5] and a Jew who was "very rich, having been entrusted with buying all the sultan's jewels."[6] Saladin continued this tradition of cosmopolitan toleration, and between 1172 and 1177 licensed *funduqs* in Alexandria for Venetians, Genoese, and Pisans. Venice maintained the largest presence in Alexandria; the Venetians had opened a *funduq* in Alexandria within a year after their mass arrests in Constantinople and eventually added another. But cities in Italy, France,

Cyprus, and elsewhere also were represented. A visitor from Spain, Rabbi Benjamin of Tudela, counted 28 different foreign communities in Alexandria. The largest cluster of traders may have been in Alexandria, but *funduqs* also were established in cities including Cairo, Aleppo, Damascus, Tripolis, and along the Black Sea Coast. When the Italian Giorgio Gucci visited Damascus, he was astonished how "many Christians, of almost every tongue, are there in business."[7]

Saladin's trade promotion was conspicuously successful. During the winter of 1187–1188, William of Tyre counted thirty-seven Italian ships anchored in Alexandria and during the summer trade season the number is likely to have been several hundred.[8] William noted:

> Whatever our part of the world lacks in the matter of spices, pearls, Oriental treasures, and foreign wares is brought hither from the two Indies, Saba, Arabia, and both the Ethiopias, as well as from Persia and other lands near by. All this merchandise is conveyed to Upper Egypt by way of the Red Sea, which forms the route from those races to us. It is unloaded at the city of Aidab on the shore of that same sea, and thence descends the Nile to Alexandria. Consequently, people from the East and the West flock thither in great numbers, and Alexandria is a public market for both worlds.[9]

Increasing trade volumes promoted *funduqs* that specialized in particular lines of business, such as linen, leather, candles, sweets, gold, silver, and pearls.[10] Alexandria had a *funduq* for foreign currency exchange, the *dar al-sarf*, and the financial *funduq* in Cairo dazzled Maqrizi, who there saw "chests, large and small, lining the length of the wall, leaving room only for a narrow passage down the middle; containing immense amounts of gold and silver."[11] Bankers cashed payment orders, a rudimentary form of paper currency used in daily purchases for groceries and bread. Discounting, issuing, and cashing payment orders were a standard financial service, and it was but a small step, from exchanging currencies and discounting payment instructions, to granting loans. Although the ban on paying interest remained in place, the exigencies of market practice outweighed religious reservations. The Jewish jurist Moses Maimonides was asked by his coreligionists to provide a legal opinion whether a transaction involving interest was licit and gave his conditional approval.[12] The multicultural character of Alexandria's trade community was sustained for centuries. Simon Simeonis, an Irish pilgrim passing through Alexandria in 1323, recorded:

> Thus there are fondacos of Genoa, Venice, Marseille, and of the Catalans, and others. Every merchant is obliged to betake himself, along with whatever merchandise he may have brought, to the fondaco of his respective state or region in accordance with the directions of his consul, the latter being at the head of the establishment and of all those housed in it.[13]

BUSINESS TAXES

Saladin promoted trade through fiscal incentives. No tax was levied on gold imported into Egypt that could be delivered to the sultan's mint and cast into coinage; but merchants taking gold out of the country, on the other hand, were liable for tax and thus they had an incentive to spend their money before leaving. Each *funduq* negotiated its particular tax regime individually, which gave authorities a means to differentiate between expatriate communities (much as Byzantine authorities were wont to do). Methods of tax collection were drastic. The oars and rudders of European ships were requisitioned and only returned after all taxes had been settled in full.[14] Egyptian tax collectors were intrusive, coarse, and insolent. The Italian Lionardo Frescobaldi thus described his entry in Alexandria:

> . . . they led us inside the port of Alexandria and presented us to certain officials, who had us registered and numbered like animals, and they committed us to the aforesaid consul, having first searched us carefully, even to the flesh, and having placed our things in the customs; then they cleared them, and they untied them and searched every one of our bundles and bags. And truly I doubted they would not find the six hundred ducats that I had placed in the reglet of the chest, for they would be lost, and we would have been treated worse. They made us pay two per cent on silver and gold money, and on our things, and they made us pay a ducat as tribute. Then we went with this consul to his house, which is very large and well situated.[15]

Customs officials, however disagreeable their manner, did not discriminate on grounds of religion. The Spanish Muslim Ibn Jubayr reported his coreligionist pilgrims hardly fared better:

> The day of our landing, one of the first things we saw was the coming on board of the agents of the Sultan to record all that had been brought on the ship. All the Muslims in it were brought forward one by one. And their names and descriptions, together with the names of their countries, recorded. . . . The Muslims were then ordered to take their belongings, and what remained of their provisions, to the shore, where there were attendants responsible for them and for carrying to the Customs all that they had brought ashore. There they were called one by one, and the possessions of each were produced. The Customs was packed to choking. All their goods, great and small, were searched and confusedly thrown together, while hands were thrust into their waistbands in search of what might be within. The owners were then put to oath whether they had aught else not discovered. During all this, because of the confusion of hands and the excessive throng, many possessions disappeared. After this scene of abasement and shame . . . [the pilgrims] were allowed to go.[16]

However, once travelers had the ordeal of entrance to Alexandria behind them, the city's glamour awed them and made them forget the tribulations of border passage. Ibn Jubayr exclaimed: "We have never seen a town with broader streets, or higher structures, or one more ancient and beautiful. Its markets are also magnificent."[17]

THE *KARIMI*

Saladin complemented economic liberalization inside Egypt with protectionism abroad: however permissive was his policy to European merchants seeking entry to markets in Egypt, he was unreservedly restrictive in banning anyone not a Muslim from entering markets east of Egypt. Pre-Saladinian records of trade in the Indian Ocean feature Muslims and Jews, Hindus and Christians. Post-Saladin, however, records of trade between Egypt and Asia no longer feature mentions of Jewish or Christian merchants.[18] Trade routes linking Egypt to Asia became the exclusive preserve of a Muslim merchant elite, the *karimi*. Saladin's nephew established a *funduq al-karim* in Cairo; Muslim traders established *funduqs* all along the Silk Road to China; and sent trade expeditions north of the Black Sea that reached the Baltic (whence came amber, a prized item of Islamic jewelry). Intercontinental trade was lucrative. One Abd ar Rahman (ca. 1300) had starting capital of some 500 dinars, undertook at least three voyages to China, and left an estate valued at 50,000 dinars.[19]

The specter of trade on a global scale now had become a distinct possibility and could capture the imagination of the thirteenth-century Persian author Sadi. In *Gulistan*, a book describing the author's encounters with remarkable people, the incredulous author listened to a merchant who explained how he would connect all the markets of the world known at the time through a chain of transactions that had six links: first, to export brimstone from Persia to China; second, to return with Chinese porcelain for sale in Constantinople; third, to buy Byzantine brocade and sell it in India; fourth, to return from India with steel to sell in Syria; fifth, there to buy glassware for delivery to Yemen; and sixth and at last, to close the circle by returning to Persia with Yemeni cloth.[20] *Gulistan* provided what may have been the first description of global trade arbitrage, and Sadi could not have conceived this story unless he lived in a society where the conception of global trade existed at least as a notion. Saladin's fame rests on his military and diplomatic achievements; his greatest impact, arguably, was as an economic reformer.

NOTES

1. Heyd, *Geschichte des Levantehandels*, Vol. 1, 427.

2. Lev, *Saladin in Egypt*, 125–30.
3. Ibn Jubayr, *Travels of Ibn Jubayr*, 34.
4. *Receuil des historiens des croisades*, Vol. 4, 178.
5. Naser-e Khosraw, *Book of Travels*, 55–56.
6. Naser-e Khosraw, *Book of Travels*, 58.
7. Gucci, *A Visit to the Holy Places*, 142.
8. Quoted in Heyd, *Geschichte des Levantehandels im Mittelalter*, Vol. 1, 439.
9. William of Tyre, *A History of Deeds Done Beyond the Sea*, Vol. 2, 336.
10. Labib, *Handelsgeschichte Ägyptens im Mittelalter*, 292–97.
11. Maqrizi, *Les marchés du Caire*, 136.
12. Goitein, *A Mediterranean Society*, Vol. 1, 199.
13. Quoted in Constable, *Housing the Stranger*, 112.
14. Heyd, *Geschichte des Levantehandels im Mittelalter*, Vol. 1, 439.
15. Frescobaldi, *A Visit to the Holy Places*, 38.
16. Ibn Jubayr, *Travels of Ibn Jubayr*, 31–32.
17. Ibn Jubayr, *Travels of Ibn Jubayr*, 32.
18. Goitein, "New light on the beginning of the Karimi merchants," 183; Labib, *Handelsgeschichte Ägyptens im Mittelalter*, 62. There may have been exceptions to Saladin's restrictions of Jewish participation in Asian trade: Ashtor points out some Karimi were Jewish; see "The Karimi Merchants," 55.
19. Labib, *Handelsgeschichte Ägyptens im Mittelalter*, 117–18.
20. Sadi, *Gulistan*, Chapter 3, Story 22.

Chapter Twenty-Four

Lives of the Merchants

Fortunes in the Mediterranean were won and lost by merchants who were prepared to move to wherever profits beckoned, and merchants who relocated from one trade hub to another were by no means unusual. Marco Polo, who ventured as far as China, did not seem to have thought his journey as such deserved particular notice; he only began committing his memoirs to paper when as prisoner of war in a Genoese prison he had time on his hands. Most trade centers had sizable expatriate communities. Marco Polo remarked Syrians (the generic term for Levantines) were so conspicuous in Italian cities that locals had begun to distinguish them by naming them after their native town. The name for someone from Mosul, for example, was Mosulini. But migration also headed toward the East; in the thirteenth century, the Genoese trading colony on the Crimean contained a family from Corsica named Bonaparte.[1] An immense talent pool from across a broad range of denominations and ethnicities supplied the Mediterranean economy with energetic professionals who moved to wherever their abilities could take them to positions of wealth and influence. But however splendid were rewards, there were matching risks of reversal, and medieval merchants lived on the brink between profit and perdition. The vicissitudes of medieval commercial life included exposure to bandits, pirates, and shipwreck. The immense personal costs borne by the pioneers of Mediterranean trade shine through in the biographies of representative entrepreneurs: the Catholic Romano Mairano of Venice; the Muslim Soleyman of Salerno; the Orthodox George of Antioch, and the Jewish David Maimonides of Cairo.

ROMANO MAIRANO

The Venetian Romano Mairano around 1190 retired from a business career that spanned forty years, enjoying pensions from shares in ships and property.[2] He began his career as a manager of a trade expedition, made enough money to set up as an entrepreneur, and eventually retired as an investor. But the recitation of what seems a steady career progression conceals pitfalls that threatened financial ruin and even his life. Mairano first appeared in Venetian archives in 1152, shortly after his marriage to his wife Mariota, when he borrowed money to embark on his first ventures to Thessaloniki and Constantinople. Soon he had resources to claim his own equity stakes in ventures; in 1154 his investor Valperto Gausini contributed 158 bezants, Mairano 79 bezants, but Mairano negotiated an attractive profit-sharing agreement—as the venture's manager, he claimed a 75 percent share in the business. While Mairano was abroad on business, news reached him Mariota had died. Now he made Constantinople his home, buying and letting a house there. Between 1157 and 1163, he traveled between Constantinople, Smyrna, and Accon, and his business prospered. In 1167, he raised funds from a syndicate of eight investors in Venice, who together invested 796 bezants in ventures that earned them 1,106 bezants. Business prospects were excellent, and 1169 would be a year of personal and professional fulfillment—so it seemed. The widower married again, and he and his second wife Matelda would have three children. Relations thawed between Byzantium and Venice, enticing thousands of Venetians to seek their fortunes in the East, and that very year Mairano returned to Constantinople and secured what promised to be his most profitable transaction: he leased an entire street, containing residential properties and taverns, and additionally was granted the monopoly on using weights and measures for Venetian traders.[3] Mairano should have looked forward to steady profits and his future seemed assured; however, political risks sprang disaster—Mairano had embarked on the biggest investment of his career on the very eve of the mass arrests of Venetians in Constantinople and of confiscation of their properties that took place in 1171. In the midst of this emergency, Mairano gathered Venetians aboard a ship, fled the city pursued by the Byzantine navy, and escaped to Akkon. Mairano relocated to Venice, but having lost his income in Constantinople, he unavoidably defaulted on his financial commitments. But soon, he embarked on voyages to restore his commercial position in new markets. In 1173, he sailed to Alexandria, exporting wood and returning with pepper. In 1175, reacting to news the Sicilian King William has reduced tariffs by 50 percent, he set sail for Messina. Another journey to Alexandria took place in 1182. Mairano had overcome the reversals suffered from the loss of his business in Constantinople. When he died, he left his children several properties.

SOLEYMAN OF SALERNO

Romano Mairano had not been not born to Venice's patriciate. Genoa was similarly meritocratic to Venice, offering opportunities to entrepreneurs from out of town, such as Soleyman, who moved to Genoa from Salerno. Soleyman likely was a Muslim (his name and the fact that Muslims frequently appear in his dealings point to this inference).[4] Soleyman ventured to Alexandria and Cairo in 1156, exporting saffron and silver jewelry, returning with pepper and brazil wood. Another of his convoys sailed for Alexandria in 1158, but Soleyman on this occasion appeared as an investor who deputed to others to travel on his behalf. In 1159 Soleyman bought a ship, partnering with a Christian and a Saracen, and in 1160 set out to Alexandria. Soleyman's career pattern was similar to that of Mairano except that his trade network extended into the Western Mediterranean. Soleyman's wife Eliador managed his affairs during his prolonged absence from Genoa, and the couple's finances enabled them to provide their daughter with a handsome dowry for marrying into the patrician Mallone family. In the early 1160s, however, Soleyman seems to have suffered reversals, because by 1163 he is reduced to using his daughter's substantial dowry to meet his commitments, and he had to pawn accoutrements that evinced a high standard of living, silverware and furs. The nature of his reversals is not clear from archives, however, and no further transactions are recorded after 1164—perhaps Soleyman went bankrupt.[5]

GEORGE OF ANTIOCH

George of Antioch (ca. 1100–1151), born in Syria of either Greek or Armenian parentage, made the whole of the Mediterranean a theater for his career and was famed in Catholic, Islamic, and Byzantine worlds. Ibn Khaldun noted he was "a Christian, an emigrant from the East. He had learned the [Arabic] tongue, and he excelled in accountancy."[6] George, raised a Christian orthodox, successively worked for Muslim and Catholic masters, neither of whom considered his denomination a barrier to promotion. Indeed, his first patron, sultan Temim of Tunisia, had a son who became a Pisan official. (Amicable relations between Tunisia and Pisa were of long standing; Pisa already from the ninth century may have had a Muslim quarter.)[7] After Temim's death, George, wary of Temim's son, left Tunis and offered his services to Sicily's Norman king Roger, who was only too eager to accept someone with inside knowledge of Arabic government workings. He rose to the highest levels of Sicily's government by applying Arabic fiscal, administrative, and military expertise. George oversaw tax collection, served as Roger's envoy to Egypt, and became commander of the Norman fleet. George's title *amiratus amiratorum* (whence the term *admiral*) is a Latinized version of the Arabic *emir of emirs*. In Norman service, George raided many Muslim and Byzantine cities. His targets included Tripolis (where he installed a Muslim regent), Athens, Corinth, and even Constantinople. George was keen to import skilled labor to Sicily; from one of his raids on Greece he carried away silk weavers and put them to work in Sicily. George, by denomination a Greek orthodox, had no compunction against raiding Byzantium, but his loyalty to his religion, however, was unequivocal; he endowed one of Palermo's most splendid churches, Chiesa della Martorana (still today affiliated with orthodox rite), and the inventory of its endowment gives a notion of George's spectacular wealth: the long list included ten farms and two *funduqs*.[8]

DAVID MAIMONIDES

Moses Maimonides, the philosopher, had a younger brother, David. Moses was one of most prolific scholars of his era; much less is known about his brother David, other than from letters he sent to Moses describing his journey across desert terrain to reach the Red Sea harbor Aydhab. These communications have survived, but were the last tokens of his life because David in Aydhab embarked on a ship and drowned in a storm on the Indian Ocean. We have a sense of David's personality, however, because it shines by reflection from words his brother Moses penned in remembrance:

> The greatest misfortune that has befallen me during my entire life—worse than anything else—was the demise of the saint (may his) m(emory) be b(lessed), who drowned in the Indian Sea, carrying much money belonging to me, to him, and to others, and left me with a little daughter and a widow. On the day I received that terrible news I fell ill and remained in bed for about a year, suffering from a sore boil, fever, and depression, and was almost given up. About eight years have since passed, but I am still mourning and unable to accept consolation. And how should I console myself? He grew up on my knees, he was my brother, he was my student; he traded on the markets, and earned, and I could sit safely at home. He was well versed in the Talmud and the Bible, and knew (Hebrew) grammar well, and my joy in life was to look at him. Now, all joy has gone. He has passed away and left me disturbed in my mind in a foreign country. Whenever I see his handwriting or one of his letters, my heart turns upside down and my grief awakens again.[9]

The lament of Moses for his brother David is a testimony how seaborne commerce cut short lives and careers: the rate of attrition must have been harrowing and every departure would have stoked fears of families staying at home whether this might have been the last. One ponders what conceivable allure a life of manifest fatal danger could have held for the likes of Romano

Mairano and David Maimonides, for Soleyman and George. Yet whatever the odds and again and again, merchants set sail, others were eager to follow, and with every homecoming they gave shape to a new world: the spirit of it was that of enterprise.

NOTES

1. Bratianu, *Recherches sur le commerce génois*, 226.
2. The following section follows Heynen, *Zur Entstehung des Kapitalismus in Venedig*.
3. Tafel, *Urkunden zur Älteren Handels-und Staatsgeschichte der Republik Venedig*, Vol. 1, 168 and 177; Heyd, *Geschichte des Levantehandels im Mittelalter*, Vol. 1, 239–40.
4. Abulafia, *The Two Italies*, 248–49.
5. Schaube, *Handelsgeschichte der romanischen Völker*, 157–59; Byrne, "Easterners in Genoa," 179–81.
6. Quoted in Johns, *Arabic Administration in Norman Sicily*, 83.
7. Amari, *I diplomi Arabi*, XXV.
8. Johns, *Arabic Administration in Norman Sicily*, 110.
9. Goitein, *Letters of Medieval Jewish Traders*, 207.

Chapter Twenty-Five

Early Law and Economics in Christendom

Trade with Islamic societies exposed Europeans to new products but also to new commercial practices and frameworks. In Europe there subsequently emerged two institutional innovations, forerunners of firms and of charitable trusts, which were key to evolving commercial and civil society. The first were venture capital firms, the *commenda*, that emulated the *qirâd*; the second was the *universitas*, a new legal concept with roots originating in the Islamic *waqf,* which first was used to constitute institutions of higher learning but then applied to charitable trusts and later more widely to corporations. The evolution of these two institutions crystallized in the biographies of two individuals, Leonardo Fibonacci and St. Francis of Assisi. Fibonacci showed how to apply mathematics to commercial management, which paved the way for applying quantitative approaches in wider settings. Francis, on the other hand, was not a business economist; however, his focus on the nature of ownership and the ethics of distribution of goods stimulated innovations in legal thinking. Fibonacci and Francis between them had seminal influence on advancing the analysis of the two main concerns of law and economics: economic efficiency and fair distribution. In their approaches, Fibonacci and Francis were poles apart, but by background they had much in common; Pisa and Assisi were mercantile cities and their fathers belonged to Italy's managerial elite. The most important aspect of their background, however, was that both shaped their approach to economics through encounters with Islamic economics and law.

LEONARDO FIBONACCI

Leonardo Fibonacci (ca. 1170–1240) was a seminal figure in the history of mathematics. One of his many achievements was to write the *Liber abaci*, an instruction manual on how to use arithmetic in everyday commerce that demonstrated through worked examples how numeracy helps improve business performance. Looking back to tenth-century Venice, where very few entrepreneurs were literate, let alone numerate, one can gauge how much progress had been made over the previous two centuries for Fibonacci to be able to find a receptive readership. Islamic mathematical teaching shaped Fibonacci's approach to mathematics.

Fibonacci was born in Pisa but grew up in Algeria where his father was a financial official in a Pisan *funduq*. Young Leonardo had an Arab tutor—Fibonacci remembered him in his autobiography as *magister mirabilis*—who encouraged him to continue his mathematical studies, and Fibonacci spent time in Egypt, Syria, and Greece, before advancing to an appointment in Palermo at the court of Emperor Frederick II. Fibonacci's familiarity with Arabic mathematics had immediate practical applications for his European readership. For example, Fibonacci explained why Indian numbering conventions (nine discrete digits and a placeholder called *zephyr*) simplified multiplications, compared to the Roman method of expressing numbers by letters (Romans also had not known how to perform calculations involving zeros). The *Liber abaci* showed how to calculate compound interest and profit shares, convert currencies, and perform a host of other calculations occurring in day-to-day commerce.

The *Liber abaci* was a training manual and investment primer for merchants managing *commendas* from end to end of the Mediterranean trade zone. Only a Mediterranean market that had become truly cosmopolitan could have inspired a case study such as this:

> Two men, partners in Constantinople, had together a company; one of the men went to Alexandria on business, and took with him from the common capital as much as he wished; he stayed there five years and 70 days, and his profit was a fifth of his capital each year, and his expense per year was 25 bezants. The other who remained in Constantinople had a profit in each year one seventh of his capital, and he spent 37 bezants per year . . . it is sought how much each had of their common capital. [1]

FRANCIS OF ASSISI

In Assisi, one of many cities in Italy with a cosmopolitan merchant class, there worked a silk merchant who had married a wife from France (which is why he liked to call his son Francesco, "little Frenchman"). But his son

Francis (1182–1226) did not follow in the footsteps of his father to pursue a lucrative career in commerce; instead, young Francis gave away everything he owned to live a life unburdened by material possessions. Francis's radical refusal to acquire or even to own wealth constituted a provocation of established conventions and the lifestyle he advocated was at odds with the prevailing spirit of the times. Many sections of Italy's elite, including the church, felt no compunction against owning substantial property. But Francis's assertion that the pursuit of wealth had no place in Christian ethics, in the final analysis, contained an implicit demand that the church divest all property.

Francis's idealism verged on recklessness. Such became apparent when in 1219 Francis traveled to Egypt, arriving at a time when armies of Christians and Muslims were locked in conflict, and crossed enemy lines and asked for an appointment with Egypt's ruler Al Kamil whom, he declared, he intended to convert to Christianity. It was a token of Francis's charisma that he actually succeeded in gaining access to Al Kamil. Francis persuaded Al Kamil to invite Islamic scholars to a debate on the respective merits of Christianity and Islam. There Francis, to underscore his argument of the superior truth of Christianity, volunteered to walk through fire and thus to prove God was on his side, because, he averred, God would protect him from harm, whereas any devout Muslim who dared to follow his example, on the other hand, would be consumed by flames. (According to the Franciscan Friar Bonaventure, Francis's first biographer, Francis made the following proposal to the sultan: "Our faith is beyond human reason . . . make a fire of wood, and I will go into it together with your wise men. Whichever of us is burnt, his faith is false.")[2]

Francis's debating strategy, aiming to let trial by fire be arbiter between Christianity and Islam, was in keeping with best European legal practices, because trial by fire, in medieval Europe, was the ultimate test of a plaintiff's truthfulness: it was widely held God would never let flames consume someone who spoke the truth. Al Kamil, however, rejected this suggestion, and the inconclusive encounter ended with the sultan arranging for Francis's safe return to the crusader camp. There, Christians gasped at Francis's audacity and inferred Al Kamil had ducked the challenge from fear of the outcome. But the encounter between Francis and Al Kamil was less a clash between religions than between cultures of jurisprudence. In Islam, where courts sifted evidence and assessed opposing arguments, law was guided by reasoning rather than by miracles, and trial by fire, as practiced in Europe, was not deemed due process.

Francis, rebuffed but undaunted, left Egypt for Jerusalem. There, he again he encountered institutions new to the experience of most Europeans. One such would have been *madrasas*, educational establishments that trained lawyers; these were affiliated with a particular mosque but funded by vested endowments. Franciscans also were exposed to philanthropy as practiced in Islam. Bonaventure mentioned how Muslims supported Franciscans:

> Some of the brethren went into an infidel country, and a certain Saracen, moved with pity, offered them money to buy necessary food; and when they refused it, the man marvelled greatly, seeing how poor they were. But when he understood that, having become poor for the love of God, they refused to possess anything, he was so moved with admiration that he offered to minister to them, and to provide for all their necessities, so long as he should have anything in his possession.[3]

Bonaventure was conscious Muslims had devised methods of dispensing philanthropy that were independent of Christian conceptions, and although he did not refer to *waqfs*, his account demonstrated how keenly Franciscans observed Islamic practices and how eager they were to spread information. In due course, Franciscan friars in Europe became leading advocates for the establishment of institutions that replicated *waqfs*, namely charitable trusts. The legal framework of Islamic *waqfs* derived from a subtle differentiation of Islamic property law—the fine distinction between the rights of owners as opposed to users of property. In Europe, the sphere of society where this conception was first applied was in higher education: specifically in the Inns of Court in London; in colleges in Oxford and Cambridge; and in universities in continental Europe.

FROM COLLEGES TO CORPORATIONS

Another organization with a presence straddling Europe and the Levant, the Knights Templar, was similarly keen to promote institutional innovation. The London branches of crusader orders sponsored institutions for training lawyers, the Inns of Court. There are Islamic precedents for the way the Inns of Court in London were constituted. Like *madrasas*, they were financially independent, affiliated with churches, and students were apprenticed to a master and trained in adversarial legal argumentation. From the Inns of Court issued a new approach to jurisprudence, Common Law, bringing with it procedural innovations such as trial by jury, which replicated Maliki law even in the detail of the desired number of twelve jurors (Maliki law was the Islamic school of jurisprudence dominant in Sicily, where Norman rulers had long-standing ties to the Islamic legal profession.)[4]

The Franciscan approach to the ethics of ownership caused the Vatican to undertake a radical examination of the legal nature of property. Several decades of deliberation and dispute lapsed until at last, in 1252, Pope Innocent IV cast legal provisions that accommodated the Franciscan demand for a new definition of the nature of property. Innocent IV issued a novel legal concept, the *universitas,* a legal entity with a defined set of rights and duties, including the right to own property, but one all the same not owned by its individual members. From the conception of the *universitas*, as the American philosopher John Dewey pointed out, in due course evolved the conception of corporations: "the 'fiction' theory of the personality of corporate bodies, or *universitates*, was promulgated if not originated, by Pope Innocent IV."[5]

The concept of the *universitas* was applied to constitute Europe's first universities. Contemporaneously, in 1264 in Oxford, Walter de Merton, a senior royal official with close ties to the Knights Templar, endowed Merton College, the statutes of which were copied by the oldest college of Cambridge University, Peterhouse. The statutes of Merton College, in all but name, match those of a *waqf*—a legal entity that distinguished between three parties: a donor making an irrevocable gift; a beneficiary; and managers who administered the endowment.[6] The conception of a trust was a legal innovation in English Common Law, and the historian Frederick Maitland has pointed out Franciscan friars were conspicuous during the first half of the thirteenth century as plaintiffs in legal cases that framed precedents for trusts as a legal instrument to vest property for the benefit of third parties.[7] The original impetus that led to the legal formulation of corporations tracks back to Francis's decision to divest himself of all personal property, and although Francis did not live long enough to see legal frameworks for universities emerge, by instigating a process that led to a new understanding of the nature of property rights his impact on medieval law and economics complemented that of Leonardo Fibonacci.

GOLD CURRENCIES IN EUROPE

The gold coins issued by Abd al Malik in the seventh century had helped integrate the Islamic trade zone and also projected his prestige. Centuries later, rulers in Morocco and Spain who established new power centers, took advantage of bullion from African gold mines to mint their own gold coins. The Fatimid dynasty in Egypt that emerged as the chief rival for preeminence in the Islamic realm also minted new gold coins which, however, had a reduced gold content, and consequently, once the solidity of Fatimid coins proved doubtful, the pace of commerce began to slow. But another factor undermining trust in currency standards was the launch of gold coinage issuing from the crusader states; there, Venetian merchants had acquired a monopoly to mint gold coins.

Venetians, who prior to the crusades had never minted coins, came into possession of operational mints in Palestine left behind by retreating Muslims. They secured the gold coinage monopoly in the crusader states and paid the King of Jerusalem a 15 percent tax for the privilege (a rare instance where Venetians were prepared to share profits with a government authority). Venetians and crusaders now were in a position to challenge Constantinople's traditional preserve as issuer of gold coins. (That Byzantines stopped issuance of the bezant after 1204 may have been the result of collusion by Constantinople's occupiers.) In Tyre, Venetians for the first three years did not even bother making any changes to Arab dyes (perhaps they did not know how). Venetian mints had diverse sources of supply of bullion, including the gold lamps removed from the Al Aqsa Mosque (weighing some 80 kilograms). Venetians gradually altered the appearance of Islamic coins, making changes so subtle they could easily be confused with the Arab originals. But Venetian coins—and this was critically important—had a lower gold content than their Arab competitors and so were valued less than their Islamic or Byzantine models. Consequently, crusader gold coins never crowded out the bezant or other high-quality coins. Instead, the confusion that debasement of gold coins caused among the business classes caused commerce to slow. The Byzantine historian Pachymeres observed a novel, disquieting phenomenon: prices for goods were increasing. The Egyptian Maqrizi complained, "to get a gold coin was like crossing the gates of paradise."[8] Once Venetians had palpably failed to fill the gap left by loss of the bezant, Western competitors launched rival currencies. The emperor Frederick II in Sicily minted a gold coin in 1231, and Genoa in 1252 launched the *genuino*. Seen from Rome, promoting a Genoese gold currency was apt to check Sicilian and Venetian pretensions. Vatican backing for Genoa could not be more overt: the Vatican previously had excommunicated the Sicilian king (because of laxity in pursuing crusades) and Venetian moneyers (on the grounds their coins lacked Christian iconography). The Genoese had excellent relations with the highest authorities of the Vatican. Pope Innocent IV, who was born Sinobaldo Fieschi, came from Genoa and his nephew Iacopo Fieschi belonged to a banking syndicate that minted coins.

The arrival of the *genuino* permanently altered the Mediterranean monetary system. That very year Florence followed suit with a rival gold coin, the *florin*, as with some delay did monarchs in Northern Europe. An English gold penny appeared in 1257, a French gold *ecu* in 1266, and the Venetian *ducat* in 1284. Centuries of monetary stagnation in Western Europe had ended.

NOTES

1. Fibonacci, *Fibonacci's Liber abaci*, 393.
2. Bonaventure, *The Disciple and the Master*, 118.
3. Bonaventure, *The Life of St. Francis of Assisi*, 46–7.
4. For these and many other correspondences, see George Makdisi and John Makdisi (bibliography refers).
5. Dewey, "The Historic Background of Corporate Legal Personality," 665.

6. Gaudiosi, "The Influence of the Islamic Law of Waqf on the Development of the Trust in England: The Case of Merton College."
7. Maitland, "The Origin of Uses."
8. Watson, "Back to Gold and Silver," 11.

Conclusion

Wealth has been pursued from the beginning of time. The legendary king Midas wished anything he touched be turned to gold; the Roman statesman Crassus was famous for his wealth but notorious for sharp business practices. But while from earliest history there appeared the elements of capitalism, only through the economic dynamic released in early Islam were these constituents combined and converted into a nexus that constituted capitalism. The threads of the plot how capitalism emerged in early Islam and migrated to Europe now can be pulled together.

Capitalism is a term often invoked but rarely defined. It is surprising that Adam Smith and Karl Marx, whose fame rests on their analysis of capitalism, hardly ever used the term. Gradually, the giant economic strides of the nineteenth century in full view, "capitalist" came to be a term applied to societies kept in perpetual motion through the agency of entrepreneurs. Sociologists transformed the analysis of capitalism by drawing a distinction between capitalism as such and its visible manifestations; Max Weber averred that capitalism originated in a frame of mind, fostered by Protestantism, and his assertion that capitalism follows from a particular mentality has remained dominant, although the origins of this frame of mind Werner Sombart backdated to Italy's Middle Ages.

Definitions of capitalism remain elusive because capitalism by its nature is elastic and variable and it is difficult to distinguish between causes and effects. Where definitions of capitalism agree on is that change in a capitalist society is constant and caused by quests for profit. Hence the cornerstone of a capitalist society is the market. Certain other constituents recur—such as that capital and labor are supplied by different parties; investors may allocate funds to separate ventures; and undertakings are funded through borrowings as well as investments. It follows that capitalism needs certain tools—such as money, which acts as a common denominator for the value of goods and stores up wealth for future use; agreements how providers of capital and of labor share rewards; and social approbation of wealth acquired through commerce rather than conquest. Finally, capitalism promotes certain skills and institutions—such as literacy and numeracy; freedom of travel; and a judiciary that protects property rights. Conspicuously absent from the list of enabling factors, however, is the presence of a powerful state. Capitalism in Arabia and Europe emerged in cities such as Mecca and Venice that were beyond the grip of central governments. Indeed the reason why ancient empires were of minor consequence to the evolution of markets may have been that market forces in pursuit of profit challenged the authority of a state, and hence governments had no motivation to encourage their evolution.

The seminal impact of Islam economies became clear in stages. Economic systems of Rome, Byzantium, and Islam hardly featured in Edward Gibbon's *The Decline and Fall of the Roman Empire* that set the tone for many subsequent Islamic histories: "Muhammad, with the sword in one hand and the Koran in the other, erected his throne on the ruins of Christianity and of Rome."[1] Gibbon's contemporary Adam Smith in *The Wealth of Nations* pointed out the link between the crusades and the rising prosperity of Venice:

> The cities of Italy seem to have been the first in Europe which were raised by commerce to any considerable degree of opulence. Italy lay in the center of what was at that time the improved and civilized part of the world. The Crusades too, though by the great waste of stock and destruction of inhabitants which they occasioned they must necessarily have retarded the progress of the greater part of Europe, were extremely favorable to that of some Italian cities. The great armies which marched from all parts to the conquest of the Holy Land gave extraordinary encouragement to the shipping of Venice, Genoa, and Pisa, sometimes in transporting them thither, and always in supplying them with provisions. They were the commissaries, if one may say so, of those armies; and the most destructive frenzy that ever befell the European nations, was a source of opulence to those republics.[2]

After Adam Smith pointed out wealth created in Europe derived from Italian commerce, to nineteenth-century historians early Islam's fruitful economic relations with medieval Europe became commonplace. Jacques de Mas Latrie, Michele Amari, and Wilhelm Heyd (and others) documented these ties in works that in many respects still now are not out dated. In the twentieth century, the consequences of Islam's rise on Europe's economy have been a continuing preoccupation particularly of Francophone historians. Notably, Henri Pirenne asserted Islam's expansion drove a wedge through the Mediterranean and thereby contracted Western Europe's economic sphere; Marc Bloch exposed how Europe's economic development was as constrained by lack of gold as that of Islamic realms favored by its abundance; and Maurice Lombard's encyclopedic surveys of Islam's material culture would have culminated in a definitive work, *The Golden Age of Islam*, had not his premature demise cut short his career.

That capitalism thrived in Islam was the shared opinion of two historians who by outlook were diametrically opposed, the Jesuit Henri Lammens and the Marxist Maxime Rodinson. Lammens's works brought to life Arabia's buoyant commercial culture and showed how the needs of long-distance trade instigated financial innovation. Rodinson in *Islam and Capitalism* showed in early Islam were present capitalist institutions, such as private property and lending money at interest, and in his *Préface* to Pedro Chalmeta's book on Islamic market regulation *El señor del zoco en España*, went on to trace Islamic market practices back to Babylonian times. Leone Caetani previously had opened to view the roots of Islamic commerce in ancient Mesopotamia, and the work of Karl Polanyi and Elman Service on the genesis of markets and states, while not dealing with Islam directly, supported Rodinson's intuition that socioeconomic innovation crystallized in early Islam.

Crucial factors already in place in pre-Islamic Arabia's nascent economy were the use of gold as a means of exchange; rules set by private accord for safe passage of traders; and an appreciation of a trade-off between risk and reward that guided merchants to seek out activities promising the highest profit. The Prophet of Islam, who was descended from a dynasty of entrepreneurs, strengthened this dynamic further. Muhammad established a market in Medina, and through personally appointing a *muhtasib* made consumer protection and competition policy a religious obligation. These initiatives accorded with the Koran that enjoins putting gold to productive use, endorses fair trade and investment, and supports consumer protection through banning usury and other forms of mis-selling. Muhammad's deregulation of prices—he proclaimed "prices are in the hand of God"—was a seminal innovation in market regulation.

For the emergence of Islamic law two circumstances of succession to Muhammad were catalysts. Muhammad had left no unequivocal instructions for his succession and had prohibited a priestly hierarchy, and so early Islamic society saw vigorous intellectual competition in how to regulate social life. Lawyers, rather than clerics, determined the pathway for societal evolution. Each of the first three Islamic dynasties accomplished remarkable institutional innovations: the *rashidun* introduced the world's first government pension plan; the Omayyads created an Islamic gold standard; and the Abbasids brought into being the world's first market for government debt. Caliphs supported trade with Asian and Byzantine markets; Basra was founded as a gateway to sea-lanes linking Arabia to India and China, and in Constantinople the city's Muslim merchants were afforded a mosque already in the eighth century. Saladin combined protectionism of Muslim entrepreneurs in markets east of Egypt with free trade policies in Egypt, affording European merchants *funduqs*, offshore trade centers where expatriate Europeans through immediate encounter with Islamic institutions, and under the wary eyes and firm hand of Islamic authorities, acquired institutional knowledge and disseminated this knowhow in Europe. Social institutions—in commerce, scholarship, and law—that would supplant Europe's feudal order began to emerge through cross-pollination from Islamic societies.

CAPITALISM IN EUROPE

Governments contributed little to Europe's economic revival; economic dynamism in European economies had been sedate since collapse of the Roman Empire. Byzantines, Carolingians, and Normans restrained economic activity through government control. However, although the infrastructure for trade and commerce in Europe's interior regions was incomparably better than on coastlines exposed to piratical incursions, commerce in Europe stirred not in regions becalmed by central political authority but in peripheral townships on the Italian coast frequented by pirates rather than traders. Entrepreneurial innovation germinated on Europe's periphery, on coasts where nascent stability clashed with rampant anarchy. In the absence of government action, private initiative activated latent economic potential.

Italian port cities, Byzantine subjects but in practice defenseless, fostered trade relations with Muslims. Location on the periphery of great Empires gave them virtual autonomy, and when these communities discovered trade as a means to survive, a familiar economic dynamic emerged, one that replicated a pattern: in Arabia, too, trade had burgeoned once bandits turned into merchants. The process of discovering trade was more rewarding since rapine was arduous, protracted, and in some instances—such as the Arab settlement established on the French coast near St. Tropez around 890—failed utterly. But eventually, from cities such as Venice, which like Mecca lacks natural endowments and proximity to commercial centers, issued convoys traversing seas as caravans had deserts.

Piracy ruled the Mediterranean Sea, and the trusting relationships on which trade is based took generations to evolve—and even then could lapse into robbery in an instant. The Mediterranean Sea was as lawless as Arabia's deserts, but through trade was transformed into a commercial commonwealth with second round effects rippling inland. The transition from piracy to orderly commerce bestowed riches on merchants in ports on Italy's coast, and the ascent of inland republics such as Milan and Florence followed from the prosperity rippling outward from mercantile newcomers such as Amalfi and Venice. Meccan plutocrats and Venetian patricians contested markets, alternating between collaboration and conflict, but ever pursuing actions that led in the direction of profit.

Venice evolved a business model in many respects a foil to Mecca's. Both cities were situated in barren landscapes and owed their ascent to trade; Mecca's merchants traversed deserts and Venice's the seas. Venetian patricians, like Mecca's plutocrats, honed their business skills in foreign markets and could not look to authorities to protect their rights. Brigands, shipwreck, and disease imperiled a merchant before he reached his destination where he negotiated contracts in countries with foreign jurisdictions. Arabs described the dangers of desert travel with the word *azar*, Italians the hazard of losing a ship to the waves as *risicum*. Profits, though immense, were won against the odds. Venice and Mecca never became political capitals, but their mercantile elites integrated the realms of Islam and Christianity into single markets.

Markets and the rule of law that underpin them did not emerge from an unswerving linear process; the lesson that markets rely on respect for conventions and law was learned slowly and often again unlearned. In fact, markets were not intrinsically law-abiding or moral. The borders between piracy and trade were blurred and mercantile republics were no less prone to apply violence or force than despots or dynasts. States in Europe failed to foster markets; but markets, on the other hand, failed to build durable political structures. Mercantile communities waged war against each other as well as against the empires that protected them. Venice applied for concurrent trade privileges to Byzantine, Norman, and Saracen governments, fully cognizant that all three were at war against each other; acquired tax havens in Palestine during the crusades; and after Saladin had evicted crusaders from Jerusalem diverted the course of the retaliatory campaign from Palestine to Constantinople. Venice was unable to take Byzantium's place as issuer of a gold standard and the decline of her protector Byzantium—caused by her own intervention—removed the underpinning of Venetian stability. The apogee of Venetian power, when Venetians in 1204 began asset-stripping the Byzantine Empire, was the moment of its passing.

Genoa in the twelfth century generated more tax revenue than France, Palermo more than England. Italian republics were accumulating wealth at a faster rate than empires or kingdoms, and the riches of Italian patricians could begin to stand comparison with European royalty and Arab plutocrats. Italy's mercantile republics were incubators for institutions that helped capitalism flourish, such as venture capital companies, the *commenda*, and a new gold standard.

The institutional template of medieval European colleges and universities replicated that of Islamic *madrasas*, and parallels extended to how scholarship progressed in Islam and Christendom: medieval scholastics applied a methodology that resembled that of Islamic jurisprudents. Islamic law proceeded by examining a precedent, evaluating supporting testimonies, and casting judgment; European scholasticism proceeded by positing a hypothesis, advancing arguments for and against, and reaching a conclusion. Where jurisprudents discerned *pro* and *con*, scholars weighed arguments in terms of *sic et non*. Scholasticism reached its apogee in the work of Thomas Aquinas (1225–1274), a professor of the university of Naples (coincidentally founded by Sicily's king Frederick II, who endowed the university library, corresponded with Arabic scholars, and employed members of the Aquinas family at his court).

The first Europeans who visited Baghdad and observed Islamic academics in practice seem to have been two ninth-century Byzantine patriarchs, John Grammaticus and Photius, whose embassies to Baghdad are recorded. The latter, in particular, took active interest in Islamic academic life. He corresponded widely with many Islamic rulers, and in Baghdad witnessed interdenominational disputations held in public. Such events were a tradition that continued at least until the tenth century when a Spanish visitor to Baghdad witnessed public debates between representatives of all major religions (including atheists).[3] Photius was one of Europe's earliest educational reformers; he recommended students should not merely commit lessons to memory but be taught how to think independently, requiring them to evaluate the circumstances that led to a particular statement, consider how reliable were the sources, and evaluate whether alternative interpretations had merit. These recommendations, well ahead of contemporaneous European practice, replicated the methodology applied to the Islamic study of *hadiths*.

Mathematical skills that could be applied in commerce were disseminated from Italy by academics trained in Islamic institutions. Pope Sylvester II, who imported to Europe the abacus, had studied with Muslims, as did Leonardo Fibonacci. The wider application of numerical skills enabled scientific inquiry, perspectival painting, and building spherical domes. Venice, where the very style and decorations of her cathedral San Marco invited comparisons with the mosque in Damascus, was in the vanguard of importing from Islamic economies new manufacturing approaches, such as making glass and building ships in Europe's largest shipyard, the *arsenal* (the term is Arabic).

The crystallization of civil commercial society in Europe marked a milestone in 1252. The Vatican that year backed the launch of the *genuino*, Genoa's gold currency, and promulgated the legal conception of the *universitas*, an autonomous legal entity with a distinct identity that enabled the formation of corporations, civil as well as commercial. Islamic law, on the other hand, which had pioneered the concept of public charities, the *waqf*, stopped short of evolving the conception of corporations. From this moment, legal and monetary advances in Europe no longer depended on Islamic cues.

ISLAM'S ECONOMIC DECLINE

Islam's era of fruitful commercial innovation subsided for several reasons; one of these was the Mongol invasion that inflicted inestimable damage (whereas the irruption of crusader states, on the other hand, shifted trade flows from the Levant to Egypt but increased rather than reduced trade). But the decisive blow to Islamic prosperity was the discovery of new trade routes. The Portuguese by sailing around the Cape of Good Hope to reach India rendered obsolete Islamic trade routes between Asia and Europe, and finally, after Genoa's son Christopher Columbus had discovered America, Genoa became financier for the Spanish Empire as once Venice had been for Byzantium. The entire Eastern Mediterranean went into decline; Islamic economies, Venice, and Byzantium withered.

Fatal damages to Islamic economies, however, were of their own making. One in particular was government interference in markets; Egyptian rulers entered long-distance trade on their own account, distorted prices, and confiscated entrepreneurial wealth. Ibn Khaldun's warnings against government interventionism went unheeded:

> Amirs and other men in power in a country who engage in commerce and agriculture, reach a point where they undertake to buy agricultural products and goods from their owners who come to them, at prices fixed by themselves as they see fit. Then, they resell these things to the subjects under their control, at the proper times, at prices fixed by themselves. This is even more dangerous, harmful, and ruinous for the subjects.[4]

Ibn Khaldun was not alone among Islamic economists to warn against government interference in markets. Previously, Al Dimashqi had asserted, "when a regent starts trading, his subjects are lost."[5]

The expanding and rapidly prospering Islamic Empire had a voracious appetite for information and education. Caliphs and other members of the elite endowed *madrasas* that commingled Arab and foreign ways of thinking, and the benefits of assimilating expertise from other cultures showed up in improved standards of living. However, a feeling had gained ground that modernizers had led Islam astray. How could it be, it was whispered, that caliphs condoned alien ways of thought, often incompatible with revelations received from Allah? The dispute inevitably revolved around the correct approach to interpreting the Koran. The manifest contrast between the pace of cultural and institutional innovation in early Islam, and stagnation in later eras may also originate in opposing approaches to interpretation of the Koran of two antagonist schools of thought, the Mutazilites and Ashari.

The Asharis argued that God's revelation occurred outside time and place; the Mutazilites, on the other hand, that the Koran was revealed in specific circumstances of a particular moment. What on first sight appeared an arcane issue relevant only to theologians in fact had momentous implications for the way the empire would be governed. For if the Koran enunciated an eternal and therefore immutable message, then the overriding requirement on a ruler would be to adhere in perpetuity as closely as possible to Koranic precepts, however minute. But if, on the other hand, the Koran was an historical document, then its injunctions admitted adjustment as times change. Partisans of the view that man could never claim to improve on Allah's revelation found an eloquent and resolute spokesman in Ahmad ibn Hanbal (died 863). Hanbal suffered persecution, wrote Ibn Khallikan, and was pressured "to declare that the Koran was created, but would not, and although beaten and imprisoned, persisted in his refusal."[6] "The passing of Ibn Hanbal," wrote Masudi, spread shadows over the earth as thick as those which marked the Prophet's end."[7] No jurist's funeral had ever gathered so many mourners. The political ramifications of Hanbal's view were obvious to the caliph; in the final analysis, Hanbalism removed his authority to impose reforms.

Masudi in the *Meadows of Gold* provided an analogy for the debate between the Ashari and Mutazilites by comparing their outlook to that bred by two board games, backgammon and chess. In backgammon, any roll of the dice can overturn the best-laid strategy; in chess, reasoning skills map the winning game plan—fatalist Asharis excel at the former, rationalist Mutazilites at the latter game.[8] The Asharis revived a strand of thought that traced its roots to the era of the *rashidun* when materialist excess was deemed repugnant to Islam's core values, and their victory had ramifications for the development of Islamic economics; fatalism eroded entrepreneurship as a core value of Islam.

SILK AND SLAVES

A word on what goods passed between East and West. Exports to Europe included silk, spices, incense, cotton, and textiles. European exports included timber, brass, cloth, olive oil, amber, furs, and falcons. Trade inevitably gravitated to those activities that promised the highest profit margins; the most lucrative lines of business were Islamic exports of luxury goods against European exports of slaves.

Long before the advent of Islam, luxury goods commanding the highest prices in Europe were silk from China and pepper from India. These goods had to cross an immense distance until they reached their destination; their passage was grueling and perilous, profits correspondingly large, and many interested parties would have liked to bring the silk trade under control. Trade in silk attracted attention from the highest levels of Roman government. Marcus Aurelius sent a trade delegation to China that bypassed hostile

Persian territory by choosing a route along the Caspian Sea, one of repeated European efforts to gain a foothold in the silk trade, which however never met with success, until at last, some four centuries later, Chinese princesses secretly carried mulberry beetles out of the country and passed the secret of silk production to Byzantine authorities. So lucrative was the trade in silk in China, its manufacture there was an imperial monopoly; the Byzantine emperor claimed a monopoly not only on production but also on distribution. The Byzantine Civil Code specified entry points for Chinese silk (one each on the banks of the Tigris, of the Euphrates, and a third in Armenia) where trade inspectors imposed Byzantine tariffs. Consequently, anyone who avoided land routes and traveled to China by sea was in a position to undercut prices regulated by governments. Arab merchants, who already exported frankincense from Yemen and pepper from India, were quick to spot the profit potential in trade with China.

Europe's chief exports were slaves who were needed to work in farming, mining, construction, and the army; the rising standard of living in cities created demand also for female slaves in households. Exporting slaves became a flourishing business in Europe, where authorities countenanced the keeping of slaves—England's *Domesday Book* records 10 percent of the population as slaves—but considered their export reprehensible. Charlemagne confronted Pope Hadrian about the slave trade in Rome but the pope protested his innocence: "Never have we fallen into such wickedness, nor has any such deed been done with our permission."[9] However adamant were official authorities in castigating slave traders, profits were too attractive to let go of the business. The annual export of slaves from the Black Sea to a dedicated *funduq* in Alexandria has been estimated at 2,000.[10] The figure is plausible, because in Venice, where slavery was made legal, fifteenth-century fiscal returns show annual imports running at 1,000.[11] Other markets in Italy were likely to have been of similar magnitude. The slave trade brutalized its profiteers, as can be seen from the reaction of a slave's former owner to an allegation of rape where he lets the Italian trader know "you may throw her into the sea, with what she has in her belly, for it is no creature of his."[12] Italian slave imports never came to a halt until after the fall of Constantinople access to the Black Sea was blocked.

The Islamic Empire's slave population already must have been immense within decades of Muhammad's death. Substantial manpower was required for Umar to have had built a canal linking the Nile to the Red Sea; Muawiyah, only one of many substantial estate owners in Arabia, there on a single irrigation project deployed 3,000 slaves. The Omayyad caliph Abd ar Rahman III (912–961) undertook a census of his slave population in Spain, which over a fifty-year period had grown by 10,000.[13] Fatimid army recruits were imported from areas bounding the Black Sea where families were known to sell their children to Venetian and Genoese traders established on the Crimea. Judging by the size of the Fatimid armed forces—some 50,000 in Saladin's era—the Islamic Empire's demand for slaves was insatiable. The fate of slaves deserves remark.

SLAVE REBELLIONS

Slaves traded and owned in East and West came from all levels of society—the Persian author Sadi and the Spanish author Miguel de Cervantes both endured slavery and left accounts of how they suffered. The fate of slaves differed widely. The attrition rate must have been extreme for slaves working in extreme heat on farms, in mines, and in construction. But some slaves who found employment in households or as personal valets of high-ranking members of the elite sometimes enjoyed glittering careers. Several of Islam's most distinguished political leaders began their careers in bondage; the Egyptian caliph Baibars, who held to ransom King Louis IX, once had been a Mongol slave, and Roxelana, wife of Suleyman the Magnificent, was born in Bosnia.

But these were exceptions; there were many slaves who were driven to self-destruction. The slave who assassinated Umar must have known he would not survive his act of defiance; the *Arabian Nights* tell the tale of a tutor who drops his charges from a roof to their death in sight of their father before jumping after them. Conditions in Europe were no better; transport insurance policies in Italy contained exclusion clauses for suicide.[14] But individual acts of desperation did not challenge established rule, which, however, would ensue when slaves rebeled in multitude. Fear of slave revolts must have been constant and countermeasures accordingly severe; Byzantine prisoners of war rebelling on the estates of Abd al Malik were summarily executed.[15]

The most dramatic slave uprising occurred in the late ninth century when in southern Iraq a certain Ali ibn Muhammad urged the slave population to take up arms. Ali's followers worked the inhospitable fields surrounding Basra and were named Zanj after their origin on Zanzibar. To these disenfranchised, homeless, and overworked deportees Ali promised betterment, or at the very least revenge, and with nothing to lose, the Zanj followed his call. Ali took control of Basra, Mesopotamia's second largest city, and those Basrans who survived the assault now in turn had a taste of slavery. By 879, territory under Zanj control extended within seventy miles south of Baghdad. But ultimately, the imbalance between the resources of the Caliph and of Ali made for an inevitable outcome, and in 883 some 50,000 troops overran Ali's positions. Ali eluded capture, but the insurrection of the Zanj, the most successful slave rebellion since Spartacus, was over.

CAPITALISM AND RELIGION

Before closing, a final word on the uneasy relationship between religion and capitalism from the Middle Ages to the present. Although capitalism incubated within Islam and Christendom, once economic rationalism permeated the social sphere more widely, theologians alleged capitalism had lost its moorings in religion and ethics. Max Weber pointed out such animadversions were to be expected: any clerical hierarchy—irrespective of denomination—would distrust social forces unconstrained by religious ethics.[16] A remarkable convergence of religiously inspired critiques of capitalism appeared in the work of the twentieth-century Catholic and Muslim economists Amintore Fanfani and Muhammad Baqir al Sadr.

Amintore Fanfani (1908–1999), an Italian prime minister, wrote in *Catholicism, Capitalism and Protestantism*, that capitalism "is essentially a human phenomenon which came about in man, and then transformed the life of man and the structure of society."[17] For Fanfani, "the evil lies not in the possession of wealth but in making it the end of life."[18] Fanfani then concluded the Catholic ethos in the final analysis is anti-capitalist.[19] His views match those of the Grand Ayatollah Muhammad Baqir al-Sadr (1935–1980), an Islamic economist who was executed in an Iraqi prison. In *Our Economics* he confirmed early Islam endorsed but later disavowed capitalism:

> I neither deny that the individuals of the society in the age of prophethood carried on pursuing free activity and possessed economic freedom to a considerable extent. Nor do I deny that it reflected a capitalist face of Islamic economy. . . . It is true that the individual who lived in the age of prophethood seems to us to be enjoying a great deal of freedom, which [to the followers of *ijtihad* is indistinguishable from] the freedoms of the capitalism, but this imaginary fancy is dissipated and fritters away when we turn practice to . . . the legislative texts.[20]

Thus the Italian and Iraqi economists Fanfani and al Sadr were in agreement that capitalism at its origin was compatible with religion, but that that accord subsequently sundered.

This very theme engaged already the fourteenth-century Italian author Giovanni Boccaccio in a book whose very title *Decamerone* ("Greek for ten days") seems to respond to the Arabian *One Thousand and One Nights*, the alternative title for the *Arabian Nights*. Both the Arab and the Italian book feature the financial market of Alexandria where different denominations mix in trade. In one of Boccaccio's stories, Saladin approaches a Jewish banker, Melchisedek, to borrow money; both need tact and savvy if negotiations are to progress.[21] Saladin, after an exchange of politeness, tries to throw Melchisedek off balance by asking him which of the three religions claiming to be Abraham's heir—Judaism, Christianity, or Islam—he considered true and which false. Melchisedek is wary of upsetting his potential client and instead of answering direct, responds with a story: once upon a time there was a family where a father from generation to generation would bequeath a ring to his sole heir. Of a generation where a father had three sons, two copies of this ring were made; each son in the fullness of time came to possess a ring but disputes between them were forestalled as none could tell whose ring was true.[22] With this story, Melchisedek wins over Saladin and they become friends and they do business; while Boccaccio lets readers infer that religious convictions need never be at odds with flourishing markets.

NOTES

1. Edward Gibbon, *The Decline and Fall of the Roman Empire*, London, 1994, Vol. 5, 230 (beginning of chapter 50).
2. Adam Smith, *Wealth of Nations*, Book 3, chapter 3: "Of the Rise and Progress of Cities and Towns."
3. Kremer, *Geschichte der herrschenden Ideen des Islams*, 241–42.
4. Ibn Khaldun, *Muqaddimah*, Vol. 2, 96.
5. Ritter, "Ein arabisches Handbuch der Handelswissenschaft," 59.
6. Ibn Khallikan, *Biographical Dictionary*, Vol. 1, 44.
7. Masudi, *The Meadows of Gold*, 254.
8. Macoudi, *Les prairies d'or*, Vol. 8, 320.
9. Johnston, "The Mohammedan Slave Trade," 485.
10. Heyd, *Geschichte des Levantehandels im Mittelalter*, Vol. 2, 546.
11. Origo, "The Domestic Enemy," 329.
12. Origo, "The Domestic Enemy," 332.
13. Lombard, "Les bases monétaires d'une suprématie économique," 155.
14. Origo, "The Domestic Enemy," 331.
15. Kister, "The Social and Political Implications of Three Traditions," 334.
16. Weber, *Wirtschaft und Gesellschaft*, Vol. 2, 798–800.
17. Fanfani, *Catholicism. Protestantism. Capitalism*, 40.
18. Fanfani, *Catholicism. Protestantism. Capitalism*, 125.
19. Fanfani, *Catholicism. Protestantism. Capitalism*, 159.
20. Al Sadr, *Our Economics (Iqtisaduna)*, Vol. 2, Part 1, 65.
21. Boccaccio, *Decamerone*, First Day, Novel Three.
22. Giovanni Boccaccio, *The Decameron or Ten Days' Entertainment,* First Day, Novel Three.

Bibliography

ABBREVIATIONS

BSOAS	Bulletin of the School of Oriental and African Studies
DOP	Dumbarton Oaks Papers
IC	Islamic Culture
JA	Journal Asiatique
JAOS	Journal of the American Oriental Society
JASB	Journal of the Asiatic Society of Bengal
JESHO	Journal of the Economic and Social History of the Orient
JRAS	Journal of the Royal Asiatic Society of Great Britain and Ireland
MSOS	Mitteilungen des Seminars für orientalische Sprachen
SI	Studia Islamica
ZDMG	Zeitschrift der deutschen morgenländischen Gesellschaft

Abbott, Nabia. "Women and the State in Early Islam." *Journal of Near Eastern Studies* 1, No. 1 (Jan. 1942): 106–26.

Abu Yusuf. *Kitab al kharaj* (translated by Aharon ben Shemesh in *Taxation in Islam*, Vol. 3). Leiden, 1970.

Abu-Lughod, Janet. *Before European Hegemony: The World System 1250–1350*. Oxford, 1991.

Abulafia, David. *Mediterranean Encounters: Political, Religious, and Economic 1100–1550*. Aldershot, 2000.

Abulafia, David. *Frederick II: A Medieval Emperor*. Oxford, 1992.

Abulafia, David. *The Two Italies: Economic Relations between the Norman Kingdom of Sicily and the Northern Communes*. Cambridge, 1977.

Abulfeda. *The Life of Mohammed*. Elgin, ca. 1820–1825.
Académie des inscriptions et belles-lettres (ed.). *Receuil des historiens des croisades: Historiens occidentaux*. Paris, 1895.
Académie des inscriptions et belles-lettres (ed.). *Receuil des historiens des croisades: Historiens orientaux*. 5 Vols. 1872/1906.
Aghnides, Nicholas. *Mohammedan Theories of Finance*. Lahore, 1961.
Al Baghdadi. *The Eastern Key*. London, 1965.
Al Baladhuri. *The Origins of the Islamic State*. 2 Vols. New York, 1916/1924.
Al Biruni. *The Chronology of Ancient Nations*. London, 1879.
Al Fakhri. *On the Systems of Government and the Moslem Dynasties*. London, 1947.
Al Ghani. *Short Biographies of the Prophet and His Ten Companions*. Riyad, ca. 2004
Al Kindi. *The Governors and Judges of Egypt*. London, 1912.
Al Maqdisi. *La livre de la création du monde*. Vols. 4–6. Paris, 1916/1919.
Al Maqdisi. *Short Biography of the Prophet Mohammed and His Ten Companions*. Riyad, 2004.
Al Maqrizi. *Les marchés du Caire*. Cairo, 1979.
Al Maqrizi. *Description historique et topographique de l'Égypte*. Cairo, 1906–1920.
Al Maqrizi. *Le traité des famines*. Leiden, 1962.
Al Maqrizi. *History of the Ayyubid Sultans*. Boston, 1980.
Al Marghinani. *Hedaya, or Guide: A Commentary on the Musselman Laws* (translated by Charles Hamilton, 4 Vols.). London, 1870.
Al Masudi. *The Meadows of Gold*. London, 1989.
Al Mawardi. *The Laws of Islamic Governance*. London, 1996.
Al Muqaddasi. *The Best Divisions for Knowledge of the Regions*. Reading, 2001.
Al Nadim. *The Fihrist of al-Nadim*. Vol. 2. New York, 1970.
Al Sadr, Mohammed Baqir. *Our Economics (Iqtisaduna)*. Vol. 2, Part 1. Tehran, 1983.
Al Samhudi. *Geschichte der Stadt Medina*. Göttingen, 1861.
Al Suyuti. *History of the Khalifahs who Took the Right Way*. London, 1995.
Al Tabari. *The History of al-Tabari*, Vols. 6–9. Albany, 1997.
Al Tabari. *Biographies of the Prophet's Companions and Their Successors*. Albany, 1998.
Al Tirmidhi. *Jami*. Vol. 3. Riyadh, 2007.
Al Waqidi. *The Life of Muhammad*. London, 2011.
Altheim, Franz, and Ruth Stiehl. *Finanzgeschichte der Spätantike*. Frankfurt, 1957.
Amari, Michele. *I diplomi Arabi del r. archive fiorentino*. Florence, 1863. *Appendix*, 1867.
Amari, Michele. *Biblioteca Arabo-sicula*. Turin, 1880.
Amari, Michele. *Storia dei Musulmani di Sicilia*. 3 Vols. Florence, 1854/1872.
Amedroz, H. F. "The Hisba Jurisdiction in the Ahkam al-Sultaniyya of Mawardi." Part 1 *JRAS* (Jan. 1916): 77–101. Part 2 *JRAS* (Apr. 1916): 287–314.
Amedroz, H. F. "The Mazalim Jurisdiction in the Ahkam Sultaniyya of Mawardi." *JRAS* (Jul. 1911): 635–74.
Amedroz, H. F. "Tales of the Official Life from the "Tadhkira" of Ibn Hamdun, Etc." *JRAS* (Apr. 1908): 409–70.
Amitai, Reuven. "Diplomacy and the Slave Trade in the Eastern Mediterranean: A Re-examination of the Mamluk-Byzantine-Genoese Triangle in the Late Thirteenth Century in Light of the Existing Early Correspondence." *Oriente Moderno*. Nuova serie. Anno 88, No. 2: 349–68.
Anthony, Sean. "The Domestic Origins of Imprisonment." *JAOS* 129, No. 4 (Oct. 2009): 571–96.
Antoniadis-Bibicou, Hélène. *Recherches sur les douanes à Byzance*. Paris, 1963.
Arnold, Thomas. *The Caliphate*. Oxford, 1924.
Arnold, Thomas. *The Preaching of Islam*. London, 1913.
Asch-Schaibani, Abu. *Al Gami As Sagir*. Berlin, 1908.
Ashtor, Eliyahu. *A Social and Economic History of the Near East in the Middle Ages*. London, 1976.
Ashtor, Eliyahu. *Histoire des prix et des salaires dans l'orient médiéval*. Paris, 1969.
Ashtor, Eliyahu. "La recherche des prix dans l'Orient médiéval." *SI* 21 (1964): 101–44.

Ashtor, Eliyahu. "The Karimi Merchants." *JRAS*. Nos. 1 and 2. (Apr. 1956): 45–56.
Atiya, Aziz. *Crusade Commerce and Culture*. Bloomington, 1962.
Babelon, Ernest. *Du commerce des Arabes dans le nord de l'Europe avant les Croisades*. Paris, 1882.
Bacharach, Jere. "The Dinar versus the Ducat." *International Journal of Middle East Studies* 4, No. 1 (Jan. 1973): 77–96.
Baeck, Louis. *The Mediterranean Tradition in Economic Thought*. London, 1994.
Bar Hebraeus. *The Chronography of Bar Hebraeus*. Vol. 1. London, 1932.
Becker, C. H. "Die Kanzel im Kultus des alten Islam," in *Orientalische Studien*. Vol. 1. Giessen, 1906.
Behrnauer, W. "Mémoire sur les institutions de police chez les Arabes, les Persans et les Turcs." *JA* 16 (1860): 114–190 and 347–392; 1861.
Ben-David, Arye. *Talmudische Ökonomie*. Hildesheim, 1974.
Benjamin of Tudela. *The Itinerary of Benjamin of Tudela*. Oxford, 1907.
Bergmann, E. von. "Die Nominale der Münzreform des Abd al-Malik," *Sitzungsberichte der philosophisch-historischen Classe der kaiserlichen Akademie der Wissenschaften*. Vol. 56 (1870): 239–66.
Bjoerkmann, W. "Kapitalentstehung und Anlage im Islam." *MSOS* (1930): 80–98.
Bloch, Marc. "Le problème de l'or au moyen age." *Annales* 5, No. 19 (Jan. 1933): 1–34.
Bloch, Mozes Léb. *Das mosaisch-talmudische Polizeirecht*. Budapest, 1879.
Bogaert, Raymond. *Les origines antiques de la banque de dépôt*. Leiden, 1966.
Boisard, Marcel A. "On the Probable Influence of Islam on Western Public and International Law." *International Journal of Middle East Studies* 11, No. 4 (Jul. 1980): 429–50.
Bonaventure. *The Life of St. Francis of Assisi*. London, 1868.
Bonaventure. *The Disciple and the Master: St. Bonaventure's Sermons on St. Francis of Assisi*. Chicago, 1983.
Bonner, Michael. "The Kitab al-kasb Attributed to al-Shaybani: Poverty, Surplus, and the Circulation of Wealth." *JAOS* 121 No. 3 (Jul. 2001): 401–27.
Bonner, Michael. "Poverty and Economics in the Quran." *Journal of Interdisciplinary History* 35, No. 3 (Winter 2005): 391–406
Bovill, E. W. *The Golden Trade of the Moors*. Oxford, 1970.
Brand, C. M. "The Byzantines and Saladin, 1185–1192: Opponents of the Third Crusade." *Speculum* 37, No. 2 (Apr. 1962): 167–181.
Bratianu, Georges. *Recherches sur le commerce génois dans la mer noire au XIIIe siècle*. Paris, 1929.
Bratianu, Georges. *Études byzantines d'histoire économique et sociale*. Paris, 1938.
Bratianu, Georges. "L'hyperpère byzantin et la monnaie d'or des républiques italiennes au XIIIe siecle," in *Études sur l'histoire et sur l'art de Byzance*, edited by Charles Diehl. Paris (1930): 37–48.
Bratianu, Georges. *Privilèges et franchises municipals dans l'empire Byzantin*. Paris, 1936
Brehier, L. "Les colonies d'orientaux en occident au commencement du moyen age." *Byzantinische Zeitschrift* 12 (1903): 1–29.
Bretschneider, Emil. *On the Knowledge Possessed by the Ancient Chinese of the Arabs and Arabian Colonies and Other Western Countries Mentioned in Chinese Books*. London, 1871.
Brown, Horatio. "The Venetians and the Venetian Quarter in Constantinople to the Close of the Twelfth Century." *Journal of Hellenic Studies* 40, Part 1 (1920): 68–88.
Brunschvig, R. "Coup d'oeil sur l'histoire des foires à travers l'Islam," in *La foire*. Bruxelles (1953): 43–74
Brunschvig, R. "Conceptions monétaires chez les juristes musulmans (VIIIe–XII siècles)." *Arabica* 14. No. 2 (Jun. 1967): 113–43.
Bücher, Karl. *Die Entstehung der Volkswirtschaft*. Tübingen, 1908.
Buckler, F. W. *Harunu'l–Rashid and Charles the Great*. Cambridge, 1931.
Bulliet, Richard. *Conversion to Islam in the Medieval Period: An Essay in Quantitative History*. Cambridge, 1977.
Bush, George. *Life of Mohammed*. New York, 1831.

Byrne, Eugene H. "Easterners in Genoa." *JAOS* 38 (1918): 176–187.

Byrne, Eugene H. "Commercial Contracts of the Genoese in the Syrian Trade of the Twelfth Century." *Quarterly Journal of Economics* 31, No. 1 (Nov. 1916): 128–170.

Byrne, Eugene H. *Genoese Shipping in the Twelfth and Thirteenth Centuries*. Cambridge, 1930.

Caetani, Leone. *La fonction d'Islam dans l'evolution de la civilisation*. Bologna, 1912.

Caetani, Leone. *Chronografia islamica*. 5 Vols. Paris, 1912/1922.

Caetani, Leone. *Studie di storia orientale*. Vols. 1 and 3. Milan, 1911/1914.

Caetani, Leone. *Annali dell'Islam*. 10 Vols. Milan, 1905–1926.

Cahen, Claude. *Les peuples musulmans dans l'histoire médiévale*. Damascus, 1977.

Cahen, Claude. "Réflexions sur le Waqf ancien." *SI*, No. 14 (1961): 37–56.

Cahen, Claude. *Makhzumiyyat: Études sur l'histoire économique et financière de l'Égypte médiéval*. Leiden, 1970

Cahen, Claude. "Mouvements populaires et autonomisme urbain dans l'Asie musulmane du moyen âge, III." *Arabica* 6, No. 3 (Sep. 1959): 233–65.

Cahen, Claude. "A propos et autour d' 'Ein arabisches Handbuch der Handelswissenschaft.'" *Oriens* 15 (Dec. 1962): 160–71.

Cahen, Claude. "Points de vue sur la 'Révolution abbaside.'" *Revue Historique* 230, No. 2 (1963): 295–338.

Cahen, Claude. "Douanes et commerce dans les ports méditerranéens de l'Égypte médiéval d'après le Minhadj d'al-Makhzumi." *JESHO* 7, No. 3 (Nov. 1964): 217–314.

Cahen, Claude. "L'histoire économique et sociale de l'Orient musulman médiéval." *SI*, No. 3 (1955): 93–115.

Calcaschandi. *Die Geographie und Verwaltung von Ägypten*. Göttingen, 1879.

Califano, G. *Il regime dei beni "auqaf" nella storia e nel diritto dell'Islam*. Tripoli, 1913.

Casanova, Paul. *Essai de reconstitution topographique de la ville d'al Foustat ou Misr*. Cairo, 1919.

Cattan, Henry. "The Law of Waqf," in *Law in the Middle East*, edited by Liebesny et al. Vol. 1. Washington (1955): 203–222.

Chabot, J. B. (ed). *Chronique de Michel le Syrien*. 3 Vols. Paris, 1899–1904.

Chalmeta Gendrón, Pedro. *El zoco medieval: Contribución al estudio de la historia del Mercado*. Almeria, 2010.

Chalmeta, Pedro. *El señor del zoco en España: Edades media y moderna*. Madrid, 1973.

Chaney, E. "Islam and Human Capital Formation: Evidence from Pre-Modern Muslim Science," in *Handbook of the Economics of Religion*, edited by R. McCleary. Oxford, 2012.

Chau Ju-ka. *Chinese and Arab Trade*. St. Petersburg, 1911.

Chehata, Chafik. *Essai d'une theorie general de l'obligation en droit muselman*. Vol. 1. Cairo, 1936.

Cheikho et al. *Corpus scriptorum christianorum orientalium*. Paris. 1909.

Chester, Frank D. "On Early Moslem Promissory Notes." *JAOS* 16 (1896): xliii–xlvii.

Cipolla, C. *Money Prices and Civilization in the Mediterranean World*. Princeton, 1956.

Citarella, Armand O. "The Relations of Amalfi with the Arab World before the Crusades." *Speculum* 42, No. 2 (Apr. 1967): 299–312.

Citarella, Armand O. "Patterns in Medieval Trade: The Commerce of Amalfi Before the Crusades." *Journal of Economic History* 28, No. 4 (Dec. 1968): 531–55.

Clavel, Eugène. *Droit musulman*. 2 Vols. Cairo, 1896.

Clermont-Ganneau, M. "Notes d'épigraphie et d'histoire arabes." *JA* (1887): 472–97.

Coehn, Hayyim. "The Economic Background and the Secular Occupations of Muslim Jurisprudents and Traditionists in the Classical Period of Islam." *JESHO* (1970): 16–61.

Cohn, Emil. *Der Wucher (riba) in Qoran, Chadith und Fiqh*. Berlin, 1903.

Constable, Olivia R. *Trade and Traders in Muslim Spain 900–1500*. Cambridge, 1994.

Constable, Olivia R. *Housing the Stranger in the Mediterranean World: Lodging, Trade, and Travel in Late Antiquity and the Middle Ages*. Cambridge, 2003.

Constable, Olivia R. "Cross-Cultural Contracts: Sales of Land between Christians and Muslims in 12th-Century Palermo." *SI* , No. 85 (1997): 67–84.

Cook, M. A. *Studies in the Economic History of the Middle East from the Rise of Islam to the Present Day*. Oxford, 1970.

Cooperson, Michael. "Ibn Hanbal and Bishr al-Hafi: A Case Study in Biographical Traditions." *SI*, No. 86 (1997): 71–101.

Crone, P., and Cook, M. *Hagarism: The Making of the Islamic World*. Cambridge, 1977.

Crone, Patricia, and Martin Hinds. *God's Caliph: Religious Authority in the First Centuries of Islam*. Cambridge, 1986.

Crone, Patricia. "Quraysh and the Roman Army: Making Sense of the Meccan Leather Trade." *BSOAS* 70, No. 1 (2007): 63–88.

Crone, Patricia. "How Did the Quranic Pagans Make a Living?" *BSOAS* 68, No. 3 (2005): 387–99.

Crone, Patricia. *Meccan Trade and the Rise of Islam*. Princeton, 1987.

Crone, Patricia. *Slaves on Horses*. Cambridge, 1980.

Crone, Patricia. *Roman, Provincial and Islamic Law*. Cambridge, 2002.

Davis, Robert S. "Counting Slaves on the Barbary Coast." *Past and Present*, No. 172 (Aug. 2001): 87–124.

Delisle, Léopold. *Les opérations financières des Templiers*. Paris, 1889.

Della Vida, Levi. "Pre-Islamic Arabia," in *The Arab Heritage*, edited by N. A. Faris. Princeton, 1944.

Dennett, D. C. *Conversion and Poll Tax in Early Islam*. Cambridge, 1950.

Denny, Frederick M. "Ummah in the Constition of Medina." *Journal of Near Eastern Studies* 36, No. 1 (Jan. 1977): 39–47.

Denny, Frederick M. "The Will in the Quran." *Journal of Near Eastern Studies* 40, No. 3, Arabic and Islamic Studies in Honor of Nabia Abbott: Part One (Jul. 1981): 253–7.

Dewey, John. "The Historic Background of Corporate Legal Personality." *Yale Law Journal* 35, No. 6 (Apr. 1926): 655–73.

Diem, Werner. *Arabische Geschäftsbriefe des 10. bis 14. Jahrhunderts*. Wiesbaden, 1995.

Diem, Werner. *Arabische Briefe des 7. Bis 13. Jahrhunderts*. Wiesbaden, 1997.

Diem, Werner. *Arabischer Terminkauf*. Wiesbaden, 2006

Dien, Izzi. *The Theory and the Practice of Market Law in Medieval Islam*. London, 1997.

Donner, F. M. "Mecca's Food Supplies and Muhammad's Boycott." *JESHO* 20, No. 3 (Oct. 1977): 249–66.

Donner, Fred. *Mohammed and the Believers: At the Origin of Islam*. Cambridge, 2010.

Donner, Fred. *The Articulation of Early Islamic State Structures*. Burlington, 2012.

Dozy, R. *Die Israeliten zu Mekka*. Leipzig, 1864.

Duby, Georges. *The Early Growth of the European Economy*. Ithaca, 1974.

Dunbar, Charles. "The Bank of Venice." *Quarterly Journal of Economics* 6, No. 3 (Apr. 1892): 308–335.

Dunbar, Charles. "The Bank of Venice." *Quarterly Journal of Economics* 7, No. 2 (Jan. 1893): 210–216.

Duri, A. A. *Studies on the Economic Life of Mesopotamia in the 10th Century*. Baghdad, 1948(?).

Eddé, Anne-Marie. *Saladin*. Cambridge, 2011.

Egmond, Warren van. *The Commercial Revolution and the Beginings of Western Mathematics in Renaissance Florence 1300–1500*. Ann Arbor, 1976.

Ehrenkreutz, Andrew S. "The Place of Saladin in the Naval History of the Mediterranean Sea in the Middle Ages." *JAOS* 75, No. 2 (Apr. 1955): 100–116.

Ehrenkreutz, Andrew S. "The Crisis of the Dinar in the Egypt of Saladin." *JESHO* 76, No. 3 (Jul. 1956): 178–84.

Ehrenkreutz, Andrew S. "Studies in the Monetary History of the Near East in the Middle Ages." *JESHO*, Part 1: Vol. 2, No. 2 (1959): 128–61; Part 2: Vol. 6, No. 3 (1963): 243–77.

Ehrenkreutz, Andrew S. "Arabic Dinars Struck by the Crusaders: A Case of Ignorance or of Economic Subversion." *JESHO* 7, No. 2 (Jul. 1964): 167–82.

El Ali, Saleh. "The Topography of Medina." *IC* 35 (1961): 65–92.

El Ali, Saleh. "Muslim Estates in the Hidjaz in the First Century A.H." *JESHO* 2, No. 3 (Dec. 1959): 247–61.

El Bahlki. *Livre de la création et de l'histoire de el Maqdisi*. Vols. 4–6. Paris, 1907/1919.
El Bekri. "Description de l'Afrique septentrionale." *JA* 1858 (December): 499; *JA* 1859: 310–416; *JA* 1859, 14: 117–133.
Essid, Yassine. *A Critique of the Origins of Islamic Economic Thought*. Leiden, 1995.
Fabri, Felix. *The Wanderings of Felix Fabri*. New York, 1972.
Fanfani, Amintore. *Catholicism. Protestantism. Capitalism*. Sheed & Ward, 1935.
Favreau-Lilie, Marie-Luise. *Die Italiener im Heiligen Land vom ersten Kreuzzug bis zum Tode Heinrichs von Champagne (1098–1197)*. Amsterdam, 1989.
Feldman, Noah. *The Fall and Rise of the Islamic State*. Princeton, 2008.
Fibonacci, Leonardo. *Fibonacci's* Liber abaci: *A Translation into Modern English of Leonardo Pisano's Book of Calculation*. New York, 2002.
Fierro, Maribel. "Spanish Scholarship on Islamic Law." *Islamic Law and Society* 2, No. 1 (1995): 43–70.
Finley, M. I. *The Ancient Economy*. Berkeley, 1985.
Fischel, Walter. *Jews in the Economic and Political Life of Medieval Islam*. New York, 1969.
Fischel, Walter. "The Spice Trade in Mamluk Egypt: A Contribution to the Economic History of Medieval Islam." *JESHO* 1, No. 2 (Apr. 1958): 157–74.
Fischel, Walter. "The Origin of Banking in Medieval Islam: A Contribution to the Economic History of the Jews of Baghdad of the Tenth Century." *JRAS*, No. 2 (Apr. 1933): 339–52; No. 3 (Jul. 1933): 569–603.
Fitzgerald, C. P. *China: A Short Cultural History*. London, 1948.
Forand, Paul M. "The Relation of the Slave and the Client to the Master or Patron in Medieval Islam." *International Journal of Middle East Studies* 2, No. 1 (Jan. 1971): 59–66.
Foster, Benjamin. "Agoranomos and Muhtasib." *JESHO* 13, No. 2 (Apr. 1970): 128–44.
Freeland, H. W. "Gleanings from the Arabic: The Lament of Maisun, the Bedouin Wife of Muawiya." *JRAS*, New Series, Vol. 18, No. 1 (Jan. 1886): 89–91.
Frenkel, Yehoshu'a. "Political and Social Aspects of Islamic Religious Endowments ('Awqaf'): Saladin in Cairo (1169–1173) and in Jerusalem (1187–1193)." *BSOAS* 62, No. 1 (1999): 1–20.
Frescobaldi, Lionardo, Giorgio Gucci, and Sinome Sigoli. *A Visit to the Holy Places, Egypt, Palestine, and Syria in 1384*. Jerusalem, 1948.
Freytag, Georg. *Regierung des Saahd-Aldaula zu Aleppo*. Bonn, 1820.
Gabrieli, Francesco. "La politique arabe des Normands de Sicile." *SI*, No. 9 (1958): 83–96.
Gabrieli, Francesco. "Greeks and Arabs in the Central Mediterranean Area." *DOP* 18 (1964): 57–65.
Gabrieli, Francesco. "Frederick II and Moslem Culture." *East and West* 9, Nos. 1 and 2 (Mar. 1958): 53–61.
Gaiani, Alberto. "The Juridical Nature of the Moslem Qirad: An Interesting Alternative of the Associative Character of the Western Accomendacio." *East and West* 4, No. 2 (Jul. 1953): 81–6.
Gaudiosi, Monica. "The Influence of the Islamic Law of Waqf on the Development of the Trust in England: The Case of Merton College." *University of Pennsylvania Law Review* 136, No. 4 (Apr. 1988): 1231–61.
Ghazi, Farid. "Un group social: Les raffinés." *SI* 2 (1959): 37–71.
Gibb, Hamilton A. R. "Arab-Byzantine Relations under the Umayyad Caliphate." *DOP* 12 (1958): 219–33.
Gil, Moshe. "The Earliest Waqf Foundations." *Journal of Near Eastern Studies* 57, No. 2 (Apr. 1998): 125–40.
Gildmeister, J. "Die arabischen Nachrichten zur Geschichte der Harambauten." *Zeitschrift des Deutschen Palästinavereins* 13 (1890): 1–24.
Goitein, S. D. *Letters of Medieval Jewish Traders*. Princeton, 1973.
Goitein, S. D. "The Main Industries in the Mediterranean Area." *JESHO* (1961): 168–97.
Goitein, S. D. *Studies in Islamic History and Institutions*. Leiden, 1966.
Goitcin, S. D. *Jews and Arabs: Their Contacts through the Ages*. Ncw York, 1964.
Goitein, S. D. "The Exchange Rate of Gold and Silver Money in Fatimid and Ayyubid Times: A Preliminary Study of the Relevant Geniza Material." *JESHO* 8, No. 1 (Aug. 1965): 1–46.

Goitein, S. D. "The Commercial Mail Service in Medieval Islam." *JAOS* 84, No. 2 (Apr. 1964): 118–23.

Goitein, S. D. *A Mediterranean Society*. 6 Vols. Berkeley, 1967/1993.

Goitein, S. D. "New Light on the Beginnings of the Karimi Merchants." *JESHO* 1, No. 2 (Apr. 1958): 175–84.

Goitein, S. D. "Between Hellenism and Renaissance—Islam, the Intermediate Civilization." *Islamic Studies* 2, No. 2 (Jun. 1963): 217–33.

Goitein, S. D. "A Jewish Business Woman of the Eleventh Century." *Jewish Quarterly Review*, New Series, Vol. 57 (1967): 225–42.

Goitein, S. D. "Slaves and Slavegirls in the Cairo Geniza Records." *Arabica* 9, No. 1 (Jan. 1962): 1–20.

Goitein, S. D. "Bankers Accounts from the Eleventh Century A.D." *JESHO* 9, Nos. 1 and 2 (Nov. 1966): 28–66.

Goitein, S. D. "Commercial and Family Partnerships in the Countries of Medieval Islam." *IS* 3, No. 3 (Sep. 1964): 315–37.

Goldziher, Ignaz. *Muhammedanische Studien*. 2 Vols. Halle, 1889.

Gottheil, R. "An Answer to the Dhimmis." *JAOS* 41 (1921): 383–457.

Grabar, Oleg. *The Formation of Islamic Art*. New Haven, 1987.

Grabar, Oleg. "The Umayyad Dome of the Rock in Jerusalem." *Ars Orientalis* 3 (1959): 33–62.

Grabar, Oleg. *The Dome of the Rock*. Cambridge, 2006.

Grabmann, M. *Die Geschichte der scholastischen Methode*. 2 Vols. Freiburg, 1909/1911.

Graeber, David *Debt: The First 5,000 Years*. New York, 2011.

Greif, Avner. *Institutions and the Path to the Modern Economy*. Cambridge, 2006.

Greif, Avner. "Contract Enforceability and Economic Institutions in Early Trade: The Maghribi Traders' Coalition. *American Economic Review* 83, No. 3 (Jun. 1993): 525–48.

Grierson, Philip. "The Monetary Reforms of Abd al-Malik: Their Metrological Basis and Their Financial Repercussions." *JESHO* 3, No. 3 (Oct. 1960): 241–64.

Grimm, R. E. "Fibonacci Autobiography." *Fibonacci Quarterly* 5, No. 2 (Feb. 1973): 99–104.

Hallaq, Wael B. *The Origins of Islamic Law*. Cambridge, 2005.

Hallaq, Wael B. "Was al-Shafii the Master Architect of Islamic Jurisprudence?" *International Journal of Middle East Studies* 25, No. 4 (Nov. 1993): 587–605.

Hallaq, Wael B. "Was the Gate of Ijtihad Closed?" *International Journal of Middle East Studies* 16, No. 1 (Mar. 1984): 3–41.

Hamidullah, Mohammed. *Le prophète de l'Islam*. Paris, 1959.

Hamidullah, Mohammed. *Documents sur la diplomatie musulman à l'époque du prophète*. Paris, 1935.

Hamilton, Bernard. "The Impact of Crusader Jerusalem on Western Christendom." *Catholic Historical Review* 80, No. 4 (Oct. 1994): 695–713.

Hartmann, Martin. "Review of 'Le Berceau de L'Islam.'" *Die Welt des Islams* 2, No. 2 (Dec. 1914): 357–62.

Hartmann, Martin. *Der Islam*. 1909.

Haskins, Charles H. "Michael Scot and Frederick II." *Isis* 4, No. 2 (Oct. 1921): 250–75.

Haskins, Charles H. "Science at the Court of the Emperor Frederick II." *American Historical Review* 27, No. 4 (Jul. 1922): 669–94.

Haskins, Charles H. "England and Sicily in the Twelfth Century." *English Historical Review* 26, No. 103 (Jul. 1911): 433–47.

Haskins, Charles H. "Arabic Science in Western Europe." *Isis* 7, No. 3 (1925): 478–85.

Hayek, Friedrich von. "The Use of Knowledge in Society." *American Economic Review* 35, No. 4 (Sep. 1945): 519–30.

Heck, Gene. *Charlemagne, Muhammad, and the Arab Roots of Capitalism*. Berlin, 2006.

Heck, Gene. "'Arabia without Spices': An Alternate Hypothesis." *JAOS* 123, No. 3 (Jul. 2003): 547–76.

Heck, Gene. "Gold Mining in Arabia and the Rise of the Islamic State." *JESHO* 42, No. 3 (1999): 364–95.

Heck, Gene. *The Precious Metals of West Arabia and Their Role in Forging the Economic Dynamic of the Early Islamic State*. Riyadh, 2003.

Heffening, Willi. *Das islamische Fremdenrecht*. Hannover, 1925.
Heidemann, Stefan. "The Merger of Two Currency Zones in Early Islam: The Byzantine and Sasanian Impact on the Circulation in Former Byzantine Syria and Northern Mesopotamia." *Iran* 36 (1998): 95–112.
Heidemann, Stefan. "The Evolving Representation of the Early Islamic Empire and Its Religion on Coin Imagery," in *The Quran in Context*,edited by Angelika Neuwirth, Nicolai Sinai, and Michael Marx, 149–96. Leiden, 2010.
Heidemann, Stefan. "Numismatics." *The New Cambridge History of Islam*. Vol. 1: *The Formation of the Islamic World, Sixth to Eleventh Centuries*, edited by Chase Robinson, 648–663. Cambridge, 2010.
Hein, H. A. *Beiträge zur ayyubidischen Diplomatik*. Freiburg, 1968.
Hennequin, Gilles. "De la monnaie antique à la monnaie musulmane: Hommage à Maurice Lombard." *Annales* 30, No. 4 (Jul. 1975): 890–9.
Hergenröther, Josef. *Photius: Patriarch von Constantinople*. 3 Vols. Regensburg, 1867/1869.
Heyd, Wilhelm. *Geschichte des Levantehandels im Mittelalter*. 2 Vols. Hildesheim, 1984 (reprint of 1879 edition).
Heyd, Wilhelm. "Die Anfänge der italienischen Handelscolonien im byzantinischen Reich." *Zeitschrift für die gesamte Staatswissenschaft* 14, No. 4 (1858): 652–720.
Heyd, Wilhelm. "Die italienischen Handelscolonien in Ägypten." *Zeitschrift für die gesamte Staatswissenschaft* 20, No. 1 (1864): 54–138.
Heynen, R. *Zur Entstehung des Kapitalismus in Venedig*. Munich, 1905.
Hirschfeld, H. "Der Oikonomikos des Neupythagoreers 'Bryson' und sein Einfluss auf die islamische Wissenschaft." *JRAS*, No. 1 (Jan. 1929): 186–8.
Hoexter, Miriam. "Waqf Stydies in the Twentieth Century: The State of the Art." *JESHO* 41, No. 4 (1998): 474–95.
Holdsworth, W. S. "The Early History of the Contract of Insurance." *Columbia Law Review* 17, No. 2 (Feb. 1917): 85–113.
Hoover, Calvin. "Economic Forces in the Evolution of Civil and Canon Law." *Southwestern Political and Social Science Quarterly* 10 (1929): 1–14.
Hoover, Calvin. "The Sea Loan in Genoa in the 12th Century." *Quarterly Journal of Economics* 40 (1925–1926): 495–526.
Houben, Hubert. *Roger II of Sicily*. Cambridge, 2002.
Hoyland, Robert. *Seeing Islam as Others Saw It: A Survey and Evaluation of Christian, Jewish, and Zoroastrian Writings on Early Islam*. Princeton, 1997.
Hudson, Michael, and Marc van de Mieroop. *Debt and Economic Renewal in the Ancient Near East*. Bethesda, 2002.
Hudson, Michael. "How Interest Rates Were Set, 2500 BC–1000 AD: Mas, Tokos and Foenus as Metaphors for Interest Accruals." *JESHO* 43, No. 2 (2000): 132–61.
Hughes, Thomas Patrick. *A Dictionary of Islam*. London, 1885.
Hurvitz, Nimrod. "Schools of Law and Historical Context: Re-examining the Formation of the Hanbali Madhhab." *Islamic Law and Society* 7, No. 1 (2000): 37–64.
Ibn al-Athir. *The Chronicle of Ibn al-Athir for the Crusading Period.* 2 Vols. Ashgate, 2007.
Ibn Battuta. *Travels of Ibn Battuta in Asia and Africa*. London, 1829.
Ibn Hawqal. *The Oriental Geography of Ebn Haukal* (translated by W. Ouseley). London, 1800.
Ibn Ishaq. *The Life of Muhammad.* Oxford, 2006.
Ibn Jubayr. *The Travels of Ibn Jubayr*. London, 1952.
Ibn Kathir, Abu al-Fida Ismail. *The Life of the Prophet Muhammad.* 3 Vols. Reading, 1998/2000.
Ibn Khaldun. *The Muqaddimah: An Introduction to History*. 3 Vols. London, 1967.
Ibn Khallikan. *Biographical Dictionary* (translated by MacGuckin de Slane). Paris, 1842–1871.
Ibn Miskawaihi. *The Experiences of the Nations*. Vol. 1. Oxford, 1921.
Ibn Muslim, Hajjaj. *Sahih Muslim*. Vol. 4. Riyad, 2007.
Ibn Taymiyah. *Public Duties in Islam: The Institution of the Hisba*. London, 1982.
Ibrahim, Mahmood. *Merchant Capital and Islam*. Austin, 1990.

Idris, H. R. "Commerce maritime et kirad en Berbérie orientale." *JESHO* 4 (Dec. 1961): 225–39.

Imad ad Din. *Conquête de la Syrie et de la Palestine par Saladine*. Paris, 1972.

Imamuddin, S. M. "Bayt al-mal and Banks in the Medieval Muslim World." *IC* 30, No. 1 (Jan. 1961): 12–20.

Irving, Washington. *Mahomet and His Successors*. 2 Vols. 1869.

Jacob, Georg. "Die ältesten Spuren des Wechsels (a.d. Zt. Umar I)." *MSOS* 28, No. 2 (1925): 280–1.

Jacob, Georg. *Altarabisches Beduinenleben*. Hildesheim, 1967.

Jacoby, David. "The Kingdom of Jerusalem and the Collapse of Hohenstaufen Power in the Levant." *DOP* 40 (1986): 83–101.

Johns, Jeremy. *Arabic Administration in Norman Sicily*. Cambridge, 2002.

Johnston, J. H. "The Mohammedan Slave Trade." *Journal of Negro History* 13, No. 4 (Oct. 1928): 478–91.

Juster, Jean. *Les juifs dans l'empire romain*. 2 Vols. Paris, 1914.

Kallek, Cengiz. "Yahya ibn Adam's Kitab al-Kharadj: Religious Guidelines for Public Finance." *JESHO* 44, No. 2 (2001): 103–22.

Kennedy, Hugh. "Central Government and Provincial Elites in the Early Abbasid Caliphates." *BSOAS* 44. London, 1981.

Kennedy, Hugh. *The Great Arab Conquests*. London, 2007.

Khosraw, Naser-e. *Book of Travels*. Albany, 1986.

Kiernan, R. H. *The Unveiling of Arabia: The Story of Arabian Travel and Discovery*. London, 1937.

Kister, M. J. "Land Property and Jiha: A Discussion of Some Early Traditions." *JESHO* 34, No. 4 (1991): 270–311.

Kister, M. J. "The Social and Political Implications of Three Traditions in the Kitab al-Kharaj of Yayha b. Adam." *JESHO* 3, No. 3 (Oct. 1960). 326–34.

Kister, M. J. "O God, Tighten Thy grip on Mudar . . . Some Socio-Economic and Religious Aspects of an Early Hadith." *JESHO* 24, No. 3 (Oct. 1981): 242–73.

Kister, M. J. "Some Reports Concerning Mecca from Jahiliyya to Islam." *JESHO* 15, Nos. 1 and 2 (Jun. 1972): 61–93.

Kister, M. J. "Mecca and Tamim (Aspects of Their Relations)." *JESHO* 8, No. 2 (Nov. 1965): 113–63.

Kister, M. J. "The Market of the Prophet." *JESHO* 8, No. 3 (1965): 272–76.

Koder, Johannes (ed.). *Das Eparchenbuch Leons des Weisen*. Vienna, 1991.

Koder, Johannes. *Die Byzantiner und ihre Nachbarn* (translation of *Konstantinos Porphyrogenitos: De administrando imperio*). Vienna, 1995.

Koehler, Benedikt. "Female Entrepreneurship in Early Islam." *Economic Affairs* 31, No. 2 (2011): 93–5.

Koehler, Benedikt. "The Economist Mohammed Ibn Abdullah (570–632)." *Economic Affairs* 31, No. 1 (2011): 109–11.

Koehler, Benedikt. "Early Islamic Charities As Catalysts Of Institutional Innovation." *Economic Affairs* 30, No. 3 (2010): 6-8.

Koehler, Benedikt. "The Seventh-Century Islamic Gold Standard." *Economic Affairs* 30, No. 3 (2010): 72–4.

Koehler, Benedikt. "Islamic Finance as a Progenitor Of Venture Capital." *Economic Affairs* 29, No. 4 (2009): 89-91.

Kohler, Joseph. *Die Commenda im islamitischen Recht*. Würzburg, 1885.

Krauss, Samuel. *Talmudische Archäologie*. Berlin, 1910.

Krcsmárik, J. "Das Wakfrecht." *ZDMG* 65 (1891): 511–76.

Kremer, Alfred von. *Über das Einnahmebudget des Abbasiden-Reiches vom Jahre 306 H.* Vienna, 1887.

Kremer, Alfred von. *Topographie von Damascus*. Vienna, 1854.

Kremer, Alfred von. *Culturgeschichte des Orients unter den Chalifen*. 2 Vols. Vienna, 1875/1877.

Kremer, Alfred von. *Geschichte der herrschenden Ideen des Islams*. Leipzig, 1868.

Kuran, Timur. "The Absence of the Corporation in Islamic Law: Origins and Persistence." *American Journal of Comparative Law* 53, No. 4 (Fall 2005): 785–834.

Kuran, Timur. "The Provision of Public Goods under Islamic Law: Origins, Impact, and Limitations of the Waqf System." *Law & Society Review* 35, No. 4 (2001): 841–98.

Kuran, Timur. *The Long Divergence*. Princeton, 2011.

Labib, Subhi. "Geld und Kredit: Studien zur Wirtschaftschaftsgeschichte Ägyptens im Mittelalter." *JESHO* 2, No. 3 (Dec. 1959): 225–46.

Labib, Subhi. *Handelsgeschichte Ägyptens im Mittelalter*. Wiesbaden, 1965.

Labib, Subhi. "Capitalism in Medieval Islam." *JESHO* 29, No. 1 (1969): 79–96.

Lal, Deepak. *Unintended Consequences*. Cambridge, 1998.

Lammens, Henri. *L'Arabie occidentale avant l'hégire*. Beirut, 1928.

Lammens, Henri. *Études sur le Règne du Calife Omaiyade Moawia Ier*. 3 Vols. Beirut and Paris, 1906/1908

Lammens, Henri. "Mahomet fut il sincère." *Recherches de science religieuse*. Nos. 1 and 2. Paris, 1911.

Lammens, Henri. "La mecque à la veille de l'hégire," in *Mélanges de l'université Saint-Joseph*, 97–440. Beirut, 1923.

Lammens, Henri. *Études sur le siècle des Omayyades*. Beirut, 1930.

Lammens, Henri. *Le berceau de l'Islam*. Rome, 1914.

Lammens, Henri. *Le califat de Yazid Ier*. Beirut, 1912.

Lammens, Henri. *Fatima et les filles de Mahomet*. Rome, 1912.

Lammens, Henri. "L'âge de Mahomet et la chronologie de la Sira." *JA* (1911): 209–50.

Lammens, Henri. *La cité arabe de Taif à la veille de l'Hégire*. Beirut, 1922.

Lane, Frederic. *Venice: A Maritime Republic*. Baltimore, 1973.

Lane, Frederic. "The Economic Meaning of the Invention of the Compass." *American Historical Review* 68, No. 3 (Apr. 1963): 605–17.

Laoust, Henri. *Traité de droit public d'Ibn Tamiyya*. Beirut, 1948.

Laoust, Henri. *Essai sur les doctrines sociales et politiques de Takid-Din b. Taimiyya*. Cairo, 1939.

Laoust, Henri. "La biographie d'Ibn Taimiya d'après Ibn Katir." *Bulletin d'Études Orientales* 10 (1943): 115–162.

Lara, Yadira Gonzalez de. "Enforceability and Risk-Sharing in Financial Contracts: From the Sea Loan to the Commenda in Late Medieval Venice." *Journal of Economic History* 61, No. 2 (Jun. 2001): 500–504.

Lassner, Jacob. *Jews, Christians, and the Abode of Islam*. Chicago, 2012.

Lassner, Jacob. *The Topography of Baghdad in the Early Middle Ages*. Detroit, 1970.

Laum, Bernhard. *Heiliges Geld*. Tübingen, 1924.

Layish, Aharon. "The Maliki Family 'Waqf' According to Wills and 'Waqfiyyat.'" *BSOAS* 46, No. 1 (1983): 1–32.

Le Strange, Guy. *Baghdad during the Abbasid Caliphate*. Oxford, 1900.

Le Strange, Guy. *Palestine under the Moslems*. London, 1890.

Le Strange, Guy. "A Greek Embassy to Baghdad in 917 A.D." *JRAS* (Jan. 1897): 35–45.

Le Strange, Guy. "Description of Mesopotamia and Baghdad. Written about the Year 900 A.D. by Ibn Serapion." *JRAS* (Jan. 1895): 1–76.

Le Strange, Guy. "Baghdad during the Abbasid Caliphate: A Topographical Summary, with a Notice of the Contemporary Arabic and Persian Authorities." *JRAS* (Oct. 1899): 847–93.

Leemans, W. F. *The Old-Babylonian Merchant: His Business and His Social Position*. Leiden, 1950.

Lev, Yaacov. *Charity, Endowments and Charitable Institutions in Medieval Islam*. Gainesville, 2005.

Lev, Yaacov. *Saladin in Egypt*. London, 1999.

Lévi-Provencal, É. *Documents inédits sur la vie sociale et économique en occident musulman au moyen age: Trois traits hispanique de hisba*. Cairo, 1955.

Lévi-Provencal, É. *Histoire de l'Espagne musulmane*. Paris, 1950–1953

Levtzion, Nehemia. "Ibn-Hawqal, the Cheque, and Awdaghost." *Journal of African History* 9, No. 2 (1968): 223–33.

Levy, Reuben. *A Baghdad Chronicle*. Cambridge, 1929.

Lewis, Archibald. *Naval Power and Trade in the Mediterranean 500–1000*. Princeton, 1951.

Lewis, Bernard. *Race and Slavery in the Middle East*. Oxford, 1990.

Lohlker, R. *Der Handel im malekitischen Recht*. Berlin, 1991.

Lombard, Maurice. "Mahomet et Charlemagne: Le problème économique." *Annales* 3, No. 2 (Apr. 1948): 188–99.

Lombard, Maurice. "Les bases monétaires d'une suprématie économique: L'or musulman du VIIe au XIe siècle." *Annales* 2, No. 2 (Apr. 1947): 143–60.

Lombard, Maurice. "L'évolution urbaine pendant le haut moyen age." *Annales* 12, No. 1 (Jan. 1957): 7–28.

Lombard, Maurice. *The Golden Age of Islam*. Princeton, 2004.

Lopez, Robert S. "Market Expansion: The Case of Genoa." *Journal of Economic History* 24, No. 4 (Dec. 1964): 445–64.

Lopez, Robert S. "Mohammed and Charlemagne: A Revision." *Speculum* 18, No. 1 (Jan. 1943): 14–38.

Lopez, Robert S. "European Merchants in the Medieval Indies: The Evidence of Commercial Documents." *Journal of Economic History* 3, No. 2 (Nov. 1943): 164–84.

Lopez, Robert S. "Du marché temporaire à la colonie permanente: L'évolution de la politique commercial au moyen âge." *Annales* 4 (1949): 389–405.

Lopez, Robert S. "The Role of Trade in the Economic Readjustment of Byzantium in the Seventh Century." *DOP* 13 (1959): 67–85.

Lopez, Robert S. *The Three Ages of the Italian Renaissance*. Charlottesville, 1970.

Lopez, Robert S. "Harmenopoulos and the Downfall of the Bezant," in *Tomos Konstantinou Armenopoulou*, 11–125. Thessaloniki, 1952.

Lopez, Robert S. *Settecento anni fa: Il ritorno all'oro nell'occidente duecentesco*. Naples, 1955.

Lopez, Robert S. *La prima crisi della banca di Genova, 1250–1259*. Milan, 1956.

Lopez, Robert S. "An Aristocracy of Money in the Early Middle Ages." *Speculum* 28, No. 1 (Jan. 1953): 1–43.

Lopez, Robert S. "The Trade of Medieval Europe: the South," in *The Cambridge Economic History of Europe*, Vol. 2, 257–354. Cambridge, 1952.

Lopez, Robert S. *The Commercial Revolution of the Middle Ages 950–1350*. Cambridge, 1976.

Lopez, Robert S. "Les influences orientales et l'éveil économique de l'occident." *Cahiers d'histoire mondiale* 1 (1953/1954): 594–622.

Lopez, Robert S. "The Dollar of the Middle Ages." *Journal of Economic History* 11, No. 3, Part 1 (Summer 1951): 209–34.

Lopez, Robert S. "Back to Gold, 1252." *Economic History Review*, New Series, Vol. 9, No. 2 (1956): 219–40.

Lopez, Robert S. "Un texte inédit: Le plus ancien manuel italien de technique commercial." *Revue Historique* 243, No. 1 (Jan. 1970): 67–76.

Lopez, Robert S. *The Shape of Medieval Monetary History*. London, 1986.

Lopez, Robert S. "Byzantian Law in the 7th Century and Its Reception by the Germans and the Arabs." *Byzantion* 16 (1942/1943): 445–61.

Lopez, Robert S. "Silk Industry in the Byzantine Empire." *Speculum* 20, No. 1 (Jan. 1945): 1–42.

Lopez, Robert S. "European Merchants in the Medieval Indies: The Evidence of Commercial Documents." *Journal of Economic History* 3, No. 2 (Nov. 1943): 164–84.

Lopez. Robert S., and I. W. Raymond. *Medieval Trade in the Mediterranean World*. London, 1955.

Lorey, E. de, and M. van Berchem. *Les mosaiques de la mosquée des Omayyades à Damas*. Paris, 1930.

Mackensen, Ruth Stellhorn. "Four Great Libraries of Medieval Baghdad." *Library Quarterly* 2, No. 3 (Jul. 1932): 279–99.

MacKenzie, Neil. *Ayyubid Cairo: A Topographical Study*. Cairo, 1992.

Macoudi. *Les prairies d'or*. 9 Vols. Paris, 1861/1877.

Madelung, Wilferd. *The Succession to Muhammad*. Cambridge, 1997.

Maitland, F. W. "The Origin of Uses." *Harvard Law Review* 8, No. 3 (Oct. 1894): 127–37; *BSOAS* 24, No. 1 (1961): 1–56.
Makdisi, George. "Muslim Institutions of Learning in Eleventh-Century Baghdad." *BSOAS* 24, No. 1 (1961): 1–56.
Makdisi, George. "The Scholastic Method in Medieval Education: An Inquiry into Its Origins in Law and Theology." *Speculum* 49, No. 4 (Oct. 1974): 640–61.
Makdisi, George. "Madrasa and University in the Middle Ages." *SI*, No. 32 (1970): 255–64.
Makdisi, George. "Scholasticism and Humanism in Classical Islam and the Christian West." *JAOS* 109, No. 2 (Apr. 1989): 175–82.
Makdisi, George. "Legal History of Islamic Law and the English Common Law: Origins and Metamorphoses." *Cleveland State Law Review* 34 (1985/1986): 3–18.
Makdisi, George. *The Rise of Colleges: Institutions of Learning in Islam and the West.* Edinburgh, 1981.
Makdisi, John (ed.). Conference on Comparative Links Between Islamic Law and Common Law. *Cleveland State Law Review.* (1985/1986): 1–144.
Makdisi, John. "Legal Logic and Equity in Islamic Law." *American Journal of Comparative Law* 33, No. 1 (Winter 1985): 63–92.
Makdisi, John. "The Islamic Origins of the Common Law." *North Carolina Law Review* (77 N.C.L. Rev. 1635). June 1999.
Malik ibn Anas. *Al-Muwatta.* London, 1989.
Mann, Jacob. *The Jews in Egypt and Palestine under the Fatimids.* 2 Vols. Oxford, 1920/1922.
Margoliouth, D. S. "Omar's Instructions to the Kadi." *JRAS* (Apr. 1910): 307-26.
Marinez Gijon, J. "La comenda en el derecho español." *Anuario de historia de derecho espanol* 36 (1968): 369–456.
Mas Latrie, Jacques de. *Relations et commerce de l'Afrique septentrionale ou Magreb avec les nations chrétiennes au moyen âge.* Paris, 1886.
Mas Latrie, Jacques de. *Traités de paix et de commerce.* Paris, 1866.
Mas Latrie, René de. *Du droit de marque ou droit de représailles au Moyen Âge.* Paris, 1839.
Massignon, Louis. "L'influence de l'Islam au moyen age sur la foundation de l'essor des banque juives." *BEO* 1 (1931): 3–12.
Matthews, A. N. *Mishcat-ul-Masabih.* 2 Vols. Calcutta, 1810.
Mercier, Ernest. *Le code du habous ou ouakf.* Constantine, 1899.
Messier, Ronald A. "The Almoravids: West African Gold and the Gold Currency of the Mediterranean Basin." *JESHO* 17, No. 1 (Mar. 1974): 31–47.
Mez, Adam. *Die Renaissance des Islams.* Heidelberg, 1922.
Michel Syrus. *Chronique de Michel le Syrien*, edited by J. B. Chabot, 4 Vols. Paris, 1899/1910.
Mickwitz, G. "Un problème d'influence: Byzance et l'économie de l'occident médiéval." *Annales* 8, No. 37 (Jan. 1936): 21–8.
Miquel, André. "El 'señor del zoco' en España: Edades media y moderna, Contribución al studio de la historica del Mercado by Pedro Chalmeta." *Revue Historique* 254, No. 2 (Oct. 1975): 472–6.
Morand, M. *Études de droit musulman algérien.* Algiers, 1910.
Motzki, Harald. "The Role of Non-Arab Converts in the Development of Early Islamic Law." *Islamic Law and Society* 6, No. 3 (1999): 293–317.
Motzki, Harald. *Hadith: Origins and Developments.* Trowbridge, 2008.
Mueller, Reinhold C. *The Venetian Money Market: Banks, Panics, and the Public Debt 1200–1500.* Baltimore, 1997.
Muir, Edward. "The Sources of Civil Society in Italy." *Journal of Interdisciplinary History* 29, No. 3. Patterns of Social Capital: Stability and Change in Comparative Perspective: Part I (Winter 1999): 379–406.
Muir, William. *The Caliphate: Its Rise Decline and Fall.* Edinburgh, 1915.
Muir, William. *The Life of Mahomet from Original Sources.* 4 Vols. London, 1858/1861.
Muir, William. *Annals of the Early Caliphate.* London, 1883.
Neusner, Jacob. *The Economics of the Mishna.* Chicago, 1998.
Neuwirth, Angelika, et al. (ed.). *The Quran in Context.* Leiden, 2010.

Nöldeke, Theodor. "Über den Diwan des Abu Talib und den des Abu'l'aswad Adduali." *ZDMG* (1864): 228–40.

Nöldeke, Theodor. *Geschichte der Perser und Araber zur Zeit der Sasaniden*. Leiden, 1879.

Nöldeke, Theodor. *Sketches from Eastern History*. London, 1892.

Oikonomides, N. *Hommes d'affaires grecs et latins à Constantinople (XIIIe—XVe siècles)*. Montreal, Paris, 1979.

Origo, Iris. "The Domestic Enemy: The Eastern Slaves in Tuscany in the Fourteenth and Fifteenth Centuries." *Speculum* 30 No. 3 (Jul. 1955): 321–66.

Osborn, Robert. *Islam under the Khalifs of Baghdad*. London, 1878.

Peltier, Frédéric. *Le livre des ventes de Mouwatta de Malik b. Anas*. Algier, 1911.

Perceval, Caussin de. *Essai sur l'histoire des Arabes avant l'Islamisme*. Paris, 1846/1848.

Perier, Jean. *La vie d'al-Hadjdjadj*. Paris, 1904.

Petachia. *Travels of Rabbi Petachia of Ratisbon*. London, 1861.

Petry, Carl F. "From Slaves to Benefactors: The Habashis of Mamluk Cairo." *Sudanic Africa* 5 (1994): 57–66.

Petry, Carl F. "Fractionalized Estates in a Centralized Regime: The Holdings of al-Ashraf Qaytbay and Qansuh l-Ghawri According to Their Waqf Deed." *JESHO* 41, No. 1 (1998): 96–117.

Plessner, Martin. *Der Oikonomikos des Neupythaogäers "Bryson" und sein Einfluss auf die islamische Wissenschaft*. Heidelberg, 1928.

Polanyi, Karl, C. M Arensberg, and H. W. Pearson. *Trade and Markets in the Early Empires*. Glencoe, 1957.

Polanyi, Karl. "Ports of Trade in Early Society." *Journal of Economic History* 23, No. 1 (Mar. 1963): 30–45.

Polanyi, Karl. "The Economistic Fallacy." *Review (Fernand Braudel Center)* 1, No. 1 (Summer 1977): 9–18.

Postan, M. "Credit in Medieval Trade." *Economic History Review* 1, No. 2 (Jan. 1928): 234–61.

Primaudaie, F. de la. *Les Arabes en Sicilie et en Italie*. Paris, 1868.

Pryor, John H. "The Origins of the Commenda Contract." *Speculum* 52, No. 1 (Jan. 1977): 5–37.

Quatremere, E. M. "Mémoire historique sur la vie d'Abd-allah ben-Zobair." *JA* 7, No. 10 (1832): 39–82; 137–168.

Rabinowitz, Jacob J. "The Origin of the Negotiable Promissory Note." *University of Pennsylvania Law Review* 104, No. 7 (May 1956): 927–39.

Raby, Julian, and Jeremy Johns. *Bayt al-Maqdis: Abd al Malik's Jerusalem*. Oxford, 1992.

Ravid, Benjamin. "The Jewish Mercantile Settlement of Twelfth and Thirteenth Century Venice: Reality or Conjecture?" *AJS Review* 2 (1977): 201–25.

Ray, Nicholas Dylan. "The Medieval Islamic System of Credit and Banking: Legal and Historical Considerations." *Arab Law Quarterly* 12, No. 1 (1997): 43–90.

Reinaud, Joseph. *Relation des voyages faits par les Arabes et les Persans dans l'Inde et à la Chine*. Vol. 1. Paris, 1845.

Reinaud, Joseph. *Invasions des Sarrazins en France et de France en Savoie en Piémont et dans la Suisse*. Paris, 1836.

Reinaud, Joseph. *Relations politiques et commerciales de l'empire romain avec l'Asie orientale*. Paris, 1863.

Reinert, Stephen. "The Muslim Presence in Constantinople 9th–15th Centuries," in H. Ahrweiler and A. E. Laiou, *Studies on the Internal Diaspora of the Byzantine Empire*. Washington, 1998.

Riley-Smith, Jonathan. "Government in Latin Syria and Commercial Privileges of Foreign Merchants," in *Relations between East and West in the Middle Ages*, edited by Derek Baker. Edinburgh, 1973.

Ritter, H. "Ein arabisches Handbuch der Handelswissenschaft." *Der Islam* 7 (1916): 1–91.

Robinson, Chase. *Abd al-Malik*. Oxford, 2005.

Robinson, Chase. *The Formation of the Islamic World: Sixth to Eleventh Centuries*. Vol 1. Cambridge, 2010.

Rodinson, Maxime. *Islam and Capitalism*. Austin, 1978.

Rodinson, Maxime. "Préface," in *Chalmeta* (1973, see above), 15–69.

Rodinson, Maxime. *Muhammad*. London, 2002.

Roover, Florence Edler de. "Partnership Accounts in Twelfth Century Genoa." *Bulletin of the Business Historical Society* 15, No. 6 (Dec. 1941): 87–92.

Rosenthal, Franz. "The Stranger in Medieval Islam." *Arabica* 44, No. 1 (Jan. 1977): 35–77.

Rubin, Uri. "The Ilaf of Quraysh: A Study of Sura CVI." *Arabica* 31, No. 2 (Jul. 1984): 165–88.

Runciman, Steven. "Charlemagne and Palestine." *English Historical Review* 50, No. 200 (Oct. 1935): 606–19.

Sacerdoti, A. "Le colleganze nella pratica degli affari e nella legislazione veneta." *Atti del Reale Istituto Veneto* (1899): 1–46.

Sachau, Eduard. *Zur ältesten Geschichte des muhammedanischen Rechts*. Vienna, 1870.

Sachau, Eduard. *Muhammedanischs Recht nach schafitischer Lehre*. Stuttgart and Berlin, 1897.

Sadi. *Gulistan*. London, 1964.

Said, Edward. *Orientalism*. New York, 1979.

Sassoon, David S. "The History of the Jews in Basra." *Jewish Quarterly Review* 17, No. 4 (Apr. 1927): 407–69.

Sauvaget, Jean. *La mosquée omeyyade de Médine*. Paris, 1947.

Sauvaire, M. H. "Matériaux pour server à l'histoire de la numismatique et la métrologie musulmanes." *JA* (1879): 455–533.

Sayous, André. *Le commerce des Européens a Tunis de XIIe siècle jusqu'a la fin du XVIe siècle*. Paris, 1929.

Schacht, Joseph. *An Introduction to Islamic Law*. Oxford, 1982.

Schack, A. von. *Poesie und Kunst der Araber in Spanien und Sizilien*. Stuttgart, 1877.

Schaub, F. *Der Kampf gegen den Zinswucher ungerechten Preis, und unlauteren Handel im Mittelalter*. Freiburg, 1905.

Schaube, Adolf. *Handelsgeschichte der romanischen Völker*. Munich, 1906.

Scheffer-Boichorst, P. "Zur Geschichte der Syrer im Abendland." *Mitteilungen des Institut für österreichische Geschichtsforschung* 5, (1885): 520–50.

Schiltberger, Johann. *The Bondage and Travels of Johann Schiltberger*. London, 1879 (translation of *Reisen des Johannes Schiltberger*. Munich, 1859).

Schlumberger, G. *Numismatique de l'orient latin*. 2 Vols. Paris, 1878.

Schoff, H. W. (ed.). *The Periplus of the Erythaean Sea*. New York, 1912

Schulte, A. *Geschichte des mittelalterlichen Handels*. 2 Vols. Leipzig, 1900.

Sebeos. *Histoire d'Heraclius par l'eveque Sebeos*. Paris, 1904.

Serjeant, R. B. "The constitution of Medina." *IC* 3 (1964): 3–16.

Service, Elman. *Origins of the State and Civilization*. New York, 1975.

Shahid, Irfan. "Byzantium in South Arabia." *DOP* 33 (1979): 23–94.

Shatzmiller, Maya. "'Waqf khayri' in Fourteenth-Century Fez: Legal, Social, and Economic Aspects." *Anaquel de Estudios Árabes* (1991): 193–217.

Shatzmiller, Maya. "Islamic Institutions and Property Rights: The Case of the 'Public Good' Waqf." *JESHO* 44, No. 1 (2001): 44–74.

Shatzmiller, Maya. *Labour in the Medieval Islamic World*. Leiden, 1994.

Shatzmiller, Maya. "Les premiers Mérinides et le milieu religieux de Fès: L'introduction des Médersas." *SI*, No. 43 (1976): 109–18.

Sieveking, H. *Genueser Finanzwesen*. 2 Vols. Freiburg, 1898/1899.

Silberschmidt, W. *Die Commenda in ihrer frühesten Entwicklung*. Würzburg, 1889.

Silver, Morris. "Karl Polanyi and Markets in the Ancient Near East: The Challenge of the Evidence." *Journal of Economic History* 43, No. 4 (Dec. 1983): 795–829.

Simon, Robert. "Hums et ilaf." *Acta orientalia* 23, No. 2 (1970): 205–32.

Simon, Robert. *Meccan Trade and Islam*. Budapest, 1989.

Snouck Hurgronje, C. *Selected Works*. Leiden, 1957.

Sombart, Werner. *Der Bourgeois*. Munich, 1923.

Sombart, Werner. *Der moderne Kapitalismus*. 4 Vols. Munich, 1924.

Sombart, Werner. "Economic Theory and Economic History." *Economic History Review* 2, No. 1 (Jan. 1929): 1–19.
Speck, E. *Handelsgeschichte des Altertums*. 3 Vols. Leipzig, 1901.
Sprenger, Aloys. "Some Original Passages on the Early Commerce of the Arabs." *JASB* 13 (1844): 519–26.
Sprenger, Aloys. "Über das Traditionswesen bei den Arabern." *ZDMG* 10 (1856): 1–17.
Sprenger, Aloys. "On the Origin and Progress of Writing Down Historical Facts Among the Musulmans." *JASB* (1856): 303–29, 375–381.
Sprenger, Aloys. *Mohammed und der Koran*. Berlin, 1889.
Sprenger, Aloys. "Notes on Alfred von Kremer's Edition of Waqidy's Campaigns." *JASB* 25 (1856): 53–74, 199–220.
Sprenger, Aloys. *Life of Mohammed*. Allahabad, 1851.
Sprenger, Aloys. "Über die Bedeutung der edomitischen Wörter 'Alluf' in der Bibel und des arabischen Wortes 'Ylaf' im Koran." *ZDMG* 12 (1858): 315–7.
Sprenger, Aloys. "Die Schulfächer und die Scholastik der Muslime." *ZDMG* 32 (1878): 1–20.
Sprenger, Aloys. "Die Goldunze." *ZDMG* (1875): 636–7.
Sprenger, Aloys. *Die Post-und Reiserouten des Orients*. Leipzig, 1864.
Sprenger, Aloys. *Die alte Geographie Arabiens*. Bern, 1875.
Sprenger, Aloys. *Das Leben und die Lehre des Mohammad*. 3 Vols. Berlin, 1861–1865.
Sprenger, Aloys. "Die Mosaik bei den Arabern." *ZDMG* 15 (1861): 409–11.
Spuler, Bertold. *Iran in früh-islamischer Zeit*. Wiesbaden, 1952.
Stark, Freya. "Notes on the Southern Incense Route of Arabia," in *The Southern Gates of Arabia*, 289–315. London, 1930.
Starr, J. *The Jews in the Byzantine Empire*. Athens, 1939.
Stein, Siegfried. "The Development of the Jewish Law of Interest from the Biblical Period to the Expulsion of the Jews from England." *Historia Judaica* 17 (1955): 1–40.
Stuewe, Friedrich. *Handelszüge der Araber*. Berlin, 1836.
Tafel, G., and G. M. Thomas. *Urkunden zur Älteren Handels-und Staatsgeschichte der Republik Venedig mit besonderer Beziehung auf Byzanz und die Levante*. Vol. 1. Vienna, 1856.
Tanukhi, al-Muhassin ibn Ali. *The Table-Talk of a Mesopotamian Judge*. London, 1922.
Tanukhi, al-Muhassin ibn Ali. "The Table-Talk of a Mesopotamian Judge." *IC* 3 (1929): 490–552; *IC* 4 (1930): 1–28, 223–228, 363–388, 531–557; *IC* 5 (1931): 169–193, 352–371, 559–81; *IC* 6 (1932): 47–66, 184–205, 370–396.
Theophanes. *The Chronicle of Theophanes the Confessor*. Oxford, 1997.
Tischendorf, Paul von. *Das Lehnwesen in den moslemischen Staaten*. Leipzig, 1872.
Tolan, John. *Sons of Ishmael: Muslims through European Eyes in the Middle Ages*. Gainesville, 2008.
Tolan, John. *Saint Francis and the Sultan*. Oxford, 2009.
Tornauw, Nikolaus von. *Das Moslemische Recht*. Leipzig, 1855.
Tornberg, C. J. "Über muhammedanische Revolutions-Münzen." *ZDMG* (1868): 700–707.
Torrey, Charles C. "The Foundry of the Second Temple at Jerusalem." *Journal of Biblical Literature* 55, No. 4 (Dec. 1936): 247–60.
Torrey, Charles C. "The Evolution of a Financier in the Ancient Near East." *Journal of Near Eastern Studies* 2, No. 4 (Oct. 1943): 295–301.
Torrey, Charles C. *The Commercial-theological Terms in the Koran*. Leiden, 1892.
Torrey, Charles C. *The Jewish Foundation of Islam*. New York, 1933.
Tritton, A. S. *The Caliphs and Their Non-Muslim Subjects*. London, 1930.
Tritton, A. S. "Islam and the Protected Religions." *JRAS*, No. 3 (Jul. 1928): 485–508.
Tyan, Emile. *Histoire de l'organisation judiciaire en pays d'Islam*. 2 Vols. Paris, 1938.
Udovitch, Abraham. "Reflections on the Institutions of Credits and Banking in the Medieval Islamic Near East." *SI*, No. 41 (1975): 5–21.
Udovitch, Abraham. "Les échanges de marché dans l'Islam médiéval: Théorie du droit et savoir local." *Studia Islamica*, No. 65 (1987): 5–30.
Udovitch, Abraham. "At the Origins of the Western Commenda: Islam, Israel, Byzantium?" *Speculum* 37, No. 2 (Apr. 1962): 198–207.

Udovitch, Abraham. "Credit as a Means of Investment in Medieval Islamic Trade." *JAOS* 87, No. 3 (Jul. 1967): 260–4.
Udovitch, Abraham. *The Islamic Middle East*. Princeton, 1981.
Udovitch, Abraham. "Labor Partnerships in Early Islamic Law." *JESHO* 10, No. 1 (Jul. 1967): 64–80.
Udovitch, Abraham. *Partnership and Profit in Early Islam*. Princeton, 1970.
Verrier, Ramon. *Introduction à la pensée économique de l'Islam du VIIIe au XVe siècle*. Paris, 2009.
Versteegh, Kees. "The Arab Presence in France and Switzerland in the 10th Century." *Arabica* 37, No. 3 (Nov. 1990): 359–88.
Waines, David. "'Luxury Foods' in Medieval Islamic Societies." *World Archaeology* 34, No. 3 (Feb. 2003): 571-80.
Watson, Andrew M. "Back to Gold—and Silver." *Economic History Review*, New Series, Vol. 20, No. 1 (Apr. 1967): 1–34.
Watt, Montgomery. *The Influence of Islam on Medieval Europe*. Edinburgh, 1987.
Watt, Montgomery. *Muhammed at Mecca*. Oxford, 1953.
Watt, Montgomery. *Muhammed at Medina*. Oxford, 1956.
Weber, Max. *Wirtschaft und Gesellschaft*. 2 Vols. Tübingen, 1947.
Weil, Gustav. *Geschichte der Chalifen*. 5 Vols. Mannheim, 1846/1862.
Weil, Gustav. *Die poetische Literatur der Araber vor und unmittelbar nach Mohammed*. Stuttgart, 1837.
Weil, Gustav. *Mohammed der Prophet*. Stuttgart, 1843.
Weil, Gustav. *Historisch-kritische Einleitung in den Koran*. Bielefeld, 1844.
Wellhausen, Julius. *Reste arabischen Heidentums*. Berlin, 1897.
Wellhausen, Julius. *Das arabische Reich und sein Sturz*. Berlin, 1902 (translated as *The Arab Kingdom and Its Fall*. London, 1927).
Wellhausen, Julius. *Skizzen und Vorarbeiten*. 6 Vols. Berlin, 1884/1899.
Wellhausen, Julius. *Muhamad in Medina*. Berlin, 1882.
Wenner, Manfred. "The Arab/Muslim Presence in Medieval Central Europe." *International Journal of Middle East Studies* 12, No. 1 (Aug. 1980): 59–79.
Wiet, Gaston. "Les marchands d'épice sous les Sultans Mamlouks." *Cahiers d'histoire égyptienne* 7, No. 2 (1955): 81–147.
Wiet, Gaston. "Le Traité des famines de Maqrizi." *JESHO* 5, No. 1 (Feb. 1962): 1–90.
William of Tyre. *A History of Deeds Done beyond the Sea*. 2 Vols. New York, 1943.
Wilson, R. K. *An Introduction to Anglo-Muhammadan Law*. London, 1894.
Wolf, E. R. "The Social Organization of Mecca and the Origins of Islam." *Southwestern Journal of Anthropology* 7, No. 4 (Winter 1951): 329–56.
Wright, Thomas. *Early Travels in Palestine*. London, 1848.
Wüstenfeld, Ferdinand. *Geschichte der Fatimiden-Chalifen nach arabischen Quellen*. Göttingen, 1881.
Wüstenfeld, Ferdinand. *Die Famile el-Zubeir*. Göttingen, 1878
Wüstenfeld, Ferdinand. *Die Chroniken der Stadt Mekka* (edited and translated by Ferdinand Wüstenfeld, 4 Vols.). Leipzig, 1857/1861.
Young, M. J. L., J. D. Latham, and R. B. Serjeant. *Religion, Learning, and Science in the Abbasid Period*. Cambridge, 1991.
Zotenberg. *Invasion des Visigoths et des Arabes en France*. Toulouse, 1876.

Index

About the Author

Benedikt Koehler is editor of *A History of Financial Disasters 1857–1923* and is also the author of biographies of Ludwig Bamberger, one of the founders of Germany's Deutsche Bank, and of Adam Müller, the nineteenth-century political philosopher. *Early Islam and the Birth of Capitalism* was supported by the Institute of Economic Affairs in London and the Earhart Foundation in Ann Arbor, Michigan.